*f***P**

Ivers. The Funniest Comics, the Punkest Rockers, the Hollywood Heavyweights, the Thirty-six years of Peter Ivers. The Funniest Comics, the Punkest Rockers, the Hollywood Heavyweights, the Thirty-six years of Peter Ivers. The Funniest Comics, the Punkest Rockers, the Hollywood Heavyweights, the Thirty-six years of Peter Ivers. The Funniest Comics, the Punkest Rockers, the Hollywood Heavyweights, the Thirty-six years of Peter Ivers. The Funniest Comics, the Punkest Rockers, the Hollywood Heavyweights, the Thirty-six years of Peter Ivers. **The Funniest Comics, the Punkest Rockers, the Hollywood Heavyweights, the Thirty-six years of Peter Ivers.** The Funniest Comics, the Punkest Rockers, the Hollywood Heavyweights, the Thirty-six years of Peter Ivers. The Funniest Comics, the Punkest Rockers, the Hollywood Heavyweights, the Thirty-six years of Peter Ivers. The Funniest Comics, the Punkest Rockers, the Hollywood Heavyweights, the Thirty-six years of Peter Ivers. The Funniest Comics, the Punkest Rockers, the Hollywood Heavyweights, the Thirty-six years of Peter Ivers. The Funniest Comics, the Punkest Rockers, the Hollywood Heavyweights, the Thirty-six years of Peter Ivers. The Funniest Comics, the Punkest Rockers, the Hollywood Heavyweights, the Thirty-six years of Peter Ivers. The Funniest Comics, the

In Heaven Everything Is Fine

The Unsolved Life of Peter Ivers
and the Lost History of New Wave Theatre

Josh Frank with Charlie Buckholtz

FREE PRESS
New York London Toronto Sydney

P

Free Press
A Division of Simon & Schuster, Inc.
1230 Avenue of the Americas
New York, NY 10020

First Free Press hardcover edition August 2008

FREE PRESS and colophon are trademarks of Simon & Schuster, Inc.

For information about special discounts for bulk purchases,
please contact Simon & Schuster Special Sales at
1-800-456-6798 or business@simonandschuster.com

Designed by Julie Schroeder

Manufactured in the United States of America

10   9   8   7   6   5   4   3   2   1

Library of Congress Cataloging-in-Publication Data

Frank, Josh.
    In heaven everything is fine: the unsolved life of Peter Ivers / by Josh Frank with
Charlie Buckholtz.
        p.   cm.
    Includes bibliographical references.
    1. Ivers, Peter.   2. Rock musicians—United States—Biography.   I. Buckholtz,
Charlie.   II. Title.
    ML420.I966F73 2008
    782.42166092—dc22
    [B]   2008002943

ISBN-13: 978-1-4165-5120-1
ISBN-10:   1-4165-5120-4

For our families

For Peter

CONTENTS

ACT 1 WRESTLING WITH THE CLASSICS

ACT 2 MUSIC FOR CASH

SELECTED CAST OF CHARACTERS

THE FAMILY

David Fisher: Lucy's brother

Deb Newmyer: Lucy's cousin

Emily Fisher: Lucy's sister

Fred Jelin: Lucy's cousin

Lucy Fisher: Peter's lifelong girlfriend, movie producer

Merle Ivers: Peter's mother

Paul Ivers*: Peter's father

Ricki Lopez: Peter's sister

THE COMICS

Bill Murray*: comic, actor (*National Lampoon*, *Saturday Night Live*, *Caddyshack*, *Stripes*, *Ghostbusters*)

Chevy Chase*: comic, actor (*Saturday Night Live*, *Fletch*, *Vacation*)

Dan Aykroyd: comic, musician, actor (*Blues Brothers*, *Saturday Night Live*, Second City, *Ghostbusters*)

Doug Kenney*: Peter's close friend, *National Lampoon* cofounder, humorist, screenwriter (*Animal House*, *Caddyshack*)

Harold Ramis: friend, comic, actor, director (*National Lampoon*, *Saturday Night Live*, *Stripes*, *Groundhog Day*, *Ghostbusters*, *Analyze This*)

John Belushi*: friend, comic, musician, actor (*Blues Brothers*, *Saturday Night Live*, Second City, *Animal House*)

Judy Belushi: writer, widow of John Belushi

Mark Stumpf: college friend, writer (*Harvard Lampoon*)

Michael O'Keefe: actor (*Caddyshack*)

THE PUNKS AND ROCKERS

Charles Thompson/Frank Black: fan, musician (the Pixies)

Dave Alvin: musician (the Blasters)

Derf Scratch: musician (Fear)

Dinah Cancer: musician (45 Grave/Castration Squad)

Don Bolles: musician (the Germs, 45 Grave)

Jello Biafra: musician, spoken word (Dead Kennedys)

Jerry Casale: fan, musician (Devo)

John Cale*: friend, musician (the Velvet Underground)

Keith Morris: musician (Circle Jerks, Black Flag)

Spit Stix: musician (Fear)

Todd Homer: musician (Angry Samoans)

THE FILM DIRECTORS AND PRODUCERS

David Lynch: friend, director (*Eraserhead, Dune, The Elephant Man, Blue Velvet, Twin Peaks*)

Francis Ford Coppola*: filmmaker (*The Godfather, Apocalypse Now*)

Joe Dante: editor (*Grand Theft Auto*), filmmaker (*Gremlins, Matinee, Small Soldiers*)

John Landis: filmmaker (*Animal House, The Blues Brothers*)

Malcolm Leo: friend, producer, director (*Heroes of Rock N Roll, This Is Elvis*)

Mark Canton: producer (*Caddyshack, 300*)

Michael Shamberg: producer (*Modern Problems, The Big Chill, Pulp Fiction*)

Paula Weinstein: Lucy's friend, producer (*Analyze This, The Perfect Storm*)

Penelope Spheeris: punk documentarian and producer (*The Decline of Western Civilization*, Albert Brooks's film segments on *Saturday Night Live*)

Steve Martin: close friend, filmmaker (*Theremin: An Electronic Odyssey*)

Stuart Cornfeld: friend, producer (*The Elephant Man, The Fly, Zoolander*)

Stuart Shapiro: *Night Flight* creator-producer

FRIENDS AND COLLABORATORS: MUSIC AND THEATER

Andrew Weil: Harvard friend, author, integrative doctor

Asha Puthli: friend, collaborator, singer

Buddy Helm: friend, videographer, musician (*Tim Buckley, At Sunset*)

Buell Neidlinger: Peter's close friend and collaborator, musician, bass player, producer

Dee Dee Bridgewater: friend and singer

Durrie Parks: friend, music producer

Franne Golde: friend, collaborator, songwriter (for Christina Aguilera, Faith Hill, Whitney Houston, Jessica Simpson)

Gary Wright: musician, music producer, songwriter (*The Dreamweaver*)

George Leh: musician, collaborator, singer

Gilbert Moses: musician (Street Choir), director (*Roots*), friend

Jeff Eyrich: musician, collaborator

Kim Brody: Peter's college girlfriend, musician, performer

Larry Cohn: friend, supporter, former Vice President, Artist and Repertoire, Epic Records

Linda Perry: friend, music publisher

Marty Krystall: musician, collaborator

Paul Lenart: musician (Far Cry), collaborator

Peter Rafelson: friend, collaborator, music and film

Richard Greene: friend, bandmate, musician (Bill Monroe and the Bluegrass Boys)

Roderick Taylor: close friend, musician, screenwriter (*City of Tomorrow, The Brave One*)

Stockard Channing: girlfriend, actress (*Grease, Six Degrees of Separation, The West Wing*)

Tequila Mockingbird: friend, collaborator, vocalist, music promoter

Tim Mayer*: close friend and collaborator, stage director, poet, playwright (*My One and Only*)

Van Dyke Parks: friend, collaborator, composer, producer, songwriter (*Song Cycle, Discover America*)

Yolande Bavan: friend, collaborator, singer

FRIENDS AND COLLABORATORS

Alan Finger: Peter's yogi, founder of YogaWorks

Anne Ramis: close friend

Barbara Smith: friend, Howard's wife, Director of the American Cinematheque

Boaty Boatwright: friend, talent agent

Charlie Haas: colleague, Editorial Director, Warner Bros. Records

Chris Hart: Harvard friend

Doug Martin: friend, collaborator

Hilary Klein: friend

Howard Cutler: college friend

Howard Smith: friend, film editor (*The Abyss*)

Johanna Went: friend, performance artist

John Klein: friend, AFI filmmaker

John Leone: Harvard friend, writer

Nancy Drew: friend, early video/performance art patron

Matina Horner: friend, president of Radcliffe College

Paul Michael Glaser: friend, TV and film actor

Peter Johnson: Harvard friend

Robbie Greene: friend, business manager

Tim Hunter: friend, filmmaker (*Tex*, *The River's Edge*, *Mad Men*)

Tom Barron: Cambridge friend, musician

THE SCENESTERS

Beverly D'Angelo: actress (*Coal Miner's Daughter*, *Vacation*, *Law and Order: SVU*)

David Jove*: producer of *New Wave Theatre*

Doug Knott: colleague, lawyer, poet

Ed Ochs: colleague, *New Wave Theatre* writer

Hudson Marquez: colleague, artist (*Cadillac Ranch*)

Iris Berry: writer

Janet Cunningham: punk rock casting agent

Ken Yas: colleague, friend of David Jove, former tech specialist for George Lucas

Laurence Fishburne*: punk scene doorman, actor (*Apocalypse Now*, *Rumble Fish*, *The Matrix*)

Michael Dare: writer, performer, photographer

Paul Flattery: music video director

Pleasant Gehman: writer

Richard Skidmore: booker for *New Wave Theatre*, music producer

Robert Roll: *New Wave Theatre* performer

Wallis Nicita: casting director (*Caddyshack*, *The Falcon and the Snowman*, *The Witches of Eastwick*), producer (*Mermaid*, *Six Days and Seven Nights*)

Zachary Gertzman: New Wave Theatre announcer, musician

Zatar: owner, "the Pyramid Club"

ACQUAINTANCES

James Taylor*: singer/songwriter

Jerry Harrison: musician (Talking Heads, Modern Lovers)

Jim Tucker: loft mate, artist

John Lithgow: colleague, actor (*Terms of Endearment*, *Footloose*, *3rd Rock from the Sun*, *Dreamgirls*)

Tommy Lee Jones*: colleague, actor (*The Fugitive, Men in Black, No Country for Old Men*)

THE DETECTIVES

Clifford Shepard: Cold Case Division, Los Angeles Police Department
David Charbonneau: private detective
Hank Petrovsky: lead detective, Major Case, Los Angeles Police Department

* Not interviewed directly for the book. Stories about them are drawn from others' accounts.

WHY PETER?

Long Day's Journey into
Knight of the Blue Communion

> It is well known, what strikes the capricious mind of the
> poet is not always what affects the mass of readers. Now, while
> admiring, as others doubtless will admire, the details we have to
> relate, our main preoccupation concerned a matter to which no
> one before ourselves had given a thought.
> —*Alexandre Dumas, preface to* The Three Musketeers

You won't find Peter Ivers's albums at the record store. You can't rent his television show from your local video store or Netflix. There is no way to learn much about him and his incredible insight as an artist and pop culture visionary on the Internet, in libraries, or in news archives. His story and work have been all but forgotten.

This is a crime for many reasons. His creative brilliance, magnetic personality, and life force alone are worthy of preservation. But beyond that, Peter lived at the epicenter of a perfect storm of artistic endeavor. For a brief, magical moment in the mid 1970s and early 1980s, music, comedy, film, and theatre converged in completely new, even revolutionary ways. Peter's friends and loved ones have given me the opportunity to pluck this lost story from obscurity—Peter's role as master of ceremonies to a unique, emerging art form that today we all take for granted.

Why did I focus on Peter? It all started with five haunting words sung by a girl with unfortunate cheeks.

In the early '90s, when I first saw David Lynch's movie *Eraserhead*, I was in high school in suburban Potomac, Maryland. I was a part of the clique that survived the manicured lawns, tidy fences, football games, and homecomings by creating our own little subculture made up of all the strange, subversive pop culture we could get our hands on. One evening, inspired by Lynch's TV series, *Twin Peaks* (the only prime-time show worth watching then), some friends and I decided to check out his debut film *Eraserhead,* a grad school effort that claimed to be "a dream of dark and troubling things." The hero, Henry Spencer, lives in an abandoned building, where the lights flicker on and off, and he watches and listens to the Lady in the Radiator sing about how "in heaven, everything is fine." The film was so gritty and dark, you felt kind of perverted by the end. It was like doing something illicit without breaking the law. From that day on, I was haunted by the lady in a radiator and her five-word song.

My friends and I listened to a lot of Pixies. A few years after we watched the movie, I went to a Pixies concert and they played a song that sounded very familiar. Something about heaven . . . It hit me that they were covering the Lady in the Radiator's song. I remember thinking, "Who wrote that song?" and how cool it was that my favorite rock band was covering it, and how random. What made them do that? In the preweb world of the early '90s, I didn't have the resources to find out.

Ten years later while I was writing my first book, *Fool the World: The Oral History of a Band Called Pixies,* I discovered the composer of the song was someone named Peter Ivers.

Who was this guy? I found out a few bits and pieces. He studied classics at Harvard. He played the blues harmonica. He was a yoga master and black belt in Shotokan karate. He was a recording artist, songwriter, poet, artist, and performer. In addition to composing and singing "In Heaven," his songs have been recorded by Diana Ross, Helen Reddy, and June Pointer of the Pointer Sisters for a song in *National Lampoon's Vacation.* He wrote songs for the Roger Corman film *Grand Theft Auto* (directed by Ron Howard), the movie *Airplane!,* and the original TV series *Starsky & Hutch.* He was best known as the elfin host of the 1980s LA-based cable show *New Wave Theatre,* a precursor to MTV, where punk comedians like John Belushi came to see punk bands like the Dead Kennedys and Fear. His closest friends were the heroes of my youth: Belushi, Doug Kenney (who cofounded the *National Lampoon* and cowrote *Animal House*), writer-director Harold Ramis of *Ghostbusters* and *Vacation* fame. His life and work were cut short with his murder at age thirty-six.

But I wanted to know more than his bio. I wanted to know why everyone who met Peter seemed to fall in love with him. I wanted to know how a person described as having no enemies and being the kindest guy in the world, who had accomplished so much, ended up dead and forgotten to history. So I picked up the phone to see what I could find out.

I started with Lucy Fisher, whom Peter Ivers lived with and loved for fifteen years. Lucy has been the producer of dozens of Hollywood movies, and has served as vice chair of Columbia and TriStar. She knew Peter from his Harvard days when she was an underclasswoman at Radcliffe. They came out to Hollywood and lived together for over a decade. I called Lucy and asked her if she would talk to me about Peter. She said yes.

When I first met Lucy, I was terrified. Her stature in Hollywood was part of it, but I was more daunted because this was the woman who loved Peter and who had given her okay (as representative of the estate and Peter's mother, Merle) for me to move forward with writing his story. She was the love of his life. When we first spoke on the phone she said something that has stayed with me the entire time I worked on the book: "I have been dreading this day for a long time." It hit me then that this was not just a cool story based on five words in a weird movie I saw in high school. It was a responsibility far beyond any that I had undertaken before. This feeling was confirmed by what Lucy said next: "You have no idea what you're getting yourself into."

We met a number of times, at her office on the Sony Pictures Studios lot and at her home, where she graciously shared the personal scrapbooks of her life with Peter. She would point to a picture of her with a little girl and say, "Oh that's me and Sofia Coppola when she was eleven. Isn't she beautiful?" We looked at pictures of Peter and Doug Kenney, Lucy in the middle, both of them eyeing her adoringly.

Without Lucy, there would be no story to tell. Lucy opened her Rolodex and provided me with a list of more than one hundred people to talk to and the assurance that when they called her to check up on me she would say I was okay.

How do you go about reviving a lost-life story? With Lucy's list in hand, I followed the advice of Daryl Zero, the world's greatest fictitious private investigator (from the film *The Zero Effect*):

I can't possibly overstate the importance of good research. Everyone goes through life dropping crumbs. If you can recognize the crumbs, you can trace a path all the way from the death certificate to the dinner and movie that resulted in you in the first place. But research is an art, not a science because anyone who knows what they are doing can find the crumbs, the where, the whats, and whos. The art is in the whys. The ability to read between the crumbs (not to mix metaphors). For every event there is a cause and effect, for every crime, a motive, and for every motive, a passion. The art of research is the ability to look at the details and see the passion.

The more I researched, the more I saw of Peter's passions and the passion of his friends for him. The first person I spoke with after visiting Lucy was Steve Martin (not the comedian, although this Steve Martin is also very funny), remembered by some as one of the twins in *Fast Times at Ridgemont High*. He was a very close friend of Peter's, and has shared with Lucy the responsibility of guarding his legacy. As Steve and I ended our evening, he said, "You're going to find out who this guy was and it's going to blow your mind. And it will make the loss of him that much more profound."

A month later, I met with Harold Ramis at his Chicago office, acutely aware that I was asking him to tell me about one of his favorite people and one of his most painful memories. In addition to Peter, two other subjects of the book were friends of Harold who had died young: Doug Kenney and John Belushi. Harold was a key to this story, because in many ways he exemplified the cross-pollination of punks and comics that occurred when Peter brought these two words together. Still, I didn't know how he would feel about revisiting this difficult time. As I sat down he said, "So . . . Peter" and spoke for over an hour, openly and emotionally, as if the memories were fresh and not twenty-five years old. After a while he played me some footage from a pool party. There was Doug, Harold, and Harold's then-wife, Anne. Standing in front of them, smiling at the camera, was Peter. Living and breathing, waving at Harold and me from the past in brilliant low-def Super 8.

How did I come to understand Peter? In the end it was his friends and loved ones and the music, theatre, film, and television they created during that time that helped me read between the crumbs and come to see Peter as a whole person—the spark and the passion, the influence and impact on those who still laugh and cry trying to explain what he meant to them.

I finally visited Los Angeles County Cold Case Division detective Clifford Shepard, who remembered the case from when he was just starting out in the force as a beat cop in Peter's neighborhood. I told him what I had learned about Peter, how important he was to his friends, his family, and now to me. He explained that a lot of things bother him about unsolved investigations, but when the victim is forgotten, "That's a crime in itself." He agreed to reopen the case and test the evidence with the latest technology.

After the initial research, I asked Charlie Buckholtz, a writer and my oldest friend from my days as a young suburban outsider, to join me in my quest to tell this story. We sat up many nights, and watched many sunrises, pondering who Peter was and what he meant. Together we chipped away at the daunting task not only of interpreting a life—identifying what it was about Peter that all the people who knew him found so attractive and profound—but also communicating its essence within the confines of black ink on white paper. Peter's is a story of collaboration, and Charlie and I have put this book together in that same spirit of creative teamwork. Investigating the mysteries of his unsolved life was our primary goal.

As Peter once said, "Every decision you make is a chance to be a hero." He made a lot of decisions in his life, and many of them seemed to lead away from the success he so vitally desired. Some called him Peter Pan, the boy who refused to grow up and face facts, while others rooted for him till his last days. By choosing to live the artistic dreams that they themselves (often admittedly) had given up on, he exuded a fulfillment they could never quite achieve. With a bank account perpetually in the red, he became an unlikely role model—an icon of authenticity and a bottomless source of inspiration, emulation, and adoration—for a generation of pop culture heavyweights. Though Peter was far from perfect, the more I learned about him the more I came to understand why he was seen by so many as a hero.

Besides, perhaps as Doug Kenney once said, if you look closely enough, in the end, "You will find a subtle perfection in all [Peter] does."

Josh Frank, 2008

NOTE TO READERS

There are two things you should know.

1. About the Case Books. On August 10, 2006, I contacted the Cold Case Division of the Los Angeles Police Department to inquire about the unsolved case of Peter Ivers. I was able to persuade detective Clifford Shepard to reopen the Ivers file. The investigative case book material found herein was compiled between 2005 and 2007 during interviews I conducted while collecting information intended to assist in the investigation.

2. About certain notation in this book. While reading this book you will occasionally see at certain points in the book a symbol like this (<>) followed by a song number and title. Log on to www.Peterivers .com and navigate to the "Book Extras" "Song/Book" page where you will be able to check out Peter's songs and videos as you read about them, and to unlock "bonus features" along the way.

"Peter," she said, faltering, "are you expecting me to fly away with you?"

"Of course; that is why I have come."

"I can't come," she said apologetically, "I have forgotten how to fly."

"I'll soon teach you again."

"O Peter, don't waste the fairy dust on me."

She had risen; and now at last a fear assailed him. "What is it?" he cried, shrinking.

"I will turn up the light," she said, "and then you can see for yourself."

For almost the only time in his life that I know of, Peter was afraid. "Don't turn up the light," he cried.

—*J. M. Barrie*, Peter Pan

A *View from* The Top

February 7, 1984, 2:15p.m.

A loud trumpet call blasts over the bustling set of Channel 5 KTLA's new, highly anticipated pilot: a punk-rock variety show, a video hit parade interspersed with subversive comedy, the snarling LA punk aesthetic packaged and polished and made just palatable enough for a youthful mainstream demographic looking for a dose of danger in the comfort of their living rooms. In short, a West Coast underground *Saturday Night Live*—with an edge.

Like the fanfare blasting through the set—catching off-guard the assembled mulling audience of mohawks and spikes and full-body tattoos, calling this motley troupe temporarily to attention—the fanfare accompanying the buildup to the show has been similarly grandiose. But it is far from hot air. Hosting the weekly circus will be Chevy Chase in his television homecoming, his first regular small-screen gig since leaving *SNL* in '76. Executive producing is Harold Ramis, who came up in the Second City scene and in the last five years has gained widespread recognition with the *National Lampoon* set as a writer and/or director of movies such as *Animal House*, *Meatballs*, *Caddyshack*, *Stripes*, and *National Lampoon's Vacation*. Working with Ramis are David Jove, the enigmatic force behind the cult television hit *New Wave Theatre*, of which this new pilot is a second incarnation; and Paul Flattery, a respected producer who has worked extensively in the emerging music video form. Rounding out the team is staff writer Michael Dare, a journalist, well-known local scenester, and supplier to the stars under the self-generated pseudonym "Captain Preemo." Today Dare isn't supplying the drugs, but something he hopes will be even more intoxicating and dangerous—words.

The shock of noise from the trumpet blast brings the manic bustle on the set to a halt. But what follows has no problem holding audience attention. Is that Dan Aykroyd's distinctive, oddly comforting voice blasting over the loudspeaker, resounding with twisted authority and good-natured smarm?

"UNDER NO CIRCUMSTANCES ATTEMPT TO WATCH THIS SHOW WITHOUT A WORKING TELEVISION SET."

The screen flashes quick intercuts of a star-filled sky, then a control room operated by three men wearing large papier-mâché animal masks. Then a velvety announcer booms out over the crowd:

"AND NOW, FROM HOLLYWOOD, CALIFORNIA, THE ENTERTAINMENT CAPITAL OF THE WORLD, WE WELCOME YOU TO— *THE TOP!*"

Meanwhile, backstage, Chevy Chase and David Jove wrangled over what Chevy would say and do when he walked onstage in less than fifteen seconds. Dare and Chevy had gone back and forth over possible monologues. Jove had rejected them all out of hand with a delightful cocktail of booze-filled belligerence, drug-addled paranoia, and a smug bullying egomania which he appeared to come by naturally. After all, it was his show, *New Wave Theatre*, which he had shepherded from cable-access obscurity into national distribution on the USA Network, which was the inspiration for this whole adventure. According to Jove, *New Wave Theatre* worked precisely because he wrote every word, called every shot, and controlled everything that did or did not make it onto the airwaves.

Over the last few months he had sat in writer meetings with Chevy, Ramis, Flattery, and Dare. Jove downed bottles of Bénédictine and brandy hand over fist, throwing the empties over his shoulder to shatter in a growing mound of shards. They would go around presenting their ideas, first Ramis, then Chevy, then Jove. Ramis was more concerned with the big picture, the kind of format that would strike a middle ground between satisfying the fans and keeping the network happy. Then there was Chevy, who would pace the room in sustained stream-of-consciousness rants that were some of the funniest bursts of spontaneous standup Michael Dare had ever seen. After a seven-year hiatus from television, Chevy, it seemed to Dare, had begun to feel suffocated by his movie star persona; now he was glowing with raw comedic genius. Dare took down everything that came out of Chase's mouth and saw his future lit in neon: Michael Dare, head writer of Chevy Chase's TV comeback.

Then Jove got up and, in short order, rejected each of Chase's and Ramis's suggestions. He replaced them with his own litany inspirations: frequent "behind-the-scenes" cuts to the control booth, manned by animals; a "talk show" segment featuring, exclusively, baby ducks; a duet performed by his own wife and daughter. Chevy and Harold listened to Jove's ideas and rejected each in turn. A great, ominous silence ensued. One by one, each of *The Top*'s founding geniuses ventured a thought and was summarily rejected—Ramis and Chase by Jove, and vice versa.

Then Chevy floated an idea based on a suggestion Dare had made to him before the meeting. Dare spoke up to second Chase and flesh out the gag. Then he noticed Jove, who had pulled his shirt up just enough to reveal a firearm stuffed into his pants. Dare didn't know Jove well enough to know what he was or was not capable of. Jove's past was shrouded in mystery; it was rumored that he had done jail time in Canada on drug charges, that he had fled and changed his name. ("Jove," in any event, was certainly an invention.) It was rumored that he was a narc, that he had introduced John Lennon to LSD and ratted out the Rolling Stones at the infamous Redlands bust. So Dare didn't know how serious Jove was about his gun. But he knew that Jove had been coking and drinking for the good part of the day, and that his face bore not the slightest trace of humor. So he thought better of taking a chance. Rather than risk getting shot, Dare kept quiet and let Jove shoot down yet another of Chevy's brilliant ideas.

Now, with the announcer listing tonight's guest comics and musical acts, thirteen seconds until he would have to walk out onto the stage, Chevy hardly could have been happy. He had agreed to do this in the first place only as a favor to Ramis, after Aykroyd turned him down. He didn't know anything about the LA punk scene—he was old enough to be many of these kids' father. But Ramis seemed to feel it was an untapped high-energy trend in the culture, and to package it for the mainstream could be huge. The association with the youthful counterculture could also be a refreshing reinvention and a boost to Chevy's career. Ramis was smart; Chevy knew and seemed to trust him. But he certainly didn't know David Jove, and the more a person knew Jove the less he trusted him. Chevy Chase had spent the last several months being bullied and condescended to about comedy by a person with a one-line résumé, a dubious, sketchy past, probably clinical mental instability, a messiah complex, and enough drugs in his system to carry him through the next long winter. He was both a nobody and a madman, and he was running the show.

Ramis was Chevy's connection to this, and Ramis hadn't been around all day. Shooting on *Ghostbusters* had run late, so he had arrived a few minutes ago and gone straight back to the control room. Paul Flattery knew it was a mistake to leave the talent all alone on the day of a shoot. There needed to be a person dedicated exclusively to their TLC. As with the others, it would be an understatement to say he had high hopes riding on *The Top*. The MTV Network had begun only a few years before, and it was still the only outlet for music videos on television. The field was wide open, and *The Top* was the perfect vehicle to propel him to big-time national exposure, credibility, and access. Ramis had called in some favors to get the deal made and pack the show with national talent, but it was Flattery who put up $30,000 of his own money as a guarantee to the network. In other words, it had been a mistake not to assign someone to keep Chevy happy, or at least keep him occupied. But Flattery was producing, Jove was directing, Ramis was late—and Chevy was drinking. Flattery had noticed him cradling a bottomless vodka bottle all afternoon.

Ten seconds to air, and Jove is adamant that Chevy abandon the monologues—all of them—and wing it. Chevy demurs. Jove shoves a black leather jacket with chains and a spiked Mohawk wig into Chevy's arms. Chevy throws on the costume. Jove runs back to the control room, which is in a truck five stages away from the set on which *The Top* is being shot.

The booming announcer lists the evening's guests: "FEATURING: CYNDI LAUPER! THE ROMANTICS! THE HOLLIES! SPECIAL GUESTS DAN AYKROYD, RODNEY DANGERFIELD, BILL MURRAY, LILI AND LOTUS, AND ROBERT ROLL AS GEORGE GHERKIN!"

To those around him, it is clear that Jove hates being so far away from the action. The beauty of *New Wave Theatre*, and one of the keys to its success, was his ubiquitous presence on the set. There was no stage, as punk etiquette was to play at ground level. There was also no audience, just a bunch of local punks invited by word of mouth to party with hot bands and free beer. What there was was: Jove, spending hours telling everyone where to set up. Jove, running around the stage as the main handheld camera operator, creating the show's raw, in-your-face look. Jove, taking the footage back home to his infamous Cave and editing it down to its final form with a breakneck barrage of jagged, frantic cuts.

Jove has done everything he could to re-create the raw, aggressive underground ambiance he had cultivated with *New Wave Theatre*. He has rejected the studio's many requests to see a script, insisting that they wouldn't know what they were doing until they did it. He has threatened the cast and crew, often with his gun, not to breathe a word of what was planned. He has made the stage as low to the ground as possible. He has two adjacent studios connected by an open door, one with the main set and one with a huge buffet of food and drink. The culinary abundance is in some ways a consolation prize for the studio's emphatic prohibition against alcohol on the set. Jove, who by this point is well networked in the punk scene, has managed to pack both rooms with original *New Wave Theatre* fans who know how to party, know how to dance, and have no idea how to be a proper television "audience"—which is exactly how Jove wants it.

The only thing missing is him, on the set. But that he can do nothing about. He had fought to direct from the stage, but was told that is not how "real" television works. The control room was remote, and if he wanted to be the director, that was where the directing would have to take place. The fact that he had no experience working in a real studio with a real control room didn't faze Jove—until he actually arrived. He finds himself facing three screens monitoring three stageside cameras, with no idea how to give orders to the crew on the stage. He has never ordered a cameraman, "cut to camera two," "pull into left," "camera three pull back," "give me a wide shot"; he simply doesn't know the language. So he sits back, paralyzed in a prison of mobile technology. Chevy, the punks, and the cameramen will have to sort things out for themselves while the tape rolls.

Still, Jove is expansive and on top of his game, confident that his intense preparations and insistence on total creative control have set up the show for success. This is going to be his Hollywood coronation, his shot at achieving mainstream exposure for his radical vision, at showing the industry execs he is a force to be reckoned with. He might terrify them, he might rouse their children to revolt against bourgeois values and join the punk revolution, subverting everything they thought they believed and shaking them violently awake out of their comalike slumbers. He might be hated, he might be feared. But he will not be ignored. He invited every influential person he knows in LA to the taping.

One of these guests, Hudson Marquez, ambles into the remote truck with his friend Bruce Wagner, just as the announcer wraps up his spiel. Marquez is an esteemed local artist-of-all-trades—screenwriter, painter, sculptor, maker of experimental video—who gained some renown for his involvement in the *Cadillac Ranch* installation in Amarillo, Texas, in the mid-'70s. He is friendly with Ramis and knows Jove from *New Wave Theatre*. Wagner is a talented young screenwriter and novelist. In the truck they find Jove, Ramis, and a gaggle of nervous technicians glued to the monitors. Marquez notes that Jove is higher than a kite, and Harold is being, it seems, quintessentially Harold: sitting in the eye of the hurricane, quietly chuckling to himself. Marquez tells them both it is going to be great, and makes his way to the set.

"THIS IS YOUR SUICIDAL ANNOUNCER, BILL MARTIN," concludes the intro. Meanwhile, on the screen a baby duck pecks around a tiny talk-show set. Then a family of aliens sits around their living room watching TV. The opening music kicks in.

Chevy walks out onto the stage. He looks up at the teleprompter, hoping to find at least one version of the opening monologue. But the teleprompter shows a blank screen. He stands there, silent, the opening music continuing to play—and for the first time in his life, perhaps, finds himself at a complete loss for words.

He falls back on a gag Ramis conceived, explaining in a meandering deadpan how after trying out different scenes, he had settled on becoming a punk.

On the floor, in the party, towards the back, Hudson Marquez munches on buffet while Bruce Wagner dances to the fading intro theme with Cyndi Lauper. He watches with Derf Scratch—the bassist for the band Fear, a frequent performer on *New Wave Theatre*—as beer and wine are surreptitiously distributed throughout the audience. The punks almost immediately begin heckling Chevy. One of them seems to be screaming something like, "Dance with me! Let's dance!" until Chevy finally invites him up onto the stage. A bunch of others jump up onto the stage with him and start windmilling, slam dancing, caroming violently off each other and off Chevy. Unfamiliar with the slam-dancing ritual, Chevy seems annoyed and confused. He seems to take it literally: as an attack, a provocation towards a fistfight. He seems to take it personally. And so Chevy—an athletic 6'4"—grabs the heckler and throws him forcefully off the stage.

The punks seem to take it in stride. They seem to like it: *Maybe Chevy Chase has some punk in him after all . . .* At the back of the set, Hudson and Derf look at each other, smile, and nod towards the stage. They make their way to the front of the crowd.

Back in the truck, where studio executives and Hollywood power brokers have crowded in to watch the taping, Paul Flattery tries to mask his concern. In fact, what he sees on the monitors is setting off frantic alarm bells. An experienced producer, he knows one thing above all else: do not let the shoot slip beyond your control. Improvisation is one thing. But when your host manually ejects an audience member from the stage, it is time to break. Tweaking his concern even further towards panic, he can see that one person heckling Chevy is holding a Heineken bottle, and there is certainly no Heineken at the buffet. "No booze on set"—could they have been any clearer? It is *definitely* time to break. Flattery orders Jove to call it to the crew on-stage. Jove says he wants to let the situation evolve. The truth is, he has no idea how to call anything to the crew. The gathered executives do not seem to be fooled. But Flattery has no time to argue the point. As far as he is concerned, the situation has hit Code Red. He'll pull the plug with his bare hands if he has to. He bolts out of the truck and breaks into a run towards the set.

Meanwhile, pushing his way to the stage, Derf Scratch starts screaming maniacally at Chevy: "*YOU HOMO! YOU BIG FUCK-ING HOMO!*" Part of Fear's shtick, and of punk shtick in general, is to call people homos. Derf is just playing around. Chevy does not know that.

This starts to become apparent when he shouts back at Derf, "*COME UP HERE! COME UP HERE AND SAY THAT!*" The crowd pushes Derf up onto the stage, and, in the midst of the other slam dancers, he promptly starts windmilling around Chevy, who by now has a wild, panicky look in his eyes.

Derf prances and slams around Chevy, thinking that they are working in cahoots to create good, memorable television.

One of the other punks slam dancing on the stage is Bobbi Brat, the lead singer of the band Red Scare. Brat, whose beauty is legendary in the scene, sports a lacy white bustier, white garters, and golf shoes. Her hair is short in the style of the '20s. With her on the stage is "Mad" Marc Rude, a well-known punk graphic artist in a wife-beater and head-to-toe ink. While Derf windmills around Chevy, Bobbi Brat, accidentally or not, kicks Chevy from behind. She connects with his balls. Chevy doubles over. Then he stands up, seizes Derf, and hurls him off the stage. Derf pulls himself off the floor to find Chevy waving his arms and screaming, *"IS THERE ANYONE ELSE WHO THINKS THEY CAN TAKE ME DOWN?!"*

Derf is not a large person—Chevy towers over him by a good six inches—but he is nothing if not punk rock. He charges the stage. Chevy takes a wide swing at his face. Derf ducks and rams Chevy with his head. They fall together, slamming into one of the big cameras on the way down. This gets the attention of some of the teamsters on the set. But once they see the camera is out of danger, they go back to munching their snacks.

Chevy rolls Derf into a ball and starts pounding on him. Mad Mark grabs one of Chevy's legs and starts punching it. Bobbi Brat falls on Chevy's other leg and starts zealously humping it. Mad Mark puts Chevy in a headlock, the other punks on the stage pile on, and the teamsters start maneuvering to move their cameras out of harm's way. Security rushes the stage. Derf crawls from the bottom of the pile and flees to the parking lot. Marc Rude eludes security by jumping a fence.

By the time Paul Flattery makes it to the set, Chevy is gone. Outside, Hudson Marquez wanders into the parking lot in time to catch Chevy jump into his souped-up Porsche, jam it into reverse, slam into a fence, pop the clutch shifting gears, smoke the tires, and squirrel wildly off the lot. Derf joins Marquez just in time to see Chevy squeal away. Marquez chuckles, "Jesus Christ." Derf shakes his head. "That fucking homo can't take a joke." After all, wasn't this supposed to be a punk rock show? What was more punk rock than what just happened inside? It was apparently too punk rock for Chevy. He never returned.

Security cleared the set. They reconvened a small audience a few hours later and continued taping in the docile, thinned-out studio. Cyndi Lauper performed "Time After Time." A taped segment of Rodney Dangerfield doing his "Rappin' Rodney" routine was aired, followed by a taped segment of a rambling conversation between Aykroyd and Murray, moderated by an overbearing Jove, on the *Ghostbusters* set. The full episode aired months later, with Andy Kaufman filling in as host in short taped filler segments. Kaufman had no shtick. For one of the only times in his public life, he was just himself. He died of cancer four months later. His final performance was the first and last episode of *The Top*.

In the postmortem, one name came up repeatedly. *If Peter was hosting, this never would've happened.* Peter Ivers had been the host of *New Wave Theatre*. He had dressed in outlandish costumes and mocked the punks with uncomfortably sincere questions about the meaning of life. He was frequently called a homo, sometimes threatened with violence and even death.

And yet somehow he held it all together, always remaining brightly, almost maniacally good-natured. Sincere and sardonic. Compassionate and mocking. Inscrutable and perennially unfazed.

Peter Ivers brought all his Hollywood friends to the *New Wave Theatre* tapings—Harold Ramis, Dan Aykroyd, John Belushi, Doug Kenney—and exposed them to the new counterculture of punk. Some, like Belushi, had made themselves at home, rocking out at the clubs and becoming friends with people like Derf Scratch and Lee Ving of Fear. Some, like Ramis, hung back, took vicarious hits off the uncontained thrill of these fuck-you kids and their fuck-you music and style. (Harold appreciated from a distance punk's cultural significance, while secretly swooning for the folk-light stylings of James Taylor and his reassuring ilk.)

But all of them respected punk's energy, its creativity, and its countercultural edge—so different from, and yet so redolent of, the air of '60s rebellion upon which they'd been weaned. All of them would stand around the *New Wave Theatre* set with the punks, talk with the kids, dance with the bands, laugh at the jokes. And all of them would acknowledge, with some gratitude, that it was Peter Ivers who brought them into that world. It was Peter who brought the two unlikely worlds together—the underground and the overground, as Peter would say—and managed somehow, briefly, to hold them in balance. To make them spark without catching fire, without burning everything to the ground.

Ramis exits the chaotic mobile studio just in time to catch the spoiler of Chevy's Porsche disappear into the Los Angeles afternoon smog. Undoubtedly, many holdovers from *New Wave Theatre* who are involved in *The Top* think of Peter, the originator of this experiment, the source of the shitstorm they've just witnessed and the fallout they have yet to confront. If Peter were around, this never would have happened.

March 3, 1983, 3:55 p.m.

"Who was this guy?"

The police officer floats the question half under his breath, not re-ally expecting an answer and not really caring. He sits on a stool in the center of an expansive loft space, trying to figure out which part of this situation he should be most pissed off about. Vying for first posi-tion is the pink sequined dinner jacket draped over his hand. What evil forces conspired to make *this* how he had to spend his afternoon: slog through the rain to God-forsaken downtown LA, sift through the mess of a probable squatter's den, and contemplate the identity of the kind of lowlife who'd wear a pink sequined dinner jacket?

The space is huge, twelve-foot ceilings at least, mostly unfurnished except for the bed. In other words, squatter's heaven, plenty of room to do drugs and party and whatever else, secure in the knowledge that the LAPD will look for any excuse whatsoever to avoid the drive out to Japantown. The unofficial policy is that as long as they stick to their own neighborhood, they can do whatever they want to each other and themselves. The floor is strewn with odds and ends, kids' toys, wooden contraptions that look like made-up musical instru-ments, photographs, metal objects with no obvious use. There is also an array of sound equipment: keyboards, huge PA speakers, mic stands, reel-to-reel tape machines, sheet music, a film projector. And finally, clothes, piled all over the floor, weird clothes with lots of glitter and shine. Women's clothes, suitcases' worth of dresses and capes; in some places the floor is ankle-deep with fabric, all tangled up, like a bunch of eccentric bag ladies emptied out their shopping carts all over the floor.

The officer contemplates the pink sequined dinner jacket because at least it gives him something to do. His partner didn't really hear the question he posed—"Who was this guy?"—partly because the space is so big and partly because he's too busy shouting at the teacher from the art institute for letting his students trample all over the scene. When the officers arrived, the kids, undergraduates it looked like, were buzzing like flies all over the room, some ogling the bed, craning their heads to get a look around the paramedics—no doubt trying to remember what they saw so they could paint it later—some avoiding it, picking at stuff in the room, stealing apprehensive glances every once in a while. Too spooked to get too close, but too intrigued to leave. A few students have barely made it inside the loft and are sticking close to the door.

He tries to get his partner's attention with a more specific question. "Squatter? Junkie type, you think?"

One of the artist kids pipes in, "I think he was some kind of performance artist."

The second officer turns to the kid, then back to the teacher—it turns out he lives in the loft across the hall, brought his students here on some kind of art school field trip—shouts, "Get them out of here!" and takes the opportunity to shoo away the students still loitering at the door.

With the room clear, the second officer tries to look serious and purposeful and take a mental snapshot of the place. But the truth is he doesn't know where to begin. The scene is tainted, there must have been fifteen of those kids running around when he and his partner arrived. According to procedure, they should tape off the room now. But what's the use?

Outside, the rain keeps coming down. It's been coming down since yesterday, hard warm rain, with no variation and no sign of letup. Over the weekend, the storm had gotten so bad it knocked some of the roof off the LA Convention Center. The wind has mostly subsided. Now it's just the rain.

"Performance artist." Neither of them has any idea what that means. They know that over the past year or so some "artsy types" have been migrating into this part of town. Partly because it's cheap, and partly, no doubt, to get an experience of "real life"—see how the other half lives and then become rich and famous presenting it to the rest of the world.

For the local element, the junkies and winos and hookers and pimps, "artsy" is just another word for easy prey. The artists were always getting mugged and broken into and burgled, harassed and beaten and shot and stabbed, for drug money and sometimes just for fun. Some of the artists were junkies and thieves themselves. Either way, for many cops, "artsy" is just another word for a crappy trip downtown and a whole caseload of unpleasant extra work.

The two officers called to 321 East 3rd Street are no exception. They pace around the apartment lamenting the loss of a perfectly good afternoon. It's getting dark, and the detectives haven't even radioed to say when they'll arrive. A heater next to the bed emits a low steady buzz. For a while, that and the rain are the room's only sounds.

Then the phone rings, the sound exploding into the loft.

The machine picks it up. A high, nasal, upbeat voice delivers the outgoing message. *"Hi, I'm in an ultra heavy writing mode. What's your frame? If you need me, you can find me. Love, Peter."* The incoming message is a woman who sounds half-nervous, half-confused, and half-annoyed.

"Hey, it's Franne. We're supposed to be in the studio for 'He's My Kind.' Everybody's waiting. Where are you?"

The officers give each other a look. Around the corner, in the smaller adjacent loft that makes an *L* with this one, Jim Tucker, the neighbor who called it in, sits in shock on his bed. Every once in a while he curses out loud, to no one in particular. He's even more pissed off than the cops—he *really* wasn't supposed to be here. He came home early from a vacation in Seattle with friends he hadn't seen in years. They'd hung out in a big loft watching the new "music videos" he had been editing and distributing to club owners, who would project them onto the wall while people danced. In the past year or so, a tight community of artists and A/V types had moved downtown to take advantage of big industrial loft spaces rented on the cheap. They worked on projects together, shared ideas, and helped each other get work. At night they partied together at the same handful of bars. The work they were doing was right at the edge, experimenting with new ways of combining music and video; no one anywhere else was doing anything like it. His Seattle friends, also artists, were appropriately blown away. They sat and watched and nodded their heads. It was exactly the kind of work he wanted to become known for.

Now there was nothing to do but sit around wondering why he

had to come back early. Why did he have to be the one to find this, the one to call the cops? He had a strong, queasy feeling that he would be lugging this day around with him for the rest of his life: the kind of thing *nobody* wants to become known for. He wasn't even supposed to be here! One thing was certain, he wasn't going anywhere anytime soon. The cops took his statement in their notebook, which as far as he could tell was the only thing they'd done right so far today. Now for him, too, there's nothing to do but wait for the detectives.

Meanwhile, the second officer spots an ashtray on the floor, mangled butts piled to the brim. He picks it up and sits with it at the foot of the bed.

Looking up from the sequined jacket, the first officer says, "Hey, that's evidence."

The second officer holds it up. "It's an ashtray."

Something on the floor catches his attention. He picks up what looks like a small pile of photographs peeking out from under a chiffon dress. He motions to the first officer, who drops the jacket and joins him on the foot of the bed. They flip through the photos together.

"Who was this guy?" the second officer asks.

The pictures show a man in his early thirties. In some of the pictures he's dressed in flamboyant costumes or women's clothes, in some he's in a photo booth with his face pressed up side by side with another guy. In others he's in a shower with a different guy, both wearing clothes. In some of the pictures he's naked, jumping around dancing or in bizarre painful-looking yoga poses or just standing there, looking as comfortable and natural as a baby or an animal in the wild.

The phone rings again. *"Peter, fucker, where are you? It's Doug, I've been trying you all day. We were supposed to film at your place this morning! I'm with Steve in his office, we got all these pissed-off people here. It's probably too late to do anything today, but get back to me so we can reschedule and I can let all these people go."*

"Maybe he's not a squatter after all," the first officer says. "Sounds like one of these 'artists.' "

"Well," his partner replies, "you got these wholesome photographs, you got 'He's My Kind,' you got Doug and Steve waiting to shoot some film with a bunch of people in an empty loft. Yeah, sure, sounds like a regular Francis Ford Coppola."

"Well, it means he has friends," says the first officer. "Maybe even family. And a film crew."

"You see this place?" says his partner. "Who knows what a guy like this was into."

The rain keeps coming down.

They sit on the edge of the bed as the sun goes down, waiting for the detectives to arrive.

It is almost dark, nearly two hours later, when the first set of tires screeches up to the building. Jim Tucker is at his window, waiting for it. A woman jumps out the passenger side of a very nice car and bolts for the building. This is Anne Ramis, whom Tucker knows. The man she's with stands outside the car for a second, takes a breath, puts a hand through his hair, and makes his way to the door. This is Harold Ramis, whom Tucker has heard about and seen in films.

The beat cops intercept the couple in the hallway. Anne pleads with them to let her inside. The second officer asks if they know the guy who lives here, and if so, how. There's an awkward pause, and then they both offer that he was their friend. Harold adds that they also work together.

The officer tries to mask his disbelief. "You work with this guy?" He looks over to his partner. "In, ah, what capacity?"

"Movies," Harold says. "Entertainment."

Tucker steps around the corner into the big loft. Anne sees him through the door and runs across the police tape. "What did they *do* to him?" Tucker steps between her and the sightline of the bed. When she called several hours ago all jumpy and scared, Tucker hadn't thought much of it. He had seen a lot of her in the past months and she often seemed vaguely on edge. She called because she hadn't heard from Peter all morning, which apparently was unusual. But even when Tucker looked out the window and informed her that he could see Peter's car outside, and she *freaked out*, insisting he check the big loft—even then Tucker was sure he wouldn't find anything but an empty bed.

As the officers try to calm and question Harold and Anne, more cars—mostly Mercedes and Beamers—screech into the lot. Soon the hallway is packed with people shouting at the cops, demanding to know what happened and where things stand. Some make their way into the loft, some even get to the bed, and the officers, outnumbered and out of their depth, do little to stop or even discourage them.

Tucker knows who most of these people are, from seeing them around the loft and from working on the fringes of the industry. He and Peter were friendly but it didn't go much deeper than that. Every once in a while their schedules would cross and they'd sit for a late-night talk. Now, when the cops ask all these Hollywood people their relationship to Peter, almost all of them give the same answer: *He's my best friend*. The cops take all this down in their notebooks, glassy-eyed as if transcribing words they do not understand.

Then, finally, she arrives. Lucy. Tucker has never seen her before, but he knows right away it is her. Peter talked about her constantly, he couldn't stop himself. She is a pretty woman, early thirties, in a business suit. It looks like she has been crying heavily. Lucy calmly explains to the beat cops that she is going to go in the room for a while, which she does.

By the time the detectives arrive, a whole new throng of people has descended onto the loft. More Hollywood people, but mostly punks, a kid in a mohawk, leather jackets mixing in with the suits. More than forty people pushing into each other and crying and fainting, just like in a movie. The detectives take the uniformed officers' reports, yell at them for a while and order them to put the tape back up and secure a wide perimeter around the door. They have no more success at this now than they did before, and they retreat to the outer door, out back, to at least prevent more people from coming in. The detectives ignore the chaos, do some perfunctory work on the scene, then come out and start questioning people.

Then a guy careens wildly up the stairs, freaked out and likely coked-up. He zeroes in on one of the detectives, corners him, and goes to work with what proves to be an effective combination of arrogant authority and belligerent charm. Soon he has the detective laughing and nodding his head. He leaves the detective and slips into the loft; no one seems to notice or care. The detectives start questioning everyone—the more people who show up, the more questions there are to ask.

Meanwhile, the coked-up guy, who had introduced himself to the detective as David Jove, has, it seems, disappeared. Some people said they saw him take off with the blanket from the bed and maybe something else. The detectives are preoccupied, trying to figure out how things could have gotten so screwed up.

The detectives tell the beat cops to move from the back of the building and guard the front. Suddenly several cars pull up at once, Hollywood cars with people pouring out of every door. Leading the mob is a familiar face, a *very* familiar face—the most well-known law enforcement face in the country, possibly the world. The two officers feel they must be hallucinating: *What is* he *doing here?*

Paul Michael Glaser approaches the officers with a worried look. He has heard bad news about a good friend and would like to know where things stand. The scene he encounters is pandemonium and the police don't seem to be doing anything to create order, much less protect the peace. In fairness, the police are vastly outnumbered. But he would like, at least, to know what happened and if there is anything he can do.

Overwhelmed by the throng, losing once and for all whatever grasp of the situation they may have had, as the crowd crushes in around them, the two officers are hit with the full weight of the knowledge that they have no idea what this place is, who this person was, what it all means, or how to proceed. Glaser opens his mouth, but before he can get a question out, or even a word, one of the officers shouts his own question over the mob's raucous din.

"What do we do, Starsky?"

Paul Michael Glaser played Detective Dave Starsky in the hit television show *Starsky & Hutch*, from 1975 to 1979. Like the dozens of other people who have come here, he was Peter Ivers's friend.

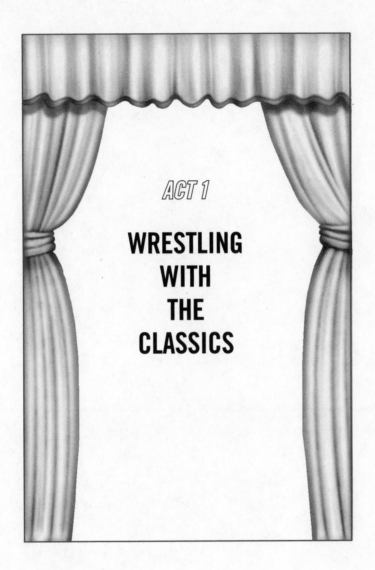

ACT 1

**WRESTLING
WITH
THE
CLASSICS**

I March Forth!

Brookline, Massachusetts, 1956, 4:15 p.m.

Merle Ivers finished up some household chores and turned to her real work of the day. Peter would be home from school soon; what music should she play for him today? She flipped through her record collection. A classical symphony, a selection of jazz standards, a Broadway show? Peter seemed to love them all as much as she did—and to appreciate them with an almost uncanny level of sophistication. In addition to music, his interests at this age included soccer and an intense preoccupation with the intricacies and nuances of human relationships. He was a small boy, but naturally active and athletic, charismatic and always well liked. And he liked the girls. It didn't hurt that he had a devastating set of what Merle had always thought of as "bedroom eyes."

Merle was open and encouraging of Peter and her daughter Ricki's interests and quirky turns of mind. She was also disciplined, at times strict, about ensuring that their minds and bodies were consistently stimulated, challenged, and engaged. She believed that children needed structure, but not because she was invested in either of her children conforming to societal norms. In a way, it was just the opposite: from her love of music she knew that structure provided the possibility for creative exploration. She felt that the right musical education would enable her children to learn this, and so she put great care into planning Peter's musical diet, carefully selecting just the right record to feed his mind and soul on any given day.

It was this core set of values, and her close relationships with her children, that had brought Merle's young family relatively unscathed through a set of very difficult years. Her first husband, Jordan Rose, was a doctor who had developed a rare cancer two years after Peter was born. They'd lived in Chicago until 1948, when the disease attacked his lungs and forced the family to relocate to Arizona, where his lungs could benefit from the clean dry air. He died a year later, a few months after Ricki's birth.

Ah, Guys and Dolls, Merle thought, sliding the show tune from the stack. *Perfect*. She held it, reconsidered, and returned it to its sleeve. *Maybe today is a better day for jazz.*

A widow at twenty-six with two young children in tow, Merle moved back in with her parents in Chicago. But she was an optimist, and she disciplined herself against despair. Only a few months after Jordan's death, she took a trip to Florida, where she met thirty-one-year-old Paul Isenstein, a former Bostonian who had retired to the bachelor's life after some early success in the textile business. Though perhaps not jazz's biggest fan—he played the reserved, conservative straight man to Merle's free spirit—Isenstein was a good man. And, most important, he was instantly and fervently *Merle's* biggest fan. Paul wanted to marry her immediately. And after getting to know him better, she was crazy for him, too. (The only thing she was not crazy for was his last name, which she found too provincial. She picked "Ivers" out of a phone book, and Paul, in his zealotry to win her over, took it on as his own.)

Nineteen-fifty—a good year for jazz, Merle thought, flipping through her records. She still had not decided what to play for Peter today.

Merle and the kids moved to Paul's apartment in Brookline, a suburb of Boston. A few years after they married, he set up his own successful business and soon moved the family into a proper house. Like his new wife, the children's education was always Paul's topmost concern.

Merle could not have been happier. Within this bubble of upper-middle-class safety and comfort, her maternal instincts took flight. She sent eight-year-old Peter and six-year-old Ricki to sleepaway camp in Maine. When Peter lost interest in recreational camping, Merle insisted he find another productive use of his time. He chose a lab-science camp. Later, when he tired of that, Merle insisted he find a job. That summer, at age fourteen, he worked at the zoo.

Paul Ivers, though by nature less demonstrative than Merle and by necessity less involved in the day-to-day parenting, was nonetheless a loving, attentive, and above all dependable father throughout Peter and Ricki's childhood years. No matter what professional responsibilities vied for his attention, he could be counted on to appear in the cheering section of any soccer game or school play.

Or, Merle mused, *maybe today is a classical day? Mendelssohn or Mozart? Symphony or sonata?*

Usually, choosing Peter's music was an almost meditative time for Merle. But today her mind was not totally at ease. A few weeks ago his fifth-grade teacher had called her in for a private conference. Swearing Merle to secrecy, the teacher pleaded with her to take Peter out of the public school system. If her advice were discovered it could mean losing her job, but she felt it would be the best thing Merle could ever do for her son. "There is no way I'm going to be able to keep him focused," she had said, "there is just not enough here to satisfy his thirst for knowledge."

Roxbury Latin was the oldest continuously running preparatory school in the country, and one of the most prestigious. The teacher felt certain that it was the only kind of environment in which Peter could truly flourish. Its entrance standards were extremely competitive, and for the last several years Harvard University had been administering aptitude tests that played a key role in the admissions process. Merle had brought both Ricki and Peter in for the test, and the results were supposed to arrive in the mail any day. Merle could frankly care less about the test per se, the status and prestige. She just wanted to provide the optimal educational environment for her kids, and she felt confident that she could get them into a good school irrespective of the results of one test.

Paul, on the other hand, saw performance on a test like this as a barometer for all future performance in life. A good score would reflect that Peter had what it took, for example, to inherit the business Paul had grown from nothing, manage it effectively, make it flourish, and provide for his family even better than Paul had been able to provide for his. Though Merle knew Paul's heart was in the right place, his anxiety over the impending test results had recently brought an edge of tension into their home.

Ah, yes, Merle thought. *This is the one. Here we go.* She drew the day's album gently out of its sleeve and blew on it lightly, clearing the dust. She fixed it in place on the player, set the needle down gently, and waited for the opening chords.

Moments later she heard Peter's footsteps tracking up the walk, through the door. When he entered the room all her worries evaporated, like ghosts exposed to daylight. His little face was so open yet so certain. Eyes voraciously curious, yet seeming to hold some profound hidden understanding. One look at him and she knew everything would be fine.

Then she realized that Peter himself did not seem totally fine, his mind appeared to be chewing on some concerns of its own. He didn't wait for her to ask what was wrong. He was worried, he told her, because he'd heard that the atomic bomb was coming and they were all going to be killed.

Merle wanted to reassure him but did not want to say something false or pat. It went against her nature and everything she believed about being a good parent. (The first and only time she had ever spanked Ricki was when, at age three, she told a lie. Peter had stood outside the house in protest, wailing, far more upset than Ricki herself.) But more important, he would see right through it. At ten, Peter had an unnervingly sharp eye for discerning falseness and authenticity. Platitudes would do nothing to calm him, but she had an idea of what would.

"Peter," Merle said. "What are you worried about? If the atomic bomb comes, we're all going to go. You won't be alone. If you go, I'm going, too. We'll all be together."

Peter focused his eyes and nodded slowly. Finally his mouth opened into a grin.

Later that afternoon, as mother and son chatted about his day to a soundtrack of jazz standards, Paul burst through the front door waving a piece of mail high in the air, his face lit up by a radiant smile.

"He's a genius!" Paul proclaimed. "Harvard says Peter is a genius!"

HEADLINES:

New York City, Alice Tully Hall, Lincoln Center, 1969

Mr. Ivers performed to a well-dressed Lincoln Center audience in what appeared to be quite a handsome pair of polka-dot pajamas and bunny-eared slippers.
        —New York Times, *1969*

PETER JOHNSON, friend from Harvard
"He would show up and wear his pajamas and play. He was outside the box. He was very short, five-two maybe, but boy, he was a dynamo. So he would come out on stage looking like a little kid in his pajamas. And he looked like a little kid, too, if you see him in pictures. So he was just working with people's expectations, and showing them life and reality outside those expectations."

MERLE IVERS
"At Lincoln Center he was asked to play the harmonica as an opening act, and it turns out he has the flu, and he's in bed with a temperature, but Stockard was there and held his hand the whole day. She was very pretty. He said, 'Mom, I've got to go, I can't not go, I have to go.' I said, 'Well, I'll make you a deal, Peter. I'll fly you over, but you have to make a deal with me that you'll fly back with me on the last plane out of New York.' He appeared in his pajamas."

BUELL NEIDLINGER, close friend, collaborator, bass player
"All the antics grew once he got to LA, from drawing circles on his nipples to opening for the New York Dolls in Hollywood with Paul Lenart."

Hollywood, The Palladium, 1974

Peter Ivers made his concert debut opening the show [for the New York Dolls]. This physically small man with a lot of energy gave an amusing performance of lighthearted comedic tunes. Gyrating up and down, he pacified an expectant audience waiting for the headliners.
        —Billboard, *1976*

PAUL LENART, musician, friend, and bandmate
"He played in diapers at this show, and he had a squirt gun in his diaper that he had gotten at a novelty shop, and it had a rubber penis on it that he put

milk in, and he would shoot it. This was in LA. This was the *Terminal Love* band, and we opened for the New York Dolls. Iggy Pop was there, others were there, we were all hanging out backstage. I was like, What am I gonna wear, if he's wearing a diaper?!"

Los Angeles, Universal Amphitheatre, 1976

STOCKARD CHANNING, college girlfriend, actress
"He went out in his diaper opening for Fleetwood Mac. I was, like, what the fuck! I didn't have any idea what to do with it, but he was like an atom, he couldn't be broken down."

> Peter Ivers filled the opening slot with a short set of hard rock plus harmonica. Ivers's stage manner was exaggerated but entertaining, the songs were distinctive and bright. "Weird" describes his effect best, probably too esoteric for the Fleetwood Mac crowd, which responded impolitely.
> —Variety, *August 30, 1976*

JELLO BIAFRA, musician, spoken-word artist, frontman for the Dead Kennedys
"Ha-Ha! [Playing in a diaper] is the kind of thing you would expect from a punk band. But number one, this was prepunk, and number two, when punk hit, his music was very different from that as well."

Los Angeles, New Wave Theatre, 1980

DURRIE PARKS, close friend, music producer
"One of my very favorite Peter Ivers memories was sitting with William Burroughs and Peter Ivers's cable show came on, the one he did in diapers. It was just a great moment. I was like, 'So, Bill, what do you think?' And he smiled."

NANCY DREW, close friend, early video/performance art patron
"Next to Andy Warhol's show, it was the most popular cable show. He and Peter were two of the most popular people."

HAROLD RAMIS, friend, comic, actor: *National Lampoon, SNL, Stripes, Ghostbusters*

"You could see it in his face, he had this kind of ironic but not hostile look. There was a lot of hostile irony at the time, especially coming from the *National Lampoon* and from New York, this kind of edgy irony. Peter was ironic without being cruel or critical, so you sort of felt kind of embraced by him."

DINAH CANCER, musician, frontwoman for 45 Grave

"Peter always asked, 'What is the meaning of life?' Asking a bunch of punk bands what the meaning of life is when they don't give a fuck about anything. I always tried to hide from him. I would get off the stage and he would run up and say, 'Hey, I want to ask you a question. What's the meaning of life?' I would say, 'I don't know! You tell me what the meaning of life is.' "

SPIT STIX, bassist for Fear

"Apparently John Belushi saw the episode where Peter comes up to Lee [Ving, Fear's frontman] and asks him what the meaning of life was. And then Lee says, 'To stay gay.' That's when John went, 'I want to meet these guys.' "

PETER IVERS INTERVIEWING LEE VING OF FEAR ON
NEW WAVE THEATRE:

PETER: What is the meaning of life?

VING: The meaning of life is . . . the meaning of life is . . . to stay gay all the way.

PETER: Well, then, you have succeeded. Lee, what do you hate least in the world?

VING: Not you.

STEVE MARTIN close friend (not to be confused with the famous actor and comedian)

"It's a fascinating detective story. Not Peter's death, but figuring out his life."

IVERS: Anyone else wanna take a crack at it . . . The meaning of life? Anyone?

chapter 2

Freshman: From the Paradise to the Gods

Cambridge, the Loeb Theater, 1965, 1:00 p.m.

Peter felt around on his work belt, found a hammer, and pounded in a nail to hang a light on the set of the latest Tim Mayer production. He called out to his friend Peter Johnson, who was working with him on the set. Nearing the end of their freshman year, they already had a nickname—"the Two Peters"—to accompany their reputation as wonder boys of technical theatre. Ivers was known for his ubiquitous carpenter's belt and his prodigious confidence. Johnson took up a position in the audience to survey the progress of their lighting arrangement.

Mayer, a junior, was a bona fide campus celebrity: a prodigy and a renegade of Harvard theatre. Some well-reviewed Gilbert and Sullivan shows his first two years had earned Mayer a reputation for insightful, professional-caliber work. Lately he had begun to take on more experimental projects. Harvard's theatre program consisted of the student-run Drama Center, which offered a fairly standard undergraduate repertoire. But now Mayer had his eye on something different, something original and uniquely his. Armed with a passionate intellect and a high-minded (if at times belligerent) charisma, he had managed to rally a core group of devotees around his self-proclaimed revolutionary dramatic vision. This group had become known around Harvard as the Tim Mayer set.

Johnson evaluated the lighting grid from the audience seating while Mayer conferred with an actress onstage, speaking closely, intimately, into her ear. Johnson nodded to Peter, who began climbing one of the frames they had built to get above the stage. He came back and joined Peter in the rafters.

The actress burst into tears.

Peter found a place in the Tim Mayer set almost as soon as he arrived at Harvard, directing the lighting design for Mayer's shows. Undaunted by the upper-class director's fearsome reputation, Peter had walked right up to him one day at the Loeb and said, "You're Mayer. I heard you're good. Real good. Well, I'm the best technical director in town." In fact, Peter had minimal background in theatre. He was, however, a natural performer with a love of all things physical, an artistic nature, and an exhibitionist streak. He spent his high school years at Roxburry Latin devouring Greek and Latin literature, writing poems, wrestling, and flirting with girls. It all came together in his love for the language and world of the ancients, whom Peter seemed to view as mentors and peers. He saw in Greek culture a purity and openness, a celebration of curiosity and frank examination of all things human that gave him something to emulate. The Greeks found wisdom in everything, and pursued it with a conspicuous lack of shame—not least in sexuality, in the wondrous pleasures of the human body. It was this classical backdrop and the cultural ethos it represented that framed and fueled Peter's passion for wrestling, which he saw as the purest sport: two bodies—in ancient times, naked bodies, perfectly sculpted human forms—grappling passionately with each other. It all struck him as beautiful and gritty, and very rock and roll. He would often tell people, "Cicero has the best rock lyrics if you can read them in the original."

He would often stage impromptu performances for his first-period class, like readings of banned Elizabethan soft porn. "Gentlemen," he would announce to a round of hormonally charged applause from his fellow students, "I present you *Fanny Hill, or Memoirs of a Woman of Pleasure,* by John Cleland, 1749." At the culmination of one such round of readings, as the heroine writhed in ecstasy and Peter's fellow students shifted restlessly in their seats, he cast his jacket off and let it fall to the floor with a commanding flourish that would have made Cicero proud. Underneath he wore a tie—and nothing else. It was a hot day, and sweat beaded down his muscular frame. His classmates rose to their feet, whistling and applauding. The class master walked in, observed the scene for a moment, and, apparently deciding he was not going to be able to beat them, joined them. It was not clear whether the standing ovation was inspired by the dirty story, the bold nonchalance of Peter's striptease, his well-toned torso, or simply the joy of watching Peter be Peter.

While a natural performer, Peter expressed only mild interest in acting and was unschooled in the technical aspects of theatre. This in part is why he had taken up lighting design to begin with: It required manual dexterity and a good eye, but little training. Lighting was a way to get involved with what to Peter seemed the most exciting thing going at Harvard. But then he met Johnson, a transfer student and a prodigy of a different sort: Johnson could build anything, do anything with his hands. In set design, as in most things he tried, Peter was a quick study. Johnson taught him how to build the most intricate sets from the most basic materials. Peter, in turn, took Johnson under his wing and introduced him around Mayer's scene. The Two Peters became a theatrical force of their own.

Peter signaled Johnson to watch the scene that was developing in the theatre below. A small crowd had formed. Mayer's plays had become so popular on campus that even his rehearsals drew spectators. The young weeping actress, Susan Stockard, composed herself and prepared to run the scene again. Two of Stockard's fellow actors, John Lithgow and Tommy Jones, big names in Harvard drama and recurring Mayer players, watched from the side. Many actors would take small roles in Mayer productions just for the sake of working with him—to be seen through his penetrating lens and cultivated under his direction. What Mayer was able to achieve onstage impressed many as extraordinary, yet so stripped down and subtle that it was difficult to isolate any particular element or technique. Many in the audience at his production of *The Tempest* walked away feeling that they had seen something unfold for the first time on any stage.

There was also an element of the grotesque built in to watching Mayer at work—or at play, or at all. A hunchback, he walked with a pronounced lurch, while chain-smoking and launching into regular coughing fits. He had an almost limp-wristed, effeminate affect and yet seemed always either to be pursuing a new (and invariably short-term) dalliance with a pretty Radcliffe girl, or bragging crudely about his latest sexual conquest. Perhaps because his physical life was so compromised, Mayer lived completely, and robustly, in the world of

letters and ideas, of uncompromising observation and verbal brinks-
manship and at times all-out psychological warfare. He could hone in
effortlessly on the dynamic in any room, on people's vulnerabilities
and strengths. Like a young superhero without control over his gifts—
but with crystal clear awareness of the power they gave him—Mayer
flung his barbed insights with wanton disregard, and at times a seeming relish, for their wounding effects. More often than not his raucous
sarcasm was also hilarious, inciting laughter from everyone except its
target.

Down on the stage, Stockard ran the scene again, again to some
point of dissatisfaction by Mayer. This time, instead of sharing his reaction privately, he spoke loudly to the assembled crowd. Peter, who
had gotten to know Stockard through the Mayer set and liked her,
swerved a spotlight down hard onto Mayer's face. In a blinding blast
of light, he called down: "Hey, Timmy, ease off—why don't you pick
on someone your father's size!"

Mayer looked up as if receiving the word of God, but unable to
quite place which sector of the heavens it was coming from.

"Ah," he said. "Mr. Ivers, master builder of the theatre. Go back
to playing with your Erector set, Mr. Ivers, and let creative souls commune in peace with the gods."

This got a big laugh from all assembled. Even Stockard laughed,
which is all Peter cared about anyway. He was one of the only people
who did not seem afraid of Mayer, freely sparring with him. And he
was one of the select few whom Mayer treated, more or less, as an
equal. Friends noted that he had a softening effect on Mayer's pronounced misanthropic tendencies. Some mutual acquaintances saw
Peter as a Peter Pan figure—a free spirit who led with his heart—to
Tim's more severe, academic Captain Hook. Peter could be as cutting
and sarcastic as Mayer, though more often than not he tended to use
his powers for good.

"Let the gods decide," Peter proclaimed with the flourish of a
diehard classics major, "which one of us is playing with himself
right now."

This got an even bigger laugh from the crowd, from Stockard and
from Mayer.

An hour later, the Two Peters had almost completed the lighting
array they'd spent the last two days setting up. Mayer was still work-

ing on the same scene with Stockard. Howard Cutler walked in, lugging a big drop he had made for the show at Peter's request. Like Peter,
Cutler, a sophomore, had found a place in the Mayer set by making
himself useful, a combination of working tech and taking minor roles
as he was needed in shows. Upon seeing Mayer's production of Brecht's
Threepenny Opera, Cutler felt that he had undergone a kind of religious conversion, a total reorientation of his aesthetic poles. Enam-
ored with the director's visionary brilliance, Cutler had no problem
accepting Mayer's imperious authority. Sometimes he would hang
back while Mayer held court in his dorm room, conducting high-level
intellectual conversations with three or four people, for three or four
hours. Mayer often held his end of the conversation from the tub,
chain-smoking and ashing into the bathwater.

The Two Peters finished their work and took another hour to help
Cutler hang his drop. Cutler had only recently gotten to know Peter. It
wasn't that Peter seemed unapproachable; he was so confident and
approachable as to seem almost larger than life. He was engaging you
and evaluating you and playing with you all at the same time, which
made him preternaturally, almost intimidatingly fun to be around—
like Mayer without the fangs.

Mayer was so engrossed in the scene with Stockard that he did not
seem to notice Cutler's new drop or the lighting set the Two Peters had
spent the last several days designing and the last several hours hanging. Peter interrupted him to get his approval on the lighting and the
drop. Mayer backed up to the edge of the stage and took it all in. After
about two and a half seconds, he cut a hand through the air.

"No, that's not right," he said. "Cut it. Make it go away."

No one missed a beat breaking down the set. As soon as it was
down, they would go back to the drawing board. Coursework would
have to wait. (It always did.) Working with Mayer might be brutal, it
might be intense, it might feel very often like a pressure cooker poised
for a violent messy scalding eruption. But it was a lot more interesting
than schoolwork. And a hell of a lot more fun.

Cambridge, Harvard Yard, 1965, 3:00 p.m.

Strolling through Harvard Yard on a perfect Cambridge spring day,
Howard Cutler drifted towards some twangy-sounding music and

discovered what seemed to be a high school jug band jamming on the stoop of Weld Hall. Cutler recently had become attuned to some of the raw, pungent sounds of Southern black music, courtesy of Tim Mayer. After rehearsal one night, Mayer had taken Cutler to Club 47 in Harvard Square to see a blues musician named Muddy Waters. Cutler was far from musically illiterate, but never in his life had he heard anything with such sheer emotional power.

Now, on the manicured Harvard grounds, he only had a moment to wonder what a group of teenagers was doing on a stoop in Harvard Yard when he noticed a familiar face among the players: Peter Ivers, on spoons. Peter was so entranced by the music that he barely seemed to notice Cutler. A kid on guitar who seemed even younger than the others motioned for Cutler to take a seat. Cutler remembered the kid—Peter sometimes brought him around the theatre, taught him tech stuff, set design, got him involved. His name was Tom Barron.

At fifteen, Barron was already known in the vibrant Cambridge music scene of 1965. Along with New York and San Francisco, Boston was one of the three pillars of the '60s American folk revival, with a heavy New Orleans influence and a strong jug band flavor. Barron had been around when Bob Dylan was discovered at Club 47; he had seen Taj Mahal get his start, and he had been with Tim Hardin when he bought his first piano. For the last two years Barron had worked stringing guitars at the Folklore Center, a bastion of Cambridge revival. His own band, the Rag Pickers, had gained some prominence around town and were featured regularly at Club 47. A jug band specializing in ragtime and blues, the Rag Pickers consisted of teenagers from a local private school. The oldest member, Dave Friedel, graduated and went to Harvard, where he was Peter's freshman-year roommate. Friedel introduced Peter to Barron, and the two struck up an instant friendship.

To Barron, Peter was someone who was always having fun, whether spontaneously striking discus-thrower poses in the middle of Harvard Square, or introducing himself to strangers with a handshake and a slogan: "My name is Peter Scott Ivers, and I take shit from no man." Peter would call Barron's house after 10:00 p.m. on a school night and invite him to join him on some spur-of-the-moment adventure. Sometimes the calls woke Barron's parents, and in any event Tom, a tenth-grader, was in for the night. But it didn't stop Peter from calling one snowy winter night from a pay phone just off Cambridge Commons. It was close to midnight, and Peter couldn't stop talking about the snowflakes; they were amazing. Tom had never known Peter to smoke pot, he'd always been a vocal opponent of drugs and alcohol and any other foreign substance that could throw off the balance of a finely tuned body and mind. But that night, Peter was either stoned or having a truly mystical, out-of-body experience—which Tom certainly would not have put past him. In a stream of consciousness that combined lyric inspiration with scientific precision, Peter explained in real time what made each falling snowflake completely unique.

"You've got to see this," Peter had said, giving play-by-play from the pay phone. "It's once in a lifetime. Here and now."

Peter took to hanging out with Barron at the Folklore Center and received a hands-on introductory workshop on Boston music. In return, he introduced Barron to the Harvard drama scene, signed him onto the tech crew, and started teaching him set design. Sometimes Peter would take him down to New York to see five plays in three days. The air of cheeky sophistication Barron sometimes saw him affect with Mayer and other Harvard friends never leaked into their relationship. Having never been trained in an instrument, Peter was more than happy to sit in with the Rag Pickers on spoons. The group's singer was a high school freshman named Kim Brody, who was dating Doug Kenney, another of Peter's dorm buddies. Kenney also sat on the stoop that day, jamming with the Rag Pickers. Like Peter, he lacked formal musical training. He was playing a comb.

Peter had plenty of reasons to feel content that day. For one, he liked Kim Brody. He liked Doug Kenney, too; they had a real ease together. Both were quick, eccentric in their own ways, and essentially uncynical and kind. Kenney was also hysterically funny, though in an almost muted way. He could communicate more with a targeted wince or mumbled, offhanded response than most people could formulate in an hour—and in doing so make a roomful of people lose their breath from laughter. He had recently been accepted on to the staff of Harvard's venerated humor magazine, the *Lampoon*.

Still, Doug would soon be going back home to the midwest for the summer. A few days after that, Tom's older brother Freddy, also a Rag Picker, was having a high school graduation party. Peter planned to ask Kim to go with him.

Another reason for Peter to feel that things were falling into place was that he had gotten into the house of his choice for next year. After freshman year, Harvard students were assigned a house for the rest of their undergraduate careers, and Adams House was known as the home for campus "artist" types.

Most important, though, was a discovery that had been brewing for a couple of months, and that Peter finally was feeling ready to fully embrace. He had discovered, he felt, an instrument—*his* instrument. Over the year, through Tom's introductions and his own breezy, comfortable way with people, he had gotten a strong taste of the local folk music and become friendly with many of its regulars. One of the musicians he had gotten to know was Al "Blind Owl" Wilson, like Peter a Boston native. One day, Wilson played Peter a blues record. The sound of the harmonica completely knocked him out: it seemed the most direct expression possible of emotion on a musical scale. Plus it was pocket-sized—just like him. His plan for the summer was to go to Tom's store, buy a harmonica, and spend every waking moment learning how to play it.

Cambridge, Harvard Dorms, 1965, 2:00 p.m.

In the spring of 1965, Peter Ivers had long hair, a scruffy beard, his eyes on a girl, and a hunger to play the blues harp. He was at the best school in the country in one of the country's hippest towns. School was almost out. His parents had a Caddy convertible and he had the keys. What else could a nineteen-year-old boy ask from summer break?

There was one nagging anxiety in his life. From the day the Harvard test crowned Peter a genius, his father's attitude towards him had changed. From Paul's perspective, being a genius carried with it certain responsibilities—in particular, academic excellence. Throughout high school, Peter excelled in the subjects that interested him and paid little attention to those that didn't. The first time Peter had brought home a C, in a high school math class, Paul took it as a personal betrayal and hung it on Peter like a scarlet letter for the rest of his high school career. "You have the IQ of a genius!" Paul had said, in what was to become the punishing refrain of their deteriorating relationship.

For Paul, there was more at stake than just Peter's intellectual growth. From his perspective, for someone of Peter's gifts anything less than straight A's bespoke laziness—a deficiency in character that Paul simply would not countenance, and that over time seemed to drive him half mad. It was only through wrought-iron diligence and an unwavering sense of responsibility to his family that Paul had managed to grow his business into what it was. And it was only because of the business that his family had everything it had. If Peter didn't feel bound by the same sense of obligation, how could he take the business over? Never mind that he did not demonstrate any interest in working in the business. This, for Paul, was the worst affront of all, but he also felt that there was time yet for Peter to come around. More immediately, a less-than-perfect academic record could have impaired Peter's chances of getting into Harvard—the only school fit for a genius, and, as Paul reminded Peter time and again, the only college he would pay for.

Paul had been happy—or at least, relieved—when his son was accepted to Harvard. But Peter's freshman-year grades were even more erratic than they'd been in high school, now that he had such demanding extracurriculars. Avid about his Greek and Latin studies—which he chose to major in partly out of passion and partly because he had read and memorized much of the classical canon throughout high school—courses in other areas received less attention. Paul saw this as a precious opportunity squandered, brazen ingratitude for his financial support, and, worst of all, confirmation of the character flaws he feared would lead Peter astray.

Then, partway through Peter's freshman year, Paul suffered a heart attack. Though he survived it, he was an almost completely changed person. His eccentricities and obsessions became intensified. His anxiety about money, for example, boiled up now to a constant roiling overflow. With Merle, he could not stop talking and worrying about the mom-and-pop stores that owed him. Merle tried with increasing stridency to remind him that they had all the money they would ever need. This was no idle speculation; Merle helped Paul in the office, she knew the books. Still, he would spend the better part of every weekend going out and making rounds to the stores, collecting on debts. Meanwhile, his anger at Peter had intensified.

But Peter wasn't thinking about Paul at the moment. He was bask-ing in his happiness in his dorm room, in the promising summer that stretched out before him—until he got a call from his mother. As soon as Peter picked up the phone he sensed something off in Merle's voice. She told him that Paul had gone to the hospital. He was stable but would have to stay for a while, no one knew exactly how long. It could be weeks. Merle paused, and Peter settled into the news with some relief. At least his father wasn't in immediate medical danger. Then: "I'm going to need your help, Peter. This summer. In the office. You're going to have to shave your beard, cut your hair, come home, put a suit on, and help me."

There was only one thing more horrific, unspeakable, and downright inconceivable than spending the summer working for his father's business. Unfortunately, that thing was saying no to his mother. So he took Kim to Freddy Barron's graduation party and wooed her, and it worked: she seemed to be wooed. And he cut his hair, and shaved his beard, and put on a suit, and went to work with his mother every day. "My perfect little gentleman," she called him. He spent the first half of the summer in the office with Merle, organizing files, before being recruited back into summer repertory theatre at the Loeb. Paul was livid; Peter was liberated; Merle was just happy he had found a constructive use of his time.

Cambridge, November 1965

No one knew where Peter had gone for the better part of the fall—only that since he came back he was different. Before stepping foot in the Loeb on his return from Brookline that summer, Peter had finally bought a harmonica. From that moment forward, any time they weren't working at the theatre, Peter and Tom Barron could be found sitting somewhere, anywhere—Peter's bedroom, Tom's parents' house, a park or random stoop—with their instruments, Tom playing licks on his guitar and Peter copying them on the harmonica.

Tom had known that Peter was smart and creative, but what he witnessed that summer was something of an entirely different order of magnitude. Peter devoured the harmonica, swallowed it whole; the process was not gradual. They would play scales over and over for hours until Peter felt he had it on his own. Nor was Peter practicing simple repetition. He did not imitate, he channeled; whatever he played he made his own. The harmonica never stood a chance. Neither did Kim Brody, who, at Peter's invitation, had come to work at the Loeb as well. The two became inseparable. Kim loved Peter's spontaneity. Sometimes they would be walking across the street, and she would turn to address Peter and find herself facing his feet: at some point, he had begun walking on his hands but continued talking normally, not missing a beat in the conversation.

Then the summer ended, sophomore year began, and a few weeks into it Peter was gone. Few people noticed, but Howard Cutler was one who did. He noticed Peter had been gone for longer than usual, and he noticed that when he got back he was different. Now, wherever he went he carried a harmonica in his pocket, and whenever he had a free second he would take it out and start playing. And the strange thing was, he could *play*. He could play Chicago blues harmonica, and he was hot. He exuded what Howard could only perceive as a kind of animal sexuality—which was not lost on many Radcliffe girls. Watching the new way women had started responding to Peter, Howard could only conclude he was getting a lot more sex than before, and a hell of a lot more sex than the rest of them. Susan Stockard was one of the few who knew where Peter had gone: to Chicago, to study and play blues harp with Muddy Waters.

This was precisely what made Peter different from the rest of the Mayer set. Sometimes, Cutler, Peter, and Mayer would go see Muddy Waters perform at Club 47. And whereas Mayer and Cutler would appreciate it deeply and expound on it for hours hence, Peter, upon the show's conclusion, would approach the bandstand and strike up a conversation with Waters—or Little Walter, or Junior Wells, or whoever was being featured that night. He would ask them about their music and about their harp technique; he would ask them where they played when they were back home in Chicago. And then, one day towards the beginning of sophomore year, he'd decided to go and find them.

close-up:

Class Acts at Harvard

Harvard's 325 years worth of alumni yearbooks fill an entire room—and yet its most famous names in popular culture fill one foot of shelf space spanning the years 1962 to 1969. These were the years that Peter and his friends graced Harvard's hallowed halls, honing their crafts and hatching their schemes to take over the theatres, cinemas, radios, televisions, and printed pages of America.

JOHN LITHGOW, colleague, actor

"It was all extracurricular—therefore, we were very full of ourselves. No one was telling us anything, we considered ourselves great geniuses. It was the most creative four years of my life. We all felt that way. I mean, anything we wanted to try, there was someone who would let us do it. There was just so much talent around, and if you wanted to do something, you could."

MARK STUMPF, college friend, *Lampoon* writer

"This is the era when John Lithgow and Stockard were big, and Tim was on top of the heap. The plays he directed were not just plays—they were events."

HOWARD CUTLER, college friend

"Peter immediately was part of this circuit, it was probably a loose coalition of around fifteen or twenty people on the theatre side. And then, through that, we would meet—here's the *Lampoon* group, and here's the newspaper guys, here's the funny guys, here's the guys who think that it's about writing novels or whatever. And we were all extremely full of ourselves, you know, I'm sure we were full of shit."

JOHN LITHGOW

"Even though Tim and I were friends, we became major figures in two different camps in Harvard theatre. Tim was much older and Brechtian, and I was more the delicate Stravinsky ballet and an operetta. He was very edgy. There were moments when we were seriously at odds with each other, but we basically stayed friends."

STOCKARD CHANNING

"I profited from being with these people like Tim, Peter, and Doug, these people that decided to dive head first into whatever they were going to dive into. They had the balls to go do it."

"I was studying Greek and Latin at Harvard, when Al Wilson of Canned Heat played me a blues record. The sound of the harmonica completely knocked me out. I picked up a harp and started playing. When Little Walter (originator of the electrified Chicago blues harp) came to town, we hung out. He told me I could never move my mouth as fast as he could move his tongue. Walter played by tongue blocking, but he was wrong. He told me to keep practicing, and I did. Before long, I was writing tunes, then lyrics. While I was looking for the right singer, I made a few demos with me singing. And people really liked the voice. It sounds like Howling Wolf, if he inhaled helium."

—*Peter Ivers, Warner Bros. Press Release*

case book part 1

DETECTIVE CLIFFORD SHEPARD, LAPD Cold Case Division
"I was living in the area at the time. In '83 I was working
at city hall, communications center. I remember hearing
over the radio as I was on my way to work that day downtown,
in Central Division. I recalled the TV program, *New Wave
Theatre*, and I remember thinking, Why would a person be
living on Skid Row where all the dope addicts are running
around? And then I didn't hear anything about it again."

* * *

DETECTIVE HANK PETROVSKY, Lead detective, Robbery/
Homicide LAPD
"They needed a guy in the robbery unit. So they hired me,
and I wasn't there a week, and my boss says he's going to
switch me over to Homicide. I say no, I don't like dead
bodies. He told me I'd get used to it. I asked him if I
couldn't take it, if I could go back to Robbery. But once
I got into it, I decided there was nothing better. The game
of catching the guy is so interesting . . .

"This happened in Central Division, the lofts over
there. I am notified by my lieutenant, get your butt over
there and handle it. Robbery homicide, we handle the high
media-type cases. That's why we got the case, because he
was an MTV-type guy.

"When I arrive at the loft, there were lots of guys
there, and we had to get them out of the place. You don't
want people walking around a crime scene. Patrol officers
are there, they secure the scene as best they can."

PETER RAFELSON, friend and collaborator
"It was absolute chaos. I was one of the first to find out
directly from the police, and they asked me to come down.
A lot of people showed up, fans, friends, word spread very

quickly and they had to basically shut down the area because it was getting out of control."

LINDA PERRY, friend, music publisher
"They let people walk through the crime scene, immediately!"

VAN DYKE PARKS, friend, collaborator, composer
"The room was contaminated."

PETER RAFELSON
"People were crying and fainting, it was just like a movie."

DETECTIVE HANK PETROVSKY
"I take small steps to see what there is from the elevator to the door, going slowly, looking for anything. Once entering the door to the loft, you are just looking around right and left. You see what you see or what you don't see. The loft itself was kind of empty, nothing fancy, you just figured it was a starving artist. It didn't seem he was well off because nothing showed me he was. It was a guy struggling to make bucks in whatever endeavor he was trying to do, but it didn't seem he had made it at that point. I figured he was an arty type because that's who lives in these lofts."

HOWARD SMITH, friend, collaborator
"It was suggested by the cops themselves that Peter was some kind of freak. That just horrified us beyond belief."

HAROLD RAMIS
"That's what [the police] wanted to believe: that he was a hippie, punk, pervert, drug user who deserved what he got."

DETECTIVE CLIFFORD SHEPARD
"Most of the time when you have a murder, the victims are doing something they shouldn't be doing, or involved in

something. Not always, but a lot of our murders have victims involved in similar activities. It's a matter of life-style."

DETECTIVE HANK PETROVSKY

"We know somebody reported this, so we want to talk to that person, like, How do you know this guy and why were you there?"

JIM TUCKER

"So I'm standing in the kitchen at noon and Anne Ramis calls. She says, I haven't heard from Peter in a while, check on him."

ANNE RAMIS

"I had been trying to get in touch with him so that we could get together, and he hadn't called. We were supposed to get together that day. I remember he used to go real early to his karate class, so I hadn't heard from him, and it just wasn't like him. It was rainy, so I was afraid he had gotten into a car accident in the rain. I kept calling the guy next door. Finally at three o'clock I got in touch with Tucker. I said I think there's something wrong, and he said, Do you have any reason to think so? And I said, Yes."

JIM TUCKER

"So I go in, and I find him, and then I call 911. And I'm standing out in front of the building, waiting for paramedics, and Barry Farr, who lived in the loft across the elevator, drives up in his caravan with his students from the art institute. I tell him what happened, and they all run upstairs and go in the room before the police get there, like, Oh my God, let's go look at it. Then the paramedics come, and I take them up, and the police come, and they chase everybody out and tape it off. Then the circus starts, all these people came, all day long, pouring in. There were forty people in there by the evening."

DETECTIVE HANK PETROVSKY
"Then from that person you ask who his friends or business associates are. They lead you to other people to talk to, and you end up talking to anybody you can that knows anything."

JIM TUCKER
"They questioned everyone that came in that night. I stood there and watched them question Harold Ramis. He was a suspect because his wife was very close to Peter. Peter gets killed, and then Harold is in the middle of this and he's like, Fuck, I've got movies to do, what is this shit?"

HAROLD RAMIS
"I learned secondhand that for the first weekend I was the number one suspect. They thought I had killed Peter because I was jealous. Very far from the truth. Even the jealousy thing. It was a mystery and a tragedy that the police couldn't solve."

DETECTIVE HANK PETROVSKY
"These lofts were so big, and you didn't have a next-door-neighbor kind of thing, but we did talk to people that lived in the building. I don't believe anyone saw or heard anything."

RICHARD GREENE, musician, collaborator, and friend
"They didn't do a damn thing. We were first on the scene, and we had all kinds of ideas and everything, and nothing was followed up."

DETECTIVE CLIFFORD SHEPARD
"When they finally get back to the station, they make what is called a murder book. They put together their notes and start the reports being made and begin a chronology."

DETECTIVE HANK PETROVSKY
"It's a looseleaf binder, one of those thick ones, and you keep a log. The first officers at the scene keep a log, like,

"Got a call at 4:00, arrived at 4:15, a log about everything that happened until we get there, and then they hand us this log of events. In the meantime, we keep a log of everything we're doing, but sometimes we wouldn't write it until getting back to the office."

PETER RAFELSON
"The investigation had begun and it was just this labyrinth, this network of people and all kinds of leads, both anonymous and discovery. I mean, it was just a cluster fuck of information surrounding this one."

chapter 3

"Undergraduates Are Not Allowed to Rent Elephants."
(FINDING THEIR INNER ELEPHANT AT HARVARD)

Cambridge, 1966, 10:00 p.m.

While happy to accept the minor celebrity garnered by his head-turning ascent on the blues harp, Peter also would have been the first one to admit he hadn't gotten there alone. First among the blues legends he had befriended was Little Walter, legendary originator of the electrified Chicago blues harp. Peter had introduced himself to Walter after a Boston show, and subsequently arranged gigs for him whenever possible at local clubs. His motivations were partially selfish: whenever Walter came in from the Windy City, he would give Peter lessons.

Only in his mid-thirties, Little Walter had already amassed a lifetime's worth of achievement and consumed several lifetimes' worth of booze. Starting in 1948 in Muddy Waters's band, he helped form what would become the most celebrated blues ensemble in history. He toured with Waters and recorded with him on his classic early-'50s albums before striking out on his own to instant, overwhelming success. His first single became the first harmonica instrumental ever to top the R&B charts, followed by fourteen Top Ten hits and three number ones. While working with Waters, Walter had experimented with holding a microphone in his hand while he played, eventually innovating (and becoming the first to record) an amplified harp sound that achieved a saxophonelike richness and nuance never heard before on the instrument. The sound became his signature, and Little Walter gained wide recognition as the best blues harmonica player of all time. He continued to work with Waters and record his own chart-topping solo hits until the ascendance of rock and roll in the late '50s eclipsed the electrified blues and sent Waters, Walter, and a whole generation of bluesmen into commercial purgatory and often, as in Walter's case, financial ruin.

By the time Peter met Walter, the bluesman was sick and frail, a physical shell whose lifelong alcoholism had begun to exact its toll in earnest. Infamous for being a mean, violent drunk whom only Muddy Waters could appease or control, he was all the more embittered for being largely forgotten, spit ashore by the brutal indifference of pop culture tides. While remaining a cult hero in blues havens like Chicago and Boston, on a national scale the once-icon had become a relative unknown.

Peter brought Walter to Boston as often as possible and treated him with the reverence due a master. He led Walter around Cambridge with the eager tenderness of a doting son, and the two would talk for hours.

Peter and Kim had become seriously involved, and their life together was filled with music in all forms. Music wasn't just something they enjoyed together, it was a soul-connecting passion, a language they shared. They would sit for hours in his dorm room listening to records, jazz, blues, which Peter would sometimes stop and play over and over until he learned it on harp. While amazed at his prowess, as far as Kim was concerned Peter's technical ability was the least of his gifts. Somehow he had managed to tap into the instrument's essence. When he played, it was performance in the richest sense: his whole body was the instrument. Something about his presence with the music made the experience of watching him play not just beautiful, but, for Kim, transporting.

Doug Kenney's Room, 1967, 4:00 a.m.

It was late at night, early-morning late, but Doug Kenney wasn't going to bed anytime soon. He had a mission, he had all the tools he needed to accomplish it—multicolored markers and a hefty supply of weed— and he was not going to rest until he found the answers he was looking for. Failure was not an option.

His mission: to figure out who was fucking whom.

It was summer in Cambridge, and the *Harvard Lampoon* staff, tasked with working on the next magazine parody, had rented a communal house. The country's oldest collegiate humor magazine, the *Lampoon* had languished in relative obscurity even among Harvard students until the previous year, when the *Harvard Lampoon Parody of Playboy*—a stand-alone issue dedicated solely to aping the iconic men's magazine—had caught fire, selling out newsstands nationally. In addition to its dead-on satire of *Playboy*'s content (including, for example, a lengthy parody of a James Bond–type thriller called "Toad-stool," and a picture of Henry Kissinger splayed out on a bearskin rug, wearing a thong), the issue had included pictorial spreads with real nudes, many of whom were friends and girlfriends of the all-male *Lampoon* staff.

Doug had joined the *Lampoon* at the beginning of his sophomore year and quickly established himself as a major force. His task for the summer was to get the next magazine parody (target: *Life* magazine) off the ground. He and about seven other Lampooners had rented the house, which in no time had become a local haven for all manner of friends, girlfriends, and hangers-on. The door was always open, and everyone seemed to be having sex with everyone else. Tonight, Doug had decided, he was going to tame the madness with a healthy dose of method. So he took out his markers, he took out his weed, and he started drawing a mural-sized graph on the wall listing all the relevant characters by name and recording who, exactly, had been with whom. He had just gotten started when someone knocked on the door. It was Peter.

Doug had not been happy to return for his sophomore year of college to find Kim, his erstwhile girlfriend, in love with Peter. Still, neither was about to let it get in the way of the friendship they had struck up the year before. It was not their brief history that kept the connection between them intact as much as a palpable sense of future potential, an intuition on both their parts of having found that rarest thing: a kindred spirit.

Peter looked up at the wall where Doug had begun his graph, and down at the unconcealed baggy on the floor. He smiled and rubbed his chin in scholarly appreciation. "Interesting." He let Doug get back to his important work and watched on in silent support.

Depending on the angle and the moment one caught a look at them, Peter and Doug could seem either an odd couple—an attraction of opposites—or a well-matched set. Kim Brody was attracted to the same things in both of them: the boyish free spirits housing minds that were subtle and searching, continuously surprising, awesomely vast and vastly, awesomely offbeat. Chris Hart, who was friends with both, saw them as rarities and geniuses whose backgrounds, intellects, and jet-fueled imaginations rendered them perennial outsiders. They were both sentimental, empathic, and openhearted, though they could also be cutting, and did not suffer ignorance, intolerance, or any form of authority gladly. When Mayer was around (he had become close friends with Kenney as well, and the three of them together were referred to in their circles as "the three musketeers"), they didn't suffer it at all.

Peter had stopped by to return some camouflage fatigues and an army helmet. He and Doug had spent much of the afternoon in the woods with Kim Brody, her little sister and brother, and a *Lampoon* photographer. The combat clothes were pint-sized. Kim's younger siblings had worn them in the shoot, for a photo spread satirizing the Vietnam War. They chatted briefly and said good night. It was late, and Doug was eager to get back to his important work.

Like Peter, Doug was gregarious and sociable. A Catholic prep school boy who'd been raised in Ohio, he seemed to Chris Hart a kind of "innocent abroad," wide-eyed and eager to take it all in. A few years younger than Doug, Hart was the son of entertainment industry royalty and had been weaned on Manhattan socialite culture. As far as he was concerned, Doug was, quite simply, the most talented person he had ever met. (As the son of award-winning playwright and screenwriter Moss Hart and Broadway legend Kitty Carlisle Hart, his assessment carried some heft: he had already met many extremely talented people in his young life.) Doug managed to make associations that to Hart indicated a subtle comic mind. His phrasing of offhand observations often left Hart feeling stunned: *How did he put those two things together in the middle of a conversation?*

The mural was coming together. Certain patterns were starting to emerge, though it was too early to say anything definitive. Well, *one* thing could be said pretty definitively: Doug was not getting a fraction of the action his housemates were getting. And Peter . . . forget about it. Of course, Peter was a musician. One couldn't really compare.

Coming from Brookline—sheltered, idyllic, Jewish—Peter was also a kind of immigrant into the world of New England WASP culture. Like Doug, he was eager to take it in and experiment with it. But if both had the capacity to operate and succeed famously in these strange new settings, their methods were essentially mirror images of one another. Doug's great strength was as a mimic. He could imitate any style, any voice, in writing and in speech, and play with it with total control. Since he joined the *Lampoon*, his dead-on parodies of the characters and institutions of campus life reflected and honed this native talent to great effect (and great response: he had already begun to build a name among students, who eagerly anticipated his next devastatingly accurate and hilarious take on their world).

But for Peter there was only one voice, his own. He wasn't trying to fit in as much as put himself all out there, sensitive to people's reactions but seemingly indifferent to their approval. Doug was a masterful chameleon; Peter was more like a peacock, feathers perpetually in full plume.

Doug's mural now took up most of the wall. Something interesting was happening. It had to do with Peter Gabel. It was amazing. But could it possibly be true?

It might be said that while Peter and Doug both encountered the world around them with great curiosity and zeal, Doug processed it from the outside in, while Peter did so from the inside out. Doug was a keen observer of the popular culture, which he consumed, digested, and regurgitated as satire through his biting fun-house lens. Peter's obscure intellectual interests, experimental nature, and soulful bent led him outside the cultural mainstream.

Doug surveyed his work. Peter Gabel—he was everywhere. The son of legendary actress and TV personality Arlene Francis and the actor Martin Gabel, Gabel held the position of ibis, the *Lampoon*'s equivalent of vice president. The previous year, he and *Lampoon* president Jonathan Cerf had appeared on the popular game show *What's My Line?* on which Peter's parents and Jonathan's father (Random House founder Bennett Cerf) were regular panelists. Gabel, who along with Chris Hart was a ready participant in the *Lampoon*'s student-populated nude photo spreads, recently had received less desirable attention when Hart returned to *Lampoon* headquarters after a phone conversation with his mother. Kitty Carlisle Hart had just taken a limo ride with her friend Truman Capote, who could barely contain his glee at being the one to inform her that he had seen her little boy naked in a nationally distributed magazine with Peter Gabel.

Whether Doug's natural mimicry reflected some deeper emptiness is a matter of speculation; what was always clear to his friends is that he was plagued by bouts of intense self-loathing. He sometimes told stories about difficulties with his parents, or about his sick brother, but those were not subjects he generally liked to talk about. He used substances (primarily marijuana) with regularity and zeal, and while there was nothing unusual about recreational drug use by the time Doug was in college, some friends saw it as a coping mechanism that masked deeper, darker currents. Chris Hart, who was in psychoanalysis at the time, suggested Doug give it a try. (He declined, fearing it might dull his creativity.) Though generally friendly and warm, Doug had sharp edges that would come out occasionally, fits of harshness that betrayed simmering frustrations and at times even rage.

It was almost dawn at *Lampoon* headquarters, morning light was filtering into the sky. The mural was done. Doug had created a clear, comprehensive graph visually documenting every *Lampoon*-associated coupling since the summer began. He stood back and surveyed his work, checking and rechecking for mistakes. But it was all there, incontrovertible.

Every arrow led to Peter Gabel.

Doug went to bed, exhausted but satisfied, at least, at having brought a modicum of order to his chaotic little corner of the world.

Adams House, 1968, 9:30 p.m.

Peter was exhausted but could not sleep. He sat up in the bed of his Adams House dorm room, the comfort of his upper-class digs not enough to quell his inner tumult. He had just returned from a family dinner where his father had brought him to tears. Paul had always made clear that he thought Peter was wasting his time at Harvard on dead languages and artsy extracurriculars. He told Peter that he was accomplishing nothing and would become nothing, that he regretted every cent he had spent on his Ivy League education. That when friends asked him about his son, he changed the subject.

Academics were not the only point of contention between them.

Paul rarely missed an opportunity to express his disapproval of the way his son dressed. During high school, Peter's personal style became increasingly flamboyant, and Paul's confusion and horror over his insistence on being "different" (rooted, at least in part, in the awareness shared by so many men of his generation of how easy it was to fall through the societal cracks, and how dire the consequences could be) came out as contempt and rage. Of course, in a time-honored father-son dynamic, this only pushed Peter further into himself. He had developed an obstinate insistence on doing things his way, consequences be damned. Anything was better than to lose himself to the strict expectations of his father, or anyone else.

The most important of Paul's expectations was the source of tonight's blowup. As he saw it, the natural step following graduation was for Peter to come work for him, learn the business, and eventually inherit it. It was an unforgivable slight that Peter seemed to have a different idea. Peter was reminded of another family dinner, freshman year, when he had stormed out in tears, threatening to join the military. It was a testament to how deeply Paul's disappointment had burrowed under his skin—and the lengths he was prepared to go to get away from it—that some part of him actually had meant it. Tonight had been no different. If Paul's strident insistence that Peter come work for him was driven in part by a desire to be close to his son, his actions had the opposite effect. They only cemented Peter's opposition to all the values he espoused, and his resolve to get as far away from him as possible.

Hamilton, Bermuda, spring 1968, 1:15 a.m.

The bar had stopped serving liquor, the band had stopped playing, and Peter and his friends were the only white people left in the club. It was Hasty Pudding Theatricals' annual spring tour to Bermuda, and this wasn't part of the official itinerary. Peter had urged everyone to come out. They had been okay, for the most part, drinking a few beers at the club. Hamilton, Bermuda's only real town, had plenty of tourists, and the tourists were out. But it was past last call, and the atmosphere seemed to be getting more . . . private. The crowd moved upstairs, to an after-hours room, where the band could keep playing.

Peter was not about to miss it. The other Puddings were wary, but his enthusiasm, as usual, proved infectious. They followed him upstairs.

The longest-running student theatrical troupe in America, Hasty Pudding Theatricals (known around campus simply as "the Pudding") was another high-powered extracurricular nexus point. The Pudding was something of a throwback, putting on a yearly musical burlesque filled with crude collegiate humor, farcical plots with quaint puns, and female parts played by actors in drag. For the students who wrote, composed, and performed the plays, though, all this retro fun was serious business.

Chris Hart was in Bermuda that spring on a trip with his family, and hooked up with the Pudding that night. He followed Peter upstairs with the rest of them. As the band alternated between jazz standards and reggae, sometimes combining different elements of the two, people danced. It was a laid-back vibe, and the students relaxed and started dancing, too. Then Peter nonchalantly stood up, approached the bandleader, pulled a harmonica out of his pocket, and asked if he could jam with them.

The Pudding contingent stopped dancing. Peter's request could be taken in any number of ways, plenty of them offensive. They were the only white people left in the place, after all, Harvard kids far away from home. *What did Peter think he was doing?* They were used to his quirky, offbeat ways on campus and around the set, but here a warm reception was much less certain. Some of them knew he dabbled in the harmonica. But could he really play? They went silent waiting for the bandleader's response. He shrugged. *Why not?*

What ensued was, Hart felt, like nothing so much as the classic movie sequence that starts out with an entire floor of dancers, until slowly the floor clears and the camera pans out to reveal a circle of awed spectators around the two breakout stars.

Because now nobody in the club was dancing. They all just stood and watched Peter play.

Cambridge, 1967–1968

Buell Neidlinger thought he must be having déjà vu. Just a month ago, around Thanksgiving, he had been approached backstage at the Boston Symphony Orchestra, for which he played bass, by a young hippie with big hair who stood out considerably among all the penguin coats and striped pants of Neidlinger's fellow players. The hippie had called him the "greatest fucking bass player in jazz" and asked if he would play with his band.

The hippie's compliment wasn't idle flattery, and it was not news to Neidlinger. At thirty-one, he was already a formidable presence in the world of instrumental music—"an animal on the instrument," in one aficionado's words. He was also sharp-tongued and egotistical, well aware of his place in the music world and quick to put others in theirs. When, as often happened, someone would attempt to pay him a compliment by telling him he was a better bassist than Paul McCartney, he'd answer coolly, "That is not saying as much as you would like it to say about me."

A cello prodigy as a child, Neidlinger had studied under some of the greatest living classical string players. In his early teens he'd discovered jazz bass, and ever since had been studying, performing, and recording with world-class musicians and composers in both fields. (Cecil Taylor, Gunther Schuller, Ornette Coleman, Igor Stravinsky, Tony Bennett, Billy Holiday, John Cage). He had only recently arrived in Boston; this was his first season with the BSO. He was teaching at the New England Conservatory of Music to make ends meet. Now Neidlinger, a world-class musician playing with a world-class symphony, was being invited to play in a basement with a scruffy hippie.

He followed the hippie to his basement.

Neidlinger was new in town, single, and loved to play. By nature he was a bohemian jazz man, married to the music and accountable to little else. So he went with the hippie to his Cambridge basement. As it turned out, the hippie's name was Victor McGill, and as it turned out his band, the Far Cry, was one of the two most popular in Cambridge.

That had been about a month ago. Now it was around Christmas, the fourth or fifth concert of the season, and here again was Victor McGill waiting for him backstage. Only this time Victor had brought a friend, not a hippie, but a clean-cut college kid. Only the college kid didn't just want to tell Neidlinger how great he was, and he didn't just want to jam with him. He wanted Neidlinger to give him music lessons. Neidlinger lived nearby, so he invited the kid over. The kid had a harmonica with him, and they played the blues together for a while.

Buell lived on the top floor of an old apartment near Fenway Park. During baseball season, every time a slugger connected they could hear the crisp crack of the bat.

The kid was Peter Ivers, and Neidlinger agreed to give him music lessons, whatever that meant. From then on Peter would come over regularly, lug his little Farfisa keyboard up in the rickety elevator, and Neidlinger would show him keyboard harmony, things like what a minor chord was, because all Peter knew was the harmonica part. He was a talented player, but his formal knowledge of music was virtually nil.

Even so, it might have seemed a strange time for Peter to start taking lessons. Musically, he was at the top of his game. The other most popular band in Cambridge besides the Far Cry was the Street Choir, in which Peter played harmonica.

Though he had been playing harp nonstop since picking it up two years ago, it hadn't occurred to him to join a band. In fact, he was "discovered" by lead guitarist John Hillman playing on the subway. A keyboardist Peter knew, Mike Tschudin, had been talking to a young, charismatic playwright he knew named Gilbert Moses about starting a band. One of the innovators of Free Southern Theatre, an activist theatre company that toured the Deep South to challenge embedded views about race, Moses was thoughtful and passionate about social change and believed theatre could play a vital role. As a musician, Moses could write, sing, and play bass. The band would play a hard, fast-driving blues rock with occasional forays into the improvisational wilds of modern jazz.

At their first public gig, an Adams House mixer—and mixer crowds were notoriously desultory in their attention to the band, viewing them essentially as suppliers of mood music to soften the stale edges around old pickup lines—90 percent of the crowd stopped dancing, stood around the stage, and just watched. A *Harvard Crimson* review of the show raved in precise and fulsome detail about the members' strengths, both as soloists and as a "pulsating unity." It described Peter as "a classics major who looks like a cross between Dennis the Menace and a Marvel superhero," his soloing as "the most aggressive, playing harp at capacity volume, punctuating his solos with sharp staccato blasts shaking him from head to toes." The set was all original, diverse arrangements ranging from blues ballads to wistful humor, with one exception. When some of the students began to get restless and make insistent requests for "Louie Louie" or "something we can dance to," the band finally relented and covered a Rolling Stones tune. At which point Peter holstered his harp and accompanied his bandmates with a running chorus—screamed directly at the audience—of "I hate this song!" Nonetheless, the *Crimson* reported that the last set was followed by a "tidal wave" of applause. That was two months ago. The more they played together, the better they got.

Though known to wield an ego in direct proportion to his considerable talent, Moses instantly fell in love with Peter, who loved him right back. In fact, it may have been at least in part his respect for Moses that prompted Peter to seek musical instruction from Buell Neidlinger in the first place—just two months into his highly successful first band, which was gaining steady momentum in both virtuosity and popularity, and no obvious end in sight. For while Peter loved to jam on the harp, there was a lot more that he wanted to say. And while he had apprenticed with some of the great blues players, he did not know a thing about composition.

Neidlinger seemed happy to help. He embraced the role of mentor not only to Peter, but to a community of younger musicians including members of the Far Cry, with whom he jammed fairly regularly. His credentials secured them local TV tapings and periodic performances at a respected concert hall.

Peter was growing as a musician. His combination of personal authenticity, raw talent, and commitment to craft had served him well throughout the previous three and a half years at Harvard. Now it made him a standout in the Cambridge music scene as well. One night he brought Merle to a gig in a cellar somewhere in town and introduced her to a friend from the scene. "Bonnie, I want you to meet my mother," he said. "Mom, this is my friend Bonnie Raitt."

Raitt looked at Merle and smiled. "Peter," she said, "you are the only person in the world I would believe when they introduce me to someone and tell me it's their mother."

Cambridge, Unicorn Club, 1968, 10:00 p.m.

It was a weeknight at the Unicorn Club, and Street Choir had finished their set. Peter sat in the audience sipping an orange soda (his drink of choice) when the next act came onstage. It was a white guy with a crew cut, older, dressed like a square and blind as a bat. Introduced as George Leh (pronounced *Lay*), he proceeded to deliver a set of the most dead-on, soul-lifting, gut-churning Georgia blues since Ray Charles, whom he seemed to be channeling. Peter approached Leh after his set to tell him how much he liked the way he sang. Leh told Peter he liked the way he played harp. A friendship was born.

George Leh was an anomaly in the hip Cambridge music scene. He just happened to love the blues and to possess a strange, incongruous gift for singing it right. He had the respect of fellow musicians but wasn't friends with them. A one-man show, disconnected from any kind of musical community, he got little feedback and did not even hold his own talent in particularly high regard. He did it because he couldn't not do it. He came to the clubs, played his sets, and went home.

Peter found this situation completely unacceptable and immediately set out to rectify it. He would invite Leh to meet for coffee and talk about music. But his real agenda was to impress upon Leh that he had something to offer that people were looking for, that they were waiting for, that they *needed*. Leh should meet this producer and work with that musician, Peter would set it up. Leh was skeptical at first. As he told Peter with a raw smile, "I may be blind, but I know what I look like." It was 1968 and George Leh had a crewcut. What else was there to say? Eventually Leh gave in and let Peter introduce him around. The response was unequivocal and swift: Leh was swooped up and cradled into the bosom of Cambridge music.

To Peter, underutilized potential was a tear in the fabric of the cosmos. He saw himself as an agent of repair, and did what he could to line up the seams. There was no clear line between being an artist, a catalyst, a collaborator, and a friend. Some of his Harvard classmates met Leh, some of his musician friends remember seeing him perform. But the image that impressed itself upon nearly everyone's memory, and would remain etched there for decades to come, was of Peter walking and talking with the blind white bluesman, accompanying him to gigs, leading him around Cambridge by the hand.

Signet Society, 1968, 9:00 p.m.

Peter unlocked the door to the Signet Society and started letting everyone in. He had managed to secure a key to the building, though no official event had been scheduled or planned. Even his friends, who were far from official, had not been given much advance notice. Peter had a pied piper's talent for organizing large groups of people to follow him on spontaneous trips. Some weekends he would decide that his entire circle of friends should take a road trip out to Western Mass, to see the mountains and the sky. A caravan would be organized within the hour.

Peter led George Leh by the arm into the Signet study, whose walls were lined with books and signed pictures of famous literary figures who had spoken there. The Signet was a student society. Only members and their guests were permitted in, and even those only during certain hours. Peter gave the guest policy a broad interpretation, and the hours he simply ignored. Neidlinger followed in behind Leh, set down his bass, and took a seat in a comfortable chair beneath a filigree plaque designed by Signet alum Edward Gorey.

Peter took a swig of his orange soda and watched the other musicians settle in. Paul Lenart, of the Far Cry, slid his guitar out of its case and took a seat.

Gil Moses came in, along with John Hillman, the Street Choir guitarist. Kim Brody showed up. Tom Barron popped in. Tim had a rehearsal, and Doug was working late on the *Lampoon,* but both said they would try and stop by later to check it out.

It might not be inaccurate to call Peter a child of the '60s, though in many ways the '60s had been lagging behind him and were finally catching up: Peter had been Peter, after all, for quite some time. Still, by the time he graduated in spring '68, the '60s were in full swing. He, Tim, and Doug never officially joined the counterculture—Peter, who maintained his body with meticulous discipline and care, was outspoken in his opposition to drugs—but they were as committed as anyone to overturning the familiar and inventing new worlds. Doug had begun working on starting a national version of the *Harvard Lampoon* to expose hypocrisy through satire. Tim had started his own theatre company, customized to his vision and accountable to no one, and it was just beginning to kick into gear. Peter seemed able to master anything he touched, and soon he would be writing his own songs.

The kids were not necessarily all taking drugs, but they were certainly taking over.

Neidlinger stood up with his bass, surveyed the room, and started a beat; the assembled musicians felt their way towards an old blues riff. As they found each other, the music gained confidence, volume, and form. Signed pictures of literary luminaries bounced and rattled on the walls. The jam went late into the night.

---
close-up:

The Three Musketeers

You, boy . . . are selfish, pig-headed, and arrogant . . . I like that . . . it reminds me of me!
  —*Porthos,* The Three Musketeers

"Tim said something about the three of them. He, Doug and Peter were like the Three Musketeers. But he said Peter was like the North Star."
  —*Anne Ramis*

THE HARVARD LAMPOON

Rich and jubilant after a tremendously successful *Playboy* parody, the Poonies hired elephants and specially designed bows and arrows to reenact the great [Battle of Hastings] right here at Cambridge-on-the-Charles. . . . What stopped the warriors from their brave encounter? They were refused permission from University Hall. . . . "Undergraduates are not allowed to rent elephants."

—*Betsy Nadas, "Salute to Times Past: The Lampoon Ibis"*
  The Crimson, *June 3, 1968*

JOHN LANDIS, filmmaker
"You know everything you need to know about Doug when you find out that he was tennis pro at a golf club in Ohio. He learned everything then. Doug was the wittiest person I think I ever met."

HOWARD CUTLER
"The *Lampoon* is a source for *The Simpsons*, and Conan O'Brien. But it's a different generation now. The president, to give you some idea how that moves, the president of the *Lampoon*, a year or two before I got there, was the guy who's now Dr. Andrew Weil."

CHRIS HART

"Doug and Peter were both just really smart, creative people, and they got each other, they saw the world in similar ways. They were hipsters who were very sweet at heart, they weren't cynical about the world. That was quite an amazing thing about them."

A Boston Sound in the Key of Peter

GEORGE LEH

"The music scene in Boston was pretty eclectic. There were lots of blues, lots of folk music, jazz was pretty much in demand, and it was kind of like a resurrection of renaissance, with bluegrass coming into fruition."

VAN DYKE PARKS

"Everyone felt he could do everything Bob Dylan could and get away with it. So we became bombarded by self-congratulatory songwriters. They had no right to self-congratulation. Everybody was playing guitar all of a sudden. I think that might have been a reason Peter would have taken a road less traveled and chosen to play the instrument he did."

MERLE IVERS

"When he was at Harvard, he decided he would like to play a musical instrument, so he called me and he said, 'I saw this fellow that plays harmonica and he told me he'd teach me how to play.' He said, 'I think it's a pretty good idea because it's so portable and it won't cost a heck of a lot of money.' And I said, 'That's wonderful dear, fine.' The next thing I knew, everyone was telling me that he had become a virtuoso over the next few years at the harmonica."

VAN DYKE PARKS

"Another thing I liked about his championing of the harmonica is that it was this fragile little relic of the quintessential American pie. He played it as a professional, not just as an afterthought. I felt like Peter really knew how to play the harmonica, and few people did at that time. It had a tremendous, melodic, haunting, emotive force when he wanted it to. He was absolutely a cut above on his harmonica."

GIL MOSES
"Peter was already one of the best harp players in the country."

PAUL LENART, Far Cry guitarist, later bandmate
"There was word out that there was this other band on [the scene] called the Street Choir, and I had heard a little bit about Peter. I ran into him a couple of times. You could never miss him because he had a swagger to him, and he was always onstage. He had a lot of confidence in himself."

HOWARD CUTLER
"You have these guys like Mayer, who are a couple of years ahead and who have been the charismatic center of it, but they aren't the ones—a little bit like Peter—they aren't the ones that become the figures in the larger culture. And, you know, one way to look at it is, you know, someone gets famous and some of them don't. Some of them are more talented and some of them aren't. But it's a more complicated story than that."

case book part 2

DETECTIVE CLIFFORD SHEPARD

"In the '70s and '80s . . . Skid Row was a violent place to be, you had a lot of different people. A lot of violent people that carry knives and guns, that's how they survived. Burglarizing, robbing, and sometimes selling drugs, all downtown. There were bars that were nothing but problems, there were shootings and stabbings all the time."

* * *

DETECTIVE HANK PETROVSKY

"Me and my partner, after seeing what we saw, we were thinking it was possibly a burglar, I believe his stereo equipment was missing, and that's the direction we were going."

HUDSON MARQUEZ, Artist, friend

"I always thought the cops treated it like any other guy downtown, like it was some kind of burglary."

JIM TUCKER

"Half the police force lives in suburbia, they aren't of the [downtown] community. They work from a completely different habitation mind-set, and I think it affects how they do their police work."

LUCY FISHER

"They consistently characterized the murder as having been the random result of a robbery by a downtown drug addict who might already be dead himself. They kept stressing that there were approximately eighty homicides in that area that year, and oftentimes the police couldn't even identify the victim, much less the perpetrator."

DETECTIVE HANK PETROVSKY

"What happened was that we started checking all burglaries in that area, and a lot of lofts had been burglarized because they weren't very secure places. We never recovered the stereo equipment. Why would a friend or associate take his stereo equipment? You could say they wanted to make it look like a burglary, but if it was in the heat of passion, you don't plan it. I don't know if there was anything there, he didn't have a lot of stuff. You get these burglars just looking to sell something for twenty or thirty bucks, so their mentality is difficult."

JOHANNA WENT

"I remember when he told me he was going to move down there, I knew the neighborhood wasn't good. The building I think had several break-ins over the months, and the security wasn't good in the building."

HUDSON MARQUEZ

"I didn't find anything particularly weird about it, because he lived downtown. I always remembered that his door was unlocked. Living downtown with your door unlocked, I find it to be, you know, foolish, very foolish. That was a mistake and it was a crime of opportunity. I totally pooh-poohed this whole silly bunch of things like, Who killed Peter Ivers?"

JIM TUCKER

"We chased a guy out of the loft one night. Anyone could just walk in, go up the staircase, onto the roof, down the fire escape, and into people's windows. That's what was happening. We heard this commotion one night, and these people from another loft were chasing this guy through the lofts, and he jumped over the side—the elevator was one of those things that has a wooden slatted door that slides up like a freight elevator—so he jumped over those and came into our kitchen. He was standing there staring at us. Then he ran out the door."

STEWART CORNFELD, friend, film producer

"I thought it was a random act of violence that would never be solved, and everyone was looking for a bigger reason. And I just always believed it was a bad neighborhood, someone broke in."

JIM TUCKER

"After the guy left, [third loftmate and landlord Peter] Taylor went, 'Man I'm going to bring this hammer and leave it in the kitchen for our protection.' Taylor had a wood shop. It was a circus tent stake-driving hammer, a big wooden mallet."

DETECTIVE HANK PETROVSKY

"We saw one alleged burglar on a ledge in a loft, real close to this one, and he falls to his death, and we thought it could be him. We didn't know it was him, but we knew guys were burglarizing the lofts."

MERLE IVERS

"I believe that it was somebody, you know, druggies looking for drugs. Looking for something to hock, to get dollars. I have a feeling they thought he was going to wake up, and they just grabbed the hammer . . ."

DETECTIVE HANK PETROVSKY

"It would be almost impossible to find out who this guy that fell is unless you find the murder book [missing since 2001 from police archives]. Back in '83, we were having eight hundred to a thousand murders a year in the city."

STEVE MARTIN

"What I told the cops was, Peter was a black belt and a yoga master and had been a champion wrestler. The distance from the front door to his bed, you had to walk across a large expanse of room. I said I found it incomprehensible that somebody could sneak up on him, could break the door open and walk all the way across the room without him knowing it. This made me extremely uncomfortable because it suggests the 'break in' was staged. It could have been someone he knew."

HOWARD SMITH

"I think in our minds we would rather it be a complete stranger that had no connection to Peter. To think it was someone who knew him is really creepy."

DETECTIVE HANK PETROVSKY

"So anyway, you do everything you can do, stuff goes into a filing cabinet until someone calls you or has more information, but most people don't."

* * *

DETECTIVE CLIFFORD SHEPARD

"Murders have no statutes of limitations, but burglaries do, so they may sometimes purge burglary files. We do follow-up reports. We do updates on the victim and the investigation, and we address the evidence too. If it goes beyond sixty days you go up to an annual report as well. We also have a chronology, some detectives are very detailed in what they do, and others are not."

chapter 4

My Father Was a Madman, and I Had No Sons: Setting the Stage with Tim and Peter

Cambridge, Agassiz Summer Theatre, August, 15, 1968, 10:00 p.m.

Tommy Lee Jones stepped downstage and squared himself for the final, climactic musical number of *Everyman*, the latest Tim Mayer masterpiece to be staged at Mayer's Agassiz Summer Theatre. The audience had just spent the last ninety minutes riveted to their seats as Jones, in the title role, following a visit by Death, searched for comrades to accompany him on the "long journey"—meeting with rejection after rejection from so-called friends with names like Fellowship, Strength, and Knowledge.

By the final scene, he is left with only two true-blue companions on the stage: Good Deeds, the only virtue willing and able to stand by Everyman through his ultimate passage; and, downstage, a group of anonymous blues musicians.

It turns out, this is all the company he needs. Good Deeds, after all, is none other than Jones's friend and Mayer's protégée, Susan Stockard (who was now Susan Channing, having married while in college). And the group of blues musicians prepared to stand by him, at least, through one last rousing tune, has a comforting, familiar face at the front: their leader, on harp, Peter Ivers.

Death—or more precisely, mortality—was not a new theme for Mayer. In addition to his physical deformity, he had been plagued by serious health problems from a young age. At nineteen, he was diagnosed with lung cancer, which surgery sent into remission. In 1967—having spent his postgraduation year in England apprenticing with the pioneering British dramatist Peter Brook, a resident director of the Royal Shakespeare Company—he produced his first original script, *Prince Eerie*, a dark paean to the underbelly of the American dream culminating with the protagonist rising from the dead to address the audience directly: "Rest easy, friends: my father was a madman, and I had no sons. Men like me are born dead. But we don't have to take it lying down."

Mayer seemed determined not to take his own looming mortality lying down, either. Shortly after *Prince Eerie*, he roused a group of talented young theatre people—stars-in-the-making like Channing, Jones, Lindsay Crouse, and Andy Weil, who had acted for Mayer as an undergrad and recently begun his first year in Harvard Med—to join in his mission of creating a new and revolutionary American National Theatre, modeled on Orson Welles's groundbreaking Mercury Theatre of the late 1930s. (Welles, who had appeared on the cover of *Time* Magazine at age twenty-three, was the standard against whom Mayer was forever judging himself.) With his partner Tom Babe, he established a summer troupe at Harvard's Agassiz Theatre.

Soon after starting at the Agassiz, Mayer noticed some bumps on his neck. He was diagnosed with lymphoma, a cancer of the lymph nodes, and scheduled for major surgery. It was then that he decided to stage *Everyman*, a play about a man condemned to death and, worse, condemned to understand how alone he is in the world.

As Jones prepared to raise his voice for the finale, Peter signaled the other instruments to quiet down to a hum. For his last act in the play—his last earthly deed—Everyman would be accompanied by one Christian virtue and one Jewish bluesman. *Everyman*'s blues score was a typical Peter invention, at once deeply soulful and aggressively physical, a powerful counterweight to Mayer's intellectual forte: his stirring symbolism, pitch-perfect dialogue, and relentless frenzy of ideas.

Howard Cutler, who by that point had become a top-shelf stage designer for Mayer in his own right, felt that Peter came increasingly to embody a visceral power that Mayer, for all his verbal intensity, would always lack. It was a power Mayer wanted more of in his productions. At the same time, Cutler gathered that Peter, who had begun to write music but still steered clear of lyrics, was in search of the right words for his composition. There was no one whose words he trusted more than Mayer's. With *Everyman*—Peter's first attempt at scoring an entire show—a creative partnership was perfected.

Peter raised the harp to his mouth as Jones began to sing a haunting, guttural rendition of "Amazing Grace." The crowd was rapt. Tim Hunter, the *Crimson* reviewer, refused to take notes or strike a pose of objectivity. The photographer claimed in earnest that the show was so good he forgot to load his camera, and Hunter, rather than calling him to task, leapt publicly to his defense. "*Everyman*'s immediacy is such that you don't take pictures and write reviews, you get very much into it instead."

The audience seemed to agree. Jones completed the song, concluding the show, and the theatre roared as the cast took its call. Only gradually, as the applause began to thin out, did it become clear that Peter hadn't stopped playing. He continued to solo on the harp as if no one else were around. The band members picked up their instruments and followed his lead. The audience, which had begun to file out, turned around and came back in.

Tim watched from the back of the theatre. He had created something, and now, with Peter's help, it was taking on a life of its own. He watched for a moment, satisfied, then exited the theatre. Onstage, the crowd danced with Peter and the band long after the curtains had fallen, long after Everyman had taken his final bow.

Cambridge Blues Club, 1968, 1:00 a.m.

Susan Channing couldn't get over the fact that she was sitting this close to the living embodiment of Chicago blues, much less watching him perform, absorbing the force of his howls and growls and thunderous beats. Though about halfway through a nearly two-decade-long commercial lull, Muddy Waters was still Muddy Waters. Peter, who'd introduced her to this music, sat next to her; he was the best person to share this experience with because he appreciated things more than anyone else she knew. Recently, he also had become her boyfriend.

At one point between songs, Muddy Waters gestured to Peter and began to speak about him. He recounted, with respect and affection, times they had played together in Chicago and Boston. Looking out over the small but devoted audience in the smoky room, Waters referred to Peter as "the greatest harp player alive."

For Peter, as for Waters, this praise must have come with a bittersweet edge. Earlier that year, Little Walter had died of head injuries sustained in a street fight. He was thirty-seven. If Peter were indeed the greatest harp player alive, he knew (and he knew Muddy knew) that it was only because Walter was no longer among the living.

Nonetheless, the public coronation from Muddy Waters was thrilling, for Peter and Channing both. For her, it was more than just the thrill of being with a musician recognized as the best by the best, in a field that prized naked soulfulness and masculine grit as much as technical skill. It was also something more personal, an exhilarating affirmation that her life was finally moving in the right direction. Because Channing had recently decided it was time to make a change.

Married at nineteen, Susan Antonia Williams Stockard had taken her husband's last name and spent the ensuing years shuttling between two lives: by day, a student and Beacon Hill housewife, by night an aspiring actress, increasingly recognized for her extraordinary talent and increasingly committed to seeing it through. Mayer, as maddening and downright cruel as he often was, had pushed her harder and believed in her more than anyone ever had, and gotten more out of her as an actress than she knew she possessed. He believed in the work they did together, and she had come to believe in it, too, as more than something she left her real life to do. Finally the tension between her two identities had come to a boil, and the desire to commit fully to acting won out. Earlier that year she had left her husband, driven to Cambridge, and paid a friend twenty-five dollars a week to stay in her spare room. She kept her ex-husband's name but reclaimed her family name as well, and Stockard Channing, professional actress, was born.

Whereas previously, Mayer had served as Channing's tough muse, now Peter was the one irritating, challenging, and inspiring her. When he stood onstage and played his harp with the Street Choir, her own creativity came bursting forth. She was essentially rediscovering herself. She had left an entire life behind and started over from scratch, a decision affirmed, in no small part, by Peter's encouragement and example. Peter was a five-foot-four Jewish kid from Brookline who had taken up the harmonica about three and a half years ago. Now he was being touted publicly by Muddy Waters as the instrument's greatest living practitioner. Faced with his example, what excuse did she have to avoid pursuing her own dream?

New York City, Office of Larry Cohn, Epic Records, 1968, 4:00 p.m.

Larry Cohn sat in his Manhattan office, acutely aware that he had his work cut out for him. Cohn had come to Epic Records as a lowly trainee, and within six months had gotten himself promoted to director of A&R. His assignment was nothing short of the label's total overhaul: to splash some mud on its all-American image, epitomized by fresh-faced crooners like Bobby Vinton and Lester Lanin, and transform it into a home for the new pastime of a culture in upheaval—rock and roll.

The first few times Larry Cohn met Peter Ivers, he did not remember his name and could not think of a reason in the world why he should. Peter was just another kid in a band that had made the pilgrimage to his New York office in search of a contract. Peter—short, rosy-cheeked, and looking about twelve years old—hung back quietly while the bandleaders, Jim Kweskin and Mel Lyman, schmoozed with Cohn.

The band was another story. Cohn didn't have to try to remember their names. Jim Kweskin's Jug Band had been one of the hottest groups to come out of the Boston folk revival, achieving national popularity and critical acclaim almost from its formation in 1963. Then, in 1968, just as they were breaking through to commercial success, Kweskin dissolved the band, shaved off the mustache that had become his trademark, and moved in with the Lyman Family, a commune that was widely thought of as a cult in a run-down neighborhood in Boston.

Kweskin's reputation was enough to pique Cohn's interest and win some highly prized office time. He had formed a new band, and the band was looking for a label. They would call themselves the Lyman Family, and while Kweskin's name would be featured prominently, it was clear to Cohn that the head of the "family," Mel Lyman, would be pulling the strings. It was Lyman who did most of the talking during the series of meetings in Cohn's office. Unfortunately, as far as Larry Cohn could tell, Lyman was insane.

Peter had gotten to know Lyman as a Boston musician. He admired his playing and counted him as an influence. Truth be told, while Peter Ivers may have been considered the greatest living blues harp player by a few small, knowing circles in Chicago and Boston, the title could well have gone to Mel Lyman. He was certainly its most recognizable public face, having achieved iconic status at the historic 1965 Newport Folk Festival—the year Bob Dylan plugged in and infuriated a generation of folk purists. Lyman had quelled the riotous mob into reverent silence with an impromptu twenty-minute harp solo of the classic spiritual "Rock of Ages." In the brochure for the festival the following year, he appeared in an ad for a new brand of harmonica customized for the blues.

By the time he arrived at Larry Cohn's office, Lyman had at various times claimed to be the living embodiment of Truth, the greatest man in the world, Jesus Christ, and an alien entity sent to Earth in human form by extraterrestrials with a mission to save the world. Nonetheless, it took a series of conversations in his office for Cohn to let Kweskin and Lyman know they were going to have to look elsewhere to be signed. But by that time, Cohn had begun to strike up a relationship with Peter, whom he'd initially written off as a hanger-on. Peter was always ready with a goofy grin and a witty line, and Cohn had to laugh at the kid's chutzpah. Sometimes Cohn would take an almost protective, paternal interest in Peter—warning him, for example, to steer clear of the likes of Mel Lyman, who regularly picked up his phone to hear one of his disciples say, "Hello, God?" and, without a trace of irony, would answer, "Speaking."

New York, Office of Larry Cohn, 1968, months later, 2 p.m.

Peter paced quietly outside Cohn's office, not so much nervous as ready to release his explosive energy. After the Kweskin deal dissolved, Peter had begun having his own meetings with Cohn. He let Cohn know that he was an artist in his own right and was looking for a contract. He had worked hard for this chance, gone through many incarnations from student, to bandmate, to bandleader. He was ready to take the next step and become a recording artist.

Cohn said he was looking for original material. Did Peter have anything original?

While the Street Choir had exposed him to a wider audience in Cambridge and honed his performance chops, the music itself was fairly straightforward Chicago blues rock. The band had been gaining in popularity and even receiving some national attention when, a few months ago, Moses suddenly had dissolved it. For Peter there were no hard feelings, as his attention had long since shifted to his musical-theatrical collaborations with Mayer. There he could draw freely on diverse influences and create uniquely textured arrangements. Classical instruments like the bassoon began to feature prominently, along with jazz riffs and driving rock guitars. Weaving through all these seemingly disparate strains and unifying them was Peter's shape-shifting harp.

Everyman's reflection on death and loneliness was followed by *The Bacchae*, a modernization of Euripides' classic protest against the cruel, capricious gods. Mayer followed *The Bacchae* with *Jesus*, then *Job*, leading another reviewer to label him—admiringly, amidst accolades and designations of greatness—"poet of the physically tormented."

Peter's scores, regularly singled out and touted on par with the productions themselves, provided haunting atmosphere, pulsing commentary, visceral amplification, and playful counterpoint to Mayer's open-veined dramatic harangues. Mayer gave words to the music, which Peter refined in response to the words; it was an ongoing conversation.

The collaboration, productive as it was, could account for only two-thirds of any song. Their songs needed a voice that could echo Peter's music through Tim's words. It was with *The Bacchae* that Peter found his first muse. Yolande Bavan was a Sri Lankan actress who had made her chops in British theatre, and then, after a chance encounter with Billie Holiday, had fallen into a career singing jazz. Her audition for *The Bacchae* consisted of coffee and a conversation with Peter and Mayer. Her previous gig had been as the latter day replacement for Annie Ross with the experimental jazz group Lambert, Hendricks, and Ross.

Peter began writing songs tailored to her voice. With Mayer's lyrics, Bavan would improvise to the music. Peter pushed her to improvise further and harder, to do things with her voice she had never tried. Mayer would listen while writing more lyrics. The collaboration became a threesome, and with Peter, at least, it became personal. Bavan, a Buddhist, felt a profound spiritual connection with Peter; they would talk about Buddhism while working on the songs. She hung out in Brookline with Peter, Mayer, and Merle and became part of the extended Ivers family.

By the end of 1968 Peter had enough original music to premier it in what he labeled a "new rock" concert at Harvard. The setup consisted of a bassoon, sax, drums, Peter on harp, and Bavan in traditional South Asian dress—"a careful balance of sounds," one *Crimson* reviewer enthused, "that managed to blend and set off the tight lash of the harp-sound with a rich, creamy-textured backing . . . Ivers's sensitive harp playing generally fused to produce a remarkable, haunting music."

This was the arsenal of original material Peter was packing as he stepped into Cohn's office at Epic. Cohn and the other execs found him, to say the least, unlike any harp player they had ever heard. Cohn was a little stunned by the visionary quality of Peter's work. Originality was what he was looking for, and here it was, standing right in his office. The musical accomplishment, the sophistication and uniqueness of this rosy-cheeked kid barely out of college was quite literally hard to believe.

Peter was offered a two-album contract with Epic. He already had much of the music towards the first. He also had a title in mind: *Knight of the Blue Communion.*

Signet Club, Lunchtime, 1969

These were Peter's first words to Lucy Fisher: "I'm the little boy that sits on his knees and gets the special dessert."

It was lunchtime at the Signet, there was a new waitress, and Peter wasted no time flirting with her. He could hardly be blamed. A skinny Radcliffe sophomore in a primped blue minidress, hair down to her waist, Lucy could have been a poster girl for late-'60s sex appeal and had fallen into the amorous sights of many a Harvard man.

Today, though, she was especially grateful for the positive attention; her first day at work was not going well. She did not know that the ad she had responded to had been a bluff on the part of the bitter old Irish steward who ran the wait staff. He'd gotten into a fight with one of the three other Radcliffe waitresses, threatened to fire her and posted the ad to rile her up. When Lucy arrived he had decided spontaneously to follow through, hiring her on the spot. Unfortunately for Lucy, the other girl had been beloved by the other waitresses and the Harvard boys, who angrily demanded explanations from Lucy as she juggled the lunch trays. Peter's kindness was a welcome reprieve. His bad-boy leather jacket and scruffy good looks made it even more welcome.

She asked him his name, though in fact she knew exactly who he was. She knew who the tall, commanding hunchback sitting next to him was, too. She knew Tim Mayer was the hottest theatre director in Boston, and Peter Ivers was a rocker with a record contract who brought blind old blues singers to the Signet to jam. She knew their faces because she had been to the Signet before, with her boyfriend.

Though raised in a family that encouraged political awareness and intellectual discussions, arriving at Radcliffe Lucy had felt very much like an innocent. In high school she had been at odds with her environment, cultivating bohemian tastes—she devoured poetry and Broadway plays, listened to folk songs and learned to play Dylan and Baez on her guitar—while attending the kind of prep school where it was expected for girls to join the Junior League. She'd excitedly looked forward to college as the place where she could finally start living her real life, bring her outside and inside worlds into line.

Lucy's first college boyfriend brought her to the Signet for an intimate literary evening with the celebrated Argentinian author Jorge Luis Borges. She was sold on the romantic literary image of the place, and because women would not be welcomed as members for some years to come, she was participating in the only available manner. Perhaps the premier (daytime) hangout for anyone with a foot in the arts, the Signet Society's sole criterion for invitation was a demonstrated involvement with the arts. This is where the people who spent most of their time running the *Crimson*, the *Lampoon*, the musical and theatrical productions, and so on met up to compare notes. It was unremarkable on a given day for Donald Graham (the *Harvard Crimson* editor-in-chief whose mother, Katharine, had recently taken over leadership of *The Washington Post*) to sit down with Peter Ivers, Doug Kenney, and Tim Mayer, who might turn to underclassman Frank Rich at another table and mercilessly ride him for his opinions on any number of topics. And this was their downtime.

The Signet's kitchen was run by a mean Irish cook named Sadie, who took shit from no one, Harvard men especially. She provided one lunch every day, on a large tray that the server would carry around to each table. Only Peter got special treatment. He often sat with his legs tucked under him, and from hard-ass Sadie received customized meals catered to meet what seemed to Lucy like an extended array of food fetishes. At the beginning of each lunch, Sadie would direct Lucy to a special tray with the instruction, "Now this is for Peter." When he described himself as "the little boy who sits on his knees and gets the special dessert," he meant it literally.

Lucy was spellbound by this eccentric, talented musician who commuted regularly to New York City to work on his major-label record. She began to anticipate her lunch shifts with great excitement; Mayer and Peter showed up virtually every day. When Peter started asking her out to plays and other cultural events, she was a goner. Peter and Tim took Lucy in and they became yet another inseparable threesome.

Eventually, the two other Signet waitresses quit, and Lucy brought in two of her best friends to replace them. At the end of the shift, Lucy and her crew would eat lunch in the kitchen, and gradually they began inviting some of the Signet regulars to continue their meals with them in the back. It became a scene unto itself, a kind of speakeasy, Lucy's private club. Her most reliable customers were Peter Ivers and Tim Mayer.

New York, in the Studio, Knight of the Blue Communion, 1969, 4:00 p.m.

Knight of the Blue Communion was recorded in one session. Peter was both frenetic and totally at ease, bouncing around the room with spontaneous directions, *You do this, and you do that man, and you, do something on top of this chorus.* His attitude seemed to be that it was all fun, and not brain surgery, while at the same time he demanded an extremely high level of improvisational skill. He would get upset when he felt the musicians were not being sufficiently responsive: *I'm giving you all the freedom, man, so just open up!* For Bavan, at least, all this laid-back looseness required nerves of steel. Eventually things began to gel, and she could feel herself and Peter's harmonica coming together like two voices.

One musician missing from the *Knight* session was Buell Neidlinger, Peter's mentor, bandmate, and friend. When Peter told Neidlinger about the contract for *Knight*, he also told him that he had another bassist in mind for the album, explaining that Buell already had a job and this guy needed a shot—which seemed to Neidlinger like a thin excuse. Following the conversation, their relationship cooled.

For the mixing session, Peter brought Peter Johnson down to New York. The two had remained close, and Peter wanted the company. They drove around the city in the white Cadillac of the Epic producer designated to work on *Knight*, and Johnson was once again struck by Peter's gift for connecting with people. The young producer seemed to feel an intense soul bond with Peter, to love him and believe in him unreservedly.

Back in the studio, Harvey Brooks, the great bassist of *Highway 61 Revisited* fame, was mixing in the next room. As far as Johnson could tell, Peter had made it.

Alexandra Garcia-Mata's New Canaan Home, Doug's Wedding, June 1970

The first time Lucy met Doug Kenney, she asked him why he was getting married. She and Peter often took trips down to New York, and on this one they stayed in the duplex Doug shared with Henry Beard. Doug and Henry had run the *Harvard Lampoon* together and brought it acclaim and cash flow with the magazine parodies. *Bored of the Rings*, a book-length parody of the Tolkien series they published just before graduating, had become a bestseller in England. Upon graduating they had licensed the Lampoon name from Harvard, struck a lucrative deal with a publishing company, and founded *National Lampoon* magazine.

By the time Lucy met Doug, he already had the duplex, a big office, an advance, and a national humor magazine that was beginning to take off. He also appeared to have a fiance, a woman from Peter and Doug's year at Radcliffe, in whom he did not seem very interested at all. To Lucy, he did not seem interested in much of anything. His current success, and the prospect of much greater success to come, seemed, more than anything, to bewilder him. He seemed constitutionally unable to absorb or appreciate his good fortune. The only thing he was visibly interested in was talking and playing with Peter. They were like two children together, able to play for hours in the sandbox without getting bored.

Marriage, though, seemed to Lucy like a very grown-up step. The wedding was planned, the date was set—and Doug had nothing good to say about any of it. Finally, Lucy was unable to contain herself. She popped the question: Why was he getting married at all?

Without hesitating Doug answered, "I have no idea."

Doug Kenney got married in a suit that looked every bit of the twenty-five dollars he paid for it at a store in inner-city Boston. He asked Peter to be his best man. Before the ceremony, Doug seemed skittish, less certain than ever why he was taking this major step. Before the procession began, Peter took him aside and told him that under no circumstances should he feel he was obligated to go through with it. In fact, he wouldn't even have to explain. He could just leave, and Peter would go out and tell everyone the wedding was off.

By this point, though, stopping the wedding probably seemed to Doug like a far more momentous decision than going through with it. One hundred and fifty guests were waiting around the other side of the house. That kind of decision would have taken a kind of clarity he was never quite able to muster.

With Peter by his side in a loud blue suit, Doug Kenney said, "I do."

New York, In the Studio, Take It Out on Me, 1970, 10:00 p.m.

Once again, Peter was taking off his clothes in public. Ever since high school, he had sought out opportunities to disrobe in front of an audience. As he and the other musicians prepared to record, he threw off his shirt, then his pants and shoes. Wearing only his underwear, he picked up his harp and began to play.

Knight of the Blue Communion had come out the year before to great critical fanfare. Peter was embraced by music aficionados as the newest, freshest thing in experimental music for his stirring and highly accomplished fusion of jazz, blues, classical, rock, folk, and even medieval and Middle Eastern modes. Critics hailed his ability to synthesize diverse strains into a sustained state of controlled chaos. "Rather than an eclectic assortment of disparate elements," one reviewer enthused, "the result of Ivers's synthesizing and directing is a unified force, moving on a new vector." Complex without being esoteric, *Knight* was that rarest of combinations, an album at once musically serious, experimental, and easy to enjoy.

Audiences, however, were less responsive. This had to do in part with the album's experimental flavor—always a hard sell—and in part with Epic's lackluster marketing. Even Larry Cohn found Peter commercially hard to position, precisely because of his visionary genius. Cohn was one of an expanding chorus of voices buzzing that Peter was ahead of his time—high praise that could also be a commercial kiss of death.

Though disappointed, Peter took *Knight*'s muted reception in stride and immediately went to work on his next album. He already had many of the songs in place and worked with the intention of making them accessible to a wider audience. As he told one interviewer, "I'm pleased with the first album, but I want the next one to be closer to the people," adding that his secondary ambition was to give his father $500,000, "so that he'll know I didn't waste any time at Harvard."

For his sophomore effort, Peter had discovered another muse. Asha Puthli had been raised by a broad-minded but tradition-bound Indian family in Bombay. Their hopes for her included both pursuing a doctorate and accepting the marriage they had arranged for her. Instead, she arrived in the United States in 1969 intent on pursuing her dream of synthesizing Indian classical music with jazz. John Hammond Sr., the mythic producer and promoter credited with signing Dylan, Springsteen, Billie Holiday, and Aretha Franklin, heard her demo and had the idea of pairing her with an interesting harmonica player he knew. Hammond brought the two together in his Sixth Avenue office, and the deal was struck.

Puthli found the *Take It Out on Me* sessions wild, eccentric, and joyful. Peter's energy inspired an enthusiasm in the other musicians. The effect was a natural adrenaline that made it possible to work for three days and three nights without sleeping. Puthli herself felt an instant bond with Peter—they were friends and collaborators who respected each other's talent and had fun with music. Notwithstanding the intense sensuality of the music itself, their friendship, she felt, had an innocent, almost childlike quality.

In the recording studio, Puthli sang from the other side of a window, inside a vocal booth. Peter had stripped down to his underwear, and was jamming on his harp almost in the buff. Paul Lenart noticed some movement in Asha's booth and looked over to find her taking her clothes off as well. She sang the rest of the session nearly naked.

John Hammond Sr. peeked into the studio briefly to see how things were going. Soon after he left, a bunch of photographers showed up and began snapping pictures. It was 1970. The band just continued to play.

Jesus on a Roof in Roxbury, Winter, 1970, 3:00 p.m.

The '60s had ended badly, and Asha Puthli was freezing cold. How did she find herself in the thick of a New England winter, on the rooftop of a burned-out factory in Roxbury (Boston's equivalent of Harlem or the South Bronx), prohibited from wearing a coat? At least she wasn't alone: the entire cast of *Jesus: A Passion Play for Americans*—a special produced by Boston's public television station and scheduled to air nationally during the upcoming Easter holiday—was freezing right along with her. Only Tim Mayer was protected from the elements, barking direction from inside a warm coat.

An executive from the station had seen Mayer's staging of *Jesus: A Passion Play for Cambridge* the previous year. Riveted by the interplay between Mayer's visual wizardry and Peter's evocative score, he felt the show was TV-ready and fast-tracked it into production.

Mayer's team took the opportunity as a sign from above and kicked into high gear. It was the affirmation of everything they had been working towards, the culmination of three years of nonstop creative work. Suddenly all Mayer's talk of creating a new movement in American theatre, with a reach that would alter the national discussion and broadly influence cultural trends, seemed prophetic. Maybe this was going to be it: their Mercury Theatre! The actors went back into rehearsal, Peter assembled a band, and Howard Cutler worked night and day scouting locations and creating new sets, which included huge freeway signs with reflective letters cobbled together to spell out "THE CRUCIFICTION."

Lucy's Dorm Room, Winter, 1970, 4:30 p.m.

Meanwhile, Peter's relationship with Lucy was taking flight. He left her funny phone messages, making dinner reservations, for instance, for two: him and his bass. He became a frequent celebrity guest at her dormitory, often stopping by when he knew she had class and leaving a bulky brick of a tape player on her pillow with a note saying, "Press Here." On the tape would be Peter's latest song, which often drew on elements and images she recognized from experiences they had shared. Sometimes, though, they seemed to come from another planet.

> *Time warp, space warp, rockin' in fury,*
> *Lost my darlin' Alpha Centauri . . .*

But however strange, when the song finished she always pressed Rewind and played it again.

Peter told Merle about the foxy new girl he was dating, though at first she didn't think much of it. With Peter, there were always girls—at her house, on the phone, usually more or less at the same time. She liked all of them but had learned not to get too attached. As always, she was happy to let Peter do his thing. And as always, she had a couple of strict rules she demanded he follow. One was never to believe them if they said they were on the Pill: use a condom at all times. The other was, get to know her mother: more likely than not, that's who she will end up turning into.

When he brought Lucy home, though, Merle did notice something different between them, a spark she had not seen with the other girls. And Peter said something about Lucy that Merle had not heard before. He said she was the smartest person he had ever known.

Peter's Apartment, 1971, 1:00 p.m.

Peter hung up the phone with Tim Hunter and began to meditate. He had gotten into Buddhism during college and now practiced meditation with the same steady focus he brought to anything he cared about. Today, though, his intention went beyond relaxation or concentration, heightened senses, or a more conscious mind—though he would need all of those things, now perhaps more than ever. After hanging up the phone with Hunter, he had a big decision to make. He closed his eyes and repeated the mantra that would help him settle into his meditative state.

Epic, as part of a broad housecleaning, had decided to drop Peter from the label. Larry Cohn still believed in Peter. He knew audiences would not understand the music at first but felt confident that as they worked with him he would come up with something that could get radio play. However, as Cohn's own career continued to take off, he had less time to work with Peter personally, and there was no other producer knowledgeable enough to direct him. Thus, he gave Peter free reign, and what he came up with, *Take It Out on Me*, was deemed too esoteric to justify the expense. The album was killed. Peter was a man without a label—a lonely, disorienting place for any musician, especially one with an album's worth of near-complete songs and ideas for hundreds more.

The TV production of *Jesus* had been a success, so well received that there was talk of making it an annual staple for the Easter holiday. Still, for Peter, things with Mayer seemed to be winding down. With the poor sales of *Knight* (all of whose lyrics were credited to Mayer), the disappointment with Epic, and the climax of *Jesus*, their collaboration had run its course. Peter found himself in transition musically, eager again to expand his control over the material he produced and ready to write his own lyrics.

On top of that, some discomfort had crept into their friendship. It had to do with Lucy. From the start, the three had been inseparable, going to plays and seeing music together, hanging out with Lucy's family, in Brookline, and at Mayer's parents' place on the Cape, or driving down to New York to visit with Doug. Mayer was a natural, aggressive flirt, and he flirted with Lucy constantly, from the first time they met, much more than Peter ever had. That Lucy had ended up with Peter did nothing to deter Mayer's thinly veiled come-ons, and that was okay, too, but only to a point. For both Peter and Lucy, it had become a bit strained.

Mayer had a late-night literary talk show on Boston's public TV station. Sometimes, when Peter was off making music with some beauty from an exotic land, Lucy would hang out with her friends Jerry Harrison and Ernie Brooks, two Harvard peers who would shortly join a local Boston oddity named Jonathan Richman to form a band called the Modern Lovers (Harrison would become a member of Talking Heads). But when they were busy, she would watch Mayer's talk show in her Somerville apartment. At the end of every show, he stared intently out into the lo-fi New England airwaves and signed off with a twist on the title line from a song he had written for Lucy: "Oh the girls that I've called on, in Chelsea and Malden, they were loveable to a lass / But none could compare with the fairest of fair / She's my someone in Somerville, Mass."

"Good night," he would say, "to my someone in Somerville, Mass." And the show would end.

Peter was not the only one for whom the comforts of Mayer's kingdom were beginning to feel confining. Paradoxically, the success of *Jesus* seemed to trigger a strange denouement for many in Mayer's set. One night around that time, Andy Weil came in for a visit from San Francisco, having recently completed Harvard Med. Throughout his years at Harvard, Weil had been a friend of Mayer's and played important roles in many of his shows. But that night, at a gathering of old friends, he told Mayer and his set that they were missing the boat. The cultural shift looming on the horizon was about raising consciousness and exploring the capacities of the human mind. The torment and angst Mayer seemed intent on foisting upon the public had outlived its value and overstayed its welcome.

Weil was not alone in his assessment that Mayer's small, incestuous, highly intellectual theatre world had become claustrophobic. Howard Cutler had been with Mayer for half a decade, a steadfast believer and faithful soldier in the cause. He'd put everything he had into the televised *Jesus*, with visions of a new Mercury Theatre dancing in his eyes. And when it was over, something about the tortured, mangled body of Jesus; the tortured lines of the gospel that Mayer had clipped and refitted for his play; Tim's own tortured body and mind, his tortured persona that increasingly risked becoming a caricature of itself; even Peter's music, the tortured tangling of all the different traditions and styles . . . All that torture and torment left Cutler and others feeling that Mayer's kingdom was perhaps not as grand as they'd imagined, and it was time for them to strike out and see the rest of the world.

Taken individually, none of these developments may have proved decisive for Peter. But looking down on them from the bird's-eye view of meditation, they seemed if not to spell out a plan, then to point clearly away from Tim Mayer.

And here, at this moment, was Tim Hunter, with an offer. Hunter had been in Peter's class at Harvard. He hung out on the fringes of Mayer's theatre circle, and, as a reviewer for the *Crimson,* had been responsible for a number of raves of Mayer's shows. Hunter's main interest, though, was film. As a freshman he had found that Harvard's two film societies were being run by graduating seniors and promptly took over both. He was always at work on his own films, and through these projects attracted a significant circle of his own. Peter's sister Ricki had performed in one of his more ambitious early efforts. Peter had done set work for one of his films and collaborated with Gil Moses for the music on another. He and Hunter had become friends.

Hunter had recently moved to Los Angeles to participate in a pres-tigious new fellowship put together by the American Film Institute (AFI), called the Center of Advanced Film Studies. The center had scoured the country to handpick its most promising young directors for its first class. Hunter was one of the chosen, and he had called Peter to ask if he consider coming out to LA and scoring his films. Before Peter awoke from his meditative state, he already knew what the answer would be.

═══════════════════════*close-up:*

The Theatrics of Tim, the Music of Peter, and a National Parody of a Giggle of a Protest

Tim's Theatre of Cruelty

HOWARD CUTLER

"So they start doing a production of Euripides' *The Bacchae* called *Oh, What a Lovely War,* and they get real notices from the Boston critics. And suddenly, the next year *The New York Times* came up and the *Sunday Times* did a piece on this theatre company. They would find a play by Aristophanes, called *Peace*—this is '68, right in the middle of the Vietnam War, right?—and they were doing Aristophanes' *Peace,* and they were setting it to rock and roll."

STOCKARD CHANNING

"The whole idea of what a rock musical is—I think there was some shit going on Broadway that was very sanitized. But Tim built this whole dark humor, theatre-of-cruelty thing."

HOWARD CUTLER

"Peter in some way, I think, wanted the intellectual power that Tim represented in his music. And so there was this kind of idea between the two of them that we could be the next really interesting thing happening musically. And it was all coming from his gut experience of a guy who's twenty-two years old and quite brilliant, and facing death."

JOHN LITHGOW

I visited [Mayer] in his loft in North Boston. I can't remember the year, but he was ill, and I just visited him as so many of us did, and he made one of his amazing dark jokes. He said, "I can die happy now, Lithgow has forgiven me."

Last night, Ivers's tightly knit band, his stylized compositions and arrangements, and extraordinary singer George Leh, came as close to stealing a show as anybody comes working with Mayer.
—*Tim Hunter, "Everyman," the* Crimson, *August 16, 1968*

HOWARD CUTLER

"Peter really went and nursed Timmy. I can remember stories of Peter going to Tim in the hospital, and he's doped up with morphine or whatever and Peter's playing the harmonica for him in the hospital room. That was part of his nature. He was helping Tim get through this thing."

STOCKARD CHANNING

"He was a catalyst in a way that I never understood at the time. Sometimes I didn't know if I'd be able to get out from under and do what I've been doing these years. When it was over [with Peter] I was very devastated by the whole situation. But when I woke up the next day, I was in this whole other place in the universe."

Doug Goes National

The *Harvard Lampoon* has recently undergone a changing of the guard while, almost simultaneously, a new magazine (founded by *Poon* alumni), *The National Lampoon*, has made its debut across the country with an initial circulation of 500,000.

—*Samuel Z. Goldhaber, "From the News Land Poons,"*
the Crimson, *April 7, 1970*

MARK STUMPF

"He had a real ear for American. The [*Harvard*] Lampoon was a very rarefied place where the humor was very intellectual. Doug's breakthrough was that he was fully attuned on that level, but also to the American idiom, and successfully crossed over in a way no one could have. Doug really is the breakthrough guy, bridging those two worlds."

MICHAEL O'KEEFE, actor (*Caddyshack*)

"They were children of the '60s, their own rebellion had led them into a world of humor as opposed to a world of demonstrations and politics, and they were trying to stir it up in the same way. Instead of ending up in an antiwar demonstration, which I would imagine they were going to anyway, they found a way to poke fun at themselves and the world around them. And a lot of people got it."

Knight of the Blue Communion, Peter's First Album

"Dark Illumination" (<>) Song #1
"Cat Scratch Fever" (<>) Song #2

Naturally, my first influences were blues harp players, but the musicians I played with while my style matured taught my ears to hear music in weird ways. I try to maximize the tension between layers to get what I think of as a sophisticated, back-alley sound.
　　—*Peter Ivers,* Knight of the Blue Communion *liner notes*

LARRY COHN
"Peter always made me laugh. I regarded him as a sixteen-year-old when I dealt with him, but he was a very bright person, always smiling, never saw him in a down moment. He was just a charming guy; he could charm the pants off the devil without trying."

This is a fine album of real avant-garde material. Peter Ivers's band is a free-swinging jazz-rock outfit quite unlike anything I've heard. They are competent craftsmen who have achieved new sounds with creative freshness. Strictly music to listen to, and not for kids.
　　—The Nichel Review, *Syracuse, NY, January 16, 1970*

LARRY COHN
"He was so far ahead, his perception of music was so far removed from the normal, let's face it, most of the rock and roll people we signed, if they could play five chords on the guitar, they were in."

Knight of the Blue Communion (Hux), is one of the most marvelously bizarre recordings ever put out by a major label, and it has lost none of its allure: the black-wind ensemble of oboe, bassoon, sax, and Ivers's graveyard-blues harp; the whoops and purrs of Yolande Bavan; the nonlinear creep of the songs by Ivers and lyricist Tim Mayer.
　　—*"As Strange as 1969 Ever Got,"* Rolling Stone, *2007*

LARRY COHN

"There was no place for him because he was so unique and new."

Take It Out on Me:
The Album for the People That Never Was

LARRY COHN

"I felt people wouldn't understand him in the beginning. But I felt that as we worked with him, he'd come up with something playable on the radio."

> "In my next album which I'm working on now, I'm tending more toward the combination of jazz, blues, rock, and classical. I'm pleased with the first album, but I want this one to be closer to the people."
> —*Peter,* Buffalo Courier-Express, *February 4, 1970*

ASHA PUTHLI

"We were all young and excited about this project. Peter's enthusiasm, energy, and humor was most contagious, and his intelligence inspiring. All of us in the studio had a bond—our eagerness to work with Peter was the bond, and there was an abundance of natural adrenaline flowing out of this and that's what kept us going for three days and three nights without any sleep till we completed recording all the songs."

> *(<>) "Clarence O'Day," Song #3*

> *Alan,*
> *I have provided two copies of seven tunes to be copyrighted for the new (second) album—Two are Ivers-Mayer, the others by me entirely—Please advise me as to disposition of 5 of my own, i.e., (cunning runt, inc.) etc.*
> *. . . In addition, to the 8 tunes on the album, I am going in next week to cut 3 tunes in search of hit teeny-bop audience.—(in an effort to match my listening audience to my sex life—)*
> *Count Peter Ivers, MBE; ESP; ABM; COCK*

LARRY COHN

"The industry had changed around '65 or '66. It became an artist-oriented industry. With Santana, and Blood, Sweat and Tears, and Jimi Hendrix and all those people, those were the years of change. Then after that it was dry cut, then we come into disco and other horror shows. The business is not a business anymore. I could be selling ladies' bras for all people care."

LUCY FISHER

"He would say, nobody knows what Peter Ivers is doing on a snowy day. On a regular day, he had his regular routines of who he would hang out with or encounter and do some creative enterprise. He had his little list with perfect block printing, and he'd write down what he was going to do, and he'd bring people off and on Peter Ivers's day. The snow would interrupt that. It was a poetic version of a snow day. It's such a kid's version of the world to even have a snow day."

case book part 3

DETECTIVE CLIFFORD SHEPARD
"Without evidence, you have to keep all these possibilities open. There are lots of people and lots of motives. Without having all the information, it's hard to say. We can only speculate."

* * *

JIM TUCKER
"At first there were fifty suspects. There was this incredible community around Ivers and they devoured each other. They ate each other alive."

MALCOLM LEO, friend, television producer
"I don't think the one that did it lived downtown. I don't think it was random. I think the opportunity for random violence wasn't on the sixth floor of a building."

HAROLD RAMIS
"That's not how strangers kill each other, that's how people intimately connected kill each other. No, this was a passionate kind of . . . ."

STUART CORNFELD, friend, film producer
"He'd been in two groups, so the rich people thought the punks did it and the punks thought the rich ones did it. The two scenes were interconnected, but there wasn't a lot of mixing, which [was] why there was a lot of finger-pointing."

FRANNE GOLDE, friend, collaborator, songwriter
"The detective wanted to talk to me. The day before, I had been at the loft, and they found my cigarette butts. A friend of Peter's went downtown with me the next day. They showed

me a picture of Peter, and I said, yes, I know him. They asked if I knew two guys in a picture that Peter had gone to Harvard with, and I didn't. They asked me questions over things that I had no idea. I was with Peter almost every day, that's what was so bizarre—I was being asked questions and I was surprised by what I didn't know."

LUCY FISHER

"When I emerged from the total shock, I found myself repeatedly at the LA Homicide Department—the last place I ever expected to ever be. But every time I climbed the stone steps to that building, I almost exploded with impotence and rage. The detectives seemed more concerned with covering up all the mistakes than in following up the potential leads constantly being thrown their way."

* * *

DETECTIVE CLIFFORD SHEPARD

"If the investigation goes well, you identify a suspect, make an arrest, talk to him, you prepare your case, run it to the DA's office, they decide about filing, and at that time, all that goes into the murder book. The death report, the victim, everything you've done to identify them and about them goes in the murder book. Sometimes you need that information later on."

ACT 2

MUSIC FOR CASH

chapter 5

Hollywood's Pet

LA, the Smiths' House, 1971, 5:00 p.m.

The knock at the door was startling; the Smiths had no reason to expect company. Granted, Peter Ivers often dropped by unexpectedly. Howard Smith had gotten to know Peter through Tim Hunter, Smith's colleague at the AFI Center. Hunter, an AFI fellow, had brought Peter out to score his movie, *Devil's Bargain,* and Peter had done such a great job and hit it off so well with the other fellows that he'd stuck around as a kind of unofficial musician-in-residence, working with various people on their projects and his own. Like many in the AFI crowd, Peter was intrigued by finding new ways of combining music and film. Since the mid-'60s, Smith had been experimenting with shooting film to go with songs he felt had cinematic possibilities.

When Peter stopped by unexpectedly, which was the only time he stopped by, he was all business and at the same time all play. For him, the line between the two was thin to nonexistent. Once in the door, he would make a beeline for the Smiths' piano and bang out his newest composition, or just press *play* on his tape recorder if the piece involved multiple instruments. He was always writing and recording new music, and he always wanted feedback. He'd play his song and they would talk about it over dinner.

But it wouldn't be Peter at the door now. He had gone back east to get his girlfriend Lucy, and they were road-tripping back across the country. They planned to stay with Howard and Barbara when they got to LA, but Peter had just called to tell the Smiths they were in Berkeley and would not be back for another couple of days.

Howard went to the door. Except for Peter, "just stopping by" was virtually unheard-of in LA. Peter seemed to take for granted that he would be welcome wherever he went, and this winning optimism more often than not made it true. Howard opened the door to a face that was unfamiliar but seemed harmless enough, even sweet. A young guy, early twenties, disheveled, shouldering a knapsack that did not seem particularly full.

"Hi, I'm Doug Kenney. Can I stay with you guys? I'm a friend of Peter's, he said you wouldn't mind."

The Smiths knew who Doug Kenney was, from Peter and from the newspaper and magazine features touting an irreverent, important, and savagely funny new satiric voice. Launched in April 1970, *National Lampoon* had spent its first year collecting the right staff, finding its editorial and graphic voice, and generally working out the kinks. Sporting provocatively themed issues (*Greed*; *Blight*; *Religion for Fun and Prophet*), mean, absurd teasers ("Is Nixon Dead?"; "Women's Lib Pinups"), and instantly iconic cover art (Richard Nixon as Moses, complete with flowing robes and horns, coming down the mountain to deliver a tablet-sized *Reader's Digest* to the awaiting throngs; a disturbingly accurate imitation of a Norman Rockwell portrait, featuring *Mad* magazine mascot Alfred E. Newman sitting in a barber's chair with a peace-sign necklace over his smock, half his head shaved down to an army-issue crew cut, the other half flowing down his back)—the *Lampoon* combined Harvard literary wit with crass schoolboy fixations and a merciless eye for hypocrisy and double-talk. For a nation suffering cultural upheaval and a brutal, endless war, this monthly injection of idol-smashing irreverence proved good medicine. By the summer of 1971, everything seemed in place. Under the steady editorial hand of Henry Beard and the bottomless output of Doug's twisted genius (his contributions regularly comprised a third of the magazine's content), a cadre of bona fide misfits had somehow managed to find each other and form a functioning staff. Subscriptions were up, ad revenues were steadily rising, and everything indicated that *National Lampoon* was on the verge of becoming both a cultural phenomenon and an extremely lucrative commercial success.

This was the moment Doug chose to skip town. He showed up at the Smiths' with a change of underwear and a *Lampoon* credit card.

He had told no one—including his wife—that he was leaving, much less where he had gone.

At the time, perhaps because of the times, none of this seemed overly strange. The Smiths, who found Doug to be a bit sheepish but extremely good-natured, welcomed him into their home. When Peter and Lucy arrived a few days later, they all settled into a familiar routine. Peter wrote music and played songs for everyone on the piano. Doug took notes for the "serious" satiric novel he planned to write (*TACOS: Teenage Commies from Outer Space*), which he hoped would establish him as a literary humorist on par with Salinger and Waugh—or at least assuage some of the encroaching shame he felt for captaining what sometimes seemed little more than a dirty comic book. It didn't help that teenage boys wrote from time to time thanking the editors effusively for various perverse images that had inspired them to repeated self-pleasure.

LA, Summer 1972

Peter, Lucy, and Doug spent a lot of time wandering around the city together, eating breakfast at Schwab's, Peter's favorite diner, and stopping in at bookstores for Doug to ask how many copies of his unwritten book they had currently in stock. Peter introduced Doug around to some of the AFI fellows as well. (One of the fellows at the time was a young director named David Lynch, who was working hard to raise money for his AFI thesis film, a surrealist nightmare set in an industrial wasteland called *Eraserhead*.)

Some days Peter, Doug, and Lucy would spend time just sitting together and reading, fiction and poetry and the occasional Sanskrit. Peter and Doug would go back and forth, often heatedly, on controversial topics in Greek and Latin literature. Every day Lucy demanded Doug tell someone, anyone, where he was, and every day he affably ignored her. There was not much more she could do. Doug looked to Lucy for the kind of nurturing feminine presence he had formerly found in Merle, and Lucy could not help but comply. It was her nature, and besides, by this point she loved Doug like a troubled little brother who despite his best intentions was always getting himself into jams. Ambitious in the extreme (having long ago determined to become both a literary star and a millionaire by age thirty), Doug had come the farthest the fastest among the three friends. And yet he seemed to lack whatever inner mechanism might allow him to appreciate or even acknowledge his success. He demanded excellence of himself and had begun to achieve some version of it with the *Lampoon*. Yet just when his gifts and efforts began to pay off, he turned tail like someone fleeing for his life.

Finally, Lucy did manage to wrench one grudging concession out of the runaway with the wounded, winning grin. She bought two postcards, addressed one to the *Lampoon* and the other to Doug's wife, and stood over Doug until he scribbled something down. Doug filled the white space on the *Lampoon* card with one long, looping scrawl: "Next time, try a Yalie!" The message to his wife was similarly informative and concise.

Though concerned, Peter and Lucy did not consider the possibility that Doug might be having an actual nervous breakdown. At the time, psychotherapy was still a relative novelty, and clinical names for psychological conditions were far from household terms. Such conditions were known mainly by more colloquial, disparaging nicknames that tended to curb the likelihood of open discussion. Doug was doubly lucky to have been branded a creative genius; otherwise he just would have been considered nuts.

Besides which, Peter was only twenty-five years old, and Lucy, twenty-two. They knew nothing about nervous breakdowns. They just knew that their friend needed to be around friends, and they were the friends he had chosen. So, even though all three of them had graduated from school, they treated that summer like summer vacation: read books, saw movies, went camping, and took road trips to Mexico together. They went to Disneyland, rode the rides, watched the shows. Peter tried to pick up Minnie Mouse (who seemed, momentarily, to exhibit some interest), and Doug asked the Pirates of the Caribbean if they wanted some magazines for their bonfire (they ignored him).

And then, when the weather cooled and the trees began to turn everywhere in the world except LA, Doug returned east to make another tentative stab at embracing what was not only his stated ambition, but seemed increasingly to be his fate: exerting massive impact on mainstream culture while achieving unfathomable financial success.

Lucy went back, too. When her father died, she and her mother had planned to travel to Europe together, and the trip was coming up. Also, frankly, she wasn't sure she was ready to move to LA. Sure, Peter had a dream and a plan—he was the only person she knew who did. The rock-star girlfriend routine had worked for her in college, but college was over. She had no idea what she might do in LA.

LA, Duke's, Tropicana Motel, 1972, 9:00 a.m.

Dear Alan,

Sorry I've been so remiss. I am definitely one of the greatest closet composers in history. The American Film Institute is a kamikaze flight into oblivion. I just got a score for a sexploitation flick, but we haven't discussed money or points. I'll let you know. Larry Cohn, who signed me to Epic, has been made executive vice president of Playboy Records and called me last week. I may ask for an A&R job as well as present him with a plan for a new record. He seems the type that might repeat his mistakes.

To find me just put a stethoscope on the heartbeat of Hollywood.

I'll be in touch,

Peter Ivers

Peter sat in his regular seat and ordered the same breakfast he always ordered at his regular coffee shop, Duke's, which was next to the Tropicana Motel. For all his random, unexpected drop-ins at the homes and offices of friends, Peter plotted each day thoughtfully, even rigorously. Since Lucy and Doug left, a chunk of each day was taken up with the carpentry job he had found at NBC building sets for *The Tonight Show* and other productions. Lately, though, he'd had to cut down his hours because the sawdust was triggering allergies and making him sick. This gave him more time at his own office—Duke's—where he could throw his considerable energies into mapping out his frontal attack on Hollywood.

As the usual waitress across the room smiled over at him, Peter scribbled his end game objective down on a napkin: *Become a rock star.* No one could argue with the venue he had chosen from which to stage his assault. While not much to look at—not much more, really, than a run-down motel court on Santa Monica Boulevard in West Hollywood—the Tropicana had a storied history of housing rock legends at seminal stages of their careers, such as Jim Morrison and Frank Zappa. Peter had moved in as soon as Doug and Lucy moved out. He still spent plenty of time with the Smiths and their piano, and he'd scored Howard's AFI film. But the Tropicana was where he needed to lay his head. Just as he had immersed himself in Boston's homey folk clubs and found his way into Chicago's grittiest blues houses, now he wanted to absorb the spirit of LA rock mythology by planting himself at ground zero. He designed a business card that summed up his immediate goal succinctly:

PETER IVERS

MUSIC FOR CASH

TROPICANA MOTEL

652-5720

Peter spent the better part of each day getting these cards into the hands of potential collaborators. At Duke's, at AFI, at the clubs and parties he'd begun to play around town; everyone knew about Music for Cash. This morning, though, Peter was not handing out any cards. He was writing his daily letter to Lucy. He was asking her, again, when she'd be back—although she had made it clear that she would not even think of returning until he had a proper place for them to live. The Tropicana may have been the perfect haven for an aspiring rock star, but it was no home for a nice Jewish girl from New Jersey, a Cliffie no less.

> *Dear Lu, say hello to Peter for me and give him a big*
> *kiss . . . Cleaning house is the first step to your return, and it*
> *does take many hours. Haven't spoken to Tim . . .*

Even while acknowledging the distressing concession he had accepted as necessary to bring her back, Peter's correspondence was characteristically optimistic, except perhaps in that last trailing-off sentence.

Something strange had happened on Lucy's mother-daughter Europe trip: Tim Mayer had tagged along. What made this strange fact even stranger was that Mayer did not fly—never, under any circumstances, period. So in the preceding weeks, when he had insisted repeatedly that he was coming on the trip, Lucy assumed he was joking. Furthermore, he had a girlfriend—a girlfriend he was always complaining about, a woman with pretensions to glamour whom Peter had nicknamed Fi Fi Latour; but a girlfriend nonetheless.

Mayer, it turned out, had not been joking. He said farewell to Fi Fi, boarded a big boat (the *Queen Mary II*), and rode it across the ocean. He found Lucy and her mother in England and made himself a fixture of their trip. Each night they would see plays together, and when, during intermission, Mayer would slip away for a drink, Lucy's mother would express her concern that he sure did seem to drink a lot. That this was news to Lucy could be attributed to her youthful inexperience and to the very specific otherness of Tim Mayer. Lucy had never been in such intimate proximity with such a flagrant, textbook WASP. It wasn't just that his father owned a huge sporting-goods company, that he was rich and preppy and had gone to fancy schools. There were a thousand details (his mother had a snuff box collection on the Cape) that made him almost a different species. Lucy knew about college drinking, but Mayer's blue-blooded New England alcoholism was something she had never noticed before.

Lucy had to admit she kind of liked the attention. This was in part because she was mad at Peter for not putting up more of a fight, for letting his best friend escort his girlfriend through the capitals of Europe and not jumping on the next flight to come and be with her himself. (Peter was sensitive and intermittently romantic but too enthralled with his own pursuits to practice chivalry with any consistency.) In part, though, it was because she had not yet realized how bizarre the situation was. Lucy assumed Mayer had some other primary reason for making the transcontinental trip. Thus, when the time came for her and her mother to fly to Ireland, she thought he would stay in England to take care of whatever business had brought him there. Instead, he bought a first-class ticket across the Irish Sea.

Lucy observed all this and reported it to Peter in letters with some amusement, some confusion, and growing surprise. Peter, reading the letters between meetings at Duke's, was not amused, not confused, and unfortunately not even surprised. He was furious and hurt, and he felt powerless. While his best friend pursued his girlfriend overseas, he worked a carpentry job, wrote songs, played gigs, and had meetings, tirelessly chipping away at his dream. He tried to put the betrayal out of his mind and stay focused on the task at hand.

He wrote his return letters to Lucy in the morning, just after breakfast, to clear his mind before launching into densely packed days that required all of his focus and energy. He tried to strike an upbeat tone but could not help but betray his increasing anxiety and bitterness.

This morning, at least, he had good news to report. In addition to his success with the AFI set, which had brought him a steady flow of paying scores and an entrée into the film business, he had recently reconnected with Neidlinger. Having moved to LA about six months ahead of Peter to take a teaching job at Cal Arts, Neidlinger was welcomed like royalty into the inner sanctum of Hollywood music. His second week in town he was invited to play in the orchestra on a feature film. Bands fought for him to sit in on their studio sessions. As in Boston, he organized the cadre of virtuoso players that assembled around him into a series of bands specializing in the diverse styles of music he liked to play. There was no shortage of gigs around town. By the force of his reputation, personality, and unparalleled playing, Neidlinger established himself immediately and forcefully as a pillar of the LA music scene.

He and Peter had parted in Boston on bad terms. Peter admitted in an interview for a Warner Bros. press kit that after he snubbed Neidlinger on *Knight*, his proud friend and mentor had threatened him with his bass." But the new setting made for a new start. Neidlinger introduced Peter to the best musicians in town (they had started gigging together again) and to his connections at labels and studios. Peter had all the songs together for a new record—words, music, harp playing, and vocals by Peter Ivers—so these were exactly the connections he needed.

One of these connections, in fact, was Peter's first appointment of the day. He put aside his unfinished letter to Lucy and prepared to meet with Van Dyke Parks. Not yet thirty, Parks was one of the music industry's reigning geniuses, having chalked up not only an impressive list of credits but a starring role in an enigmatic chapter of rock mythology. Signed to Warner Bros. in 1966 as an all-purpose hit maker—session musician, arranger, songwriter, producer, lyricist—he had played with the Byrds (and declined an invitation to join them), produced the first records of Randy Newman and Ry Cooder, worked with bands like the Everly Brothers, Arlo Guthrie, and the Grateful Dead, and, recently, won a Grammy. In 1966 he had been recruited by Brian Wilson to write the lyrics for *Smile*, the hugely anticipated follow-up to the Beach Boys' groundbreaking *Pet Sounds*. There was dissent among the other band members, about Parks's contribution. Then a fire in the studio got everyone spooked, Wilson destroyed the tapes, the project was shelved, and *Smile* went down in the annals as one of rock's great unfinished masterpieces.

Parks's main role was studio guru to Warner's stable of artists. At this he proved one of the best in the business, and his influence at the label grew. Recently he had been appointed to head up its new Audio-Visual Department, charged to make film shorts based on singles for promotional purposes. The first department of its kind at a major label, Warner Bros. Audio-Visual was created largely on Parks's initiative. He was one of a small handful of music industry people who saw the huge possibilities, artistic and commercial, in putting images to songs, and wrote a memo to Mo Ostin, the label's CEO, demanding, "I want music television." Parks had achieved the kind of oracular stature at the company that transcends any one title or job. His opinion was sought out on matters large and small. He was heavily involved in A&R decisions, answering only to Ostin.

A kind of mutual-admiration fever burned between Peter and Van Dyke. Parks admired Peter's intellectualism, his eclectic approach to songwriting, his seriousness as a musician, and his humility before other great players. Peter admired the fact that Van Dyke seemed to come by his genius so naturally; he was like an open channel of musical understanding.

Parks introduced Peter to his wife, Durrie, who produced with him in the Audio-Visual Department. Durrie introduced him to Linda Perry, their partner in a production company, who had deep connections in the music industry. Peter developed close personal relationships with all three of them—Durrie seemed particularly taken with

Peter—and they talked him up with their colleagues and introduced him around at the label. Van Dyke had already brought Peter in as a session player on a few of the records he was producing.

A few days before, while they made the rounds at the Warners office, Peter had charmed his way through Mo Ostin's secretary and literally stuck a foot in the door of the CEO's office. Ostin invited him to bring the other one in, too, but just for a minute. Once inside, Peter jumped on top of Ostin's desk, whipped out his harmonica, and played one of his new songs. Ostin didn't give him an answer, but he did seem to appreciate the breath of fresh air.

Now Van Dyke sat down across the table from Peter at Duke's, ordered a coffee—and conveyed the news that Mo Ostin had approved a demo of Peter Ivers's next album for consideration at Warner Bros. Peter gave Parks a big hug and wasted no time scrambling into action. He made an appointment with Linda Perry, who knew the industry inside and out, to talk about the business side and get advice on which studio he should use. He made an appointment with Neidlinger to decide who should be in the band.

The truth was that, musically, Linda Perry was not one of Peter's biggest fans. Her father and husband had both achieved commercial success making mainstream music, and Perry herself had produced a record back in '69 that made it onto the charts. She knew about hit records, and Peter's music did not fit the bill. If she, an aficionado, found Peter's stuff strange and didn't really get it, how were tens of thousands of average Americans to be expected to like it?

Personally, though, was another story. In her experience, musicians were narcissistic creatures. Peter, who had as much artistic passion and talent as anyone she had met, was just the opposite: when you were with him, you felt you were the most important person in that moment. Still, the persistent gap between Perry's appreciation of Peter's music and his person continued to trouble her, especially as she was being asked to use her name and contacts on his behalf. She approached Durrie, her confidante and partner-in-crime, and asked her point-blank: "Peter is wonderful, but do you really think he should have a record deal?" Without hesitating, Durrie answered "Yes." "Why?" "Because he wants it." Which suddenly, to Perry, made perfect sense.

When she showed up at Duke's later that day to meet him, Perry had more good news. At the time, Warner Bros.'s going rate for demos was $500. Tapping a powerful friend at the company, she had gotten them to triple it for Peter and give him his choice of top studios.

It was already evening when Neidlinger came by to discuss the make-up of the band. There was no question this time who would play bass. Since getting into studio work, Neidlinger had also taken an interest in the recording process, and wanted to produce the demo as well. Peter agreed.

Everything, then, was set. Now they just had to make the record that would sell a million copies and make him a rock star. Unlike Linda Perry, Peter had complete confidence that this third time would be the charm: that his new style, while tweaking some of pop's time-honored forms; had enough intelligence and sex appeal to satisfy the masses. There were others at Warners who, while perhaps somewhat more guarded in their optimism about his commercial prospects, loved Peter's music, championed him at the label, and hoped for a break-through—less for the sake of Peter's career than for their own. These were mostly the younger producers and execs, who felt the music industry had slipped into a coma of cheap sentiment and mindless beats, as reflected in the dominance of southern rock and the emergence of disco. People like Charlie Haas, an acquaintance of Tim Hunter who had found his way to Warners and become a Peter Ivers booster. Haas and his cohorts were bored to the point of embarrassment by the bland offerings their label was churning out, to say nothing of their own listless careers. Something had to come and overturn the order, wake the nation out of its haze of post-'60s escapism and shock. If not the parents, then the children: someone, something had to capture the imagination of America's youth.

Peter and Neidlinger filled out the lineup for the demo, and Neidlinger took his leave, leaving Peter in his regular seat at Duke's where some fourteen hours before he had ordered his regular breakfast, and where he ordered his regular dinner now. The cooks knew just how he liked it. As he waited the extra time it took for them to prepare the meal to his specifications, he took out the most recent letters from Lucy and this morning's unfinished return post. His pen quivered but he tried to keep it light: *"Don't flip your clit . . . Keep up the good cunt."* *"I love you,"* he professed, *"with a passion unequaled by man or midget."*

He peppered the letters with in-jokes he knew would make her laugh; but the sign-off always gave him away. He wrote every day, and every day the letter ended the same. Across the sea in London—having the time of her life—Lucy heard anger, frustration, and hurt starting to ooze off the page. It was the sheer repetition: every day, the same ending, as if the rest of the letter had just been an excuse to ask this one question, over and over again: *When are you coming home?*

He settled up at Duke's, crossed back to the Tropicana, played some music, and then read until he fell asleep, as always, fully clothed, with the lights still on.

LA, the Kleins' House, 1972

Lucy and Peter had been living with the Kleins for the good part of a year, since Lucy quit her publishing job and moved to LA. After returning from her Europe trip, she had lasted six months before deciding that she needed to be where Peter was. It rained and rained that last month in New Jersey, for twenty-six days straight. She decided that if it rained for one more day, she would take it as a sign that it was time to leave. It rained.

Her one condition for Peter remained: the Tropicana was not an option. She appreciated Peter's love for the seedy rooms, the shady characters, and the pervasive rock-and-roll romance, but she would not stay there for even one night. John Klein was a fellow at AFI, and when he and his wife Hillary had decided to rent a house in Sierra Bonita, Peter went in with them for two rooms—one for him and Lucy, and one that he soundproofed and used as a studio.

Lucy would drag Peter to NBC every morning for his carpentry job, equipped with a lunchbox and a novel by Kafka. She drove him in his orange Volkswagen that they had driven out from Boston, and then she would spend the rest of the day unsuccessfully job searching before picking him up at five. Later that year Peter bought a blue Saab, which he and Lucy shared, and on which he once forgot to set the parking brake. When it started rolling down the hill, he singlehandedly tried to stop it, banging up both the car and himself in the process in an episode he would henceforth refer to as his "Saab Story."

For the Kleins, there were times when their cozy little unit felt more like a bohemian Addams Family. As when, from time to time, the doorbell would ring after midnight, and they would open it to find a slightly menacing-looking couple all dressed in black: Van Dyke and Durrie Parks, with pressing business for Peter that apparently would not hold until dawn. (For example, Van Dyke, a *New York Times* crossword puzzle devotee, called on Peter at all hours for help with obscure ancient references—another basis for Park's admiration being that Peter was the only guy in town who knew the classics.)

Eventually Peter's allergies forced him to quit the carpentry job altogether, and he would spend the better part of each day up in his studio. At night he would come down and play the songs he had just written. While his high, nasal voice gave them pause, the Kleins thought Peter's lyrics were brilliant and his harp playing out of this world.

It was during this time that Peter recorded his third album. Warner Bros. had accepted the demo and given him a contract for the real thing. Alan Siegel, a young lawyer at a big entertainment firm in New York who represented Barbara Mandrell, had helped Peter with his Epic contract and now negotiated a good deal for him with Warner Bros. The band rehearsed and recorded in one of Hollywood's most expensive, prestigious studios, with Smokey Robinson recording across the hall. Peter had come up with a name for the album that captured its subversive pop spirit. Like much of what he wrote (or, for that matter, said—Buddy Helm, a drummer and friend, considered Peter to be master of the double, triple, and quadruple entendre), it could be understood on several different levels: *Terminal Love.*

LA, *Terminal Love* Sessions, 1974, 9 p.m.

Peter and Neidlinger barely seemed to notice the array of shiny, apparatuses that filled the spacious recording studio. They were focused on finding a special sound for a particular track, a vocal tone appropriate only for this moment of this song, never heard before and never to be replicated. They weren't going to find it in a machine. They would be lucky to find it somewhere in the room, and they scavenged around, mic in hand, bouncing Peter's voice off obscure corners and cracks, listening on the monitor for the elusive perfect tone. It was tedious but necessary. This was going to be it, the hit album, but only if they could capture on tape exactly what they heard in their heads. Neidlinger called to Peter, "Why not try it over there? We can get a bit more treble."

The *Terminal Love* sessions lasted about six months. It took so long to make because Peter's vision for the album was grandiose, even paradoxical—to make an infectious record that worked as a pop album, while at the same time undermining the whole idea of a pop album: a kind of alternative, fiercely independent brand of pop. (At the time there were few reference points for commercially successful pop with such an artistic, nonmainstream point of view. Stylistic innovators like Lou Reed and David Bowie could be pointed to as antecedents of, if not necessarily influences on, Peter's work—and while both would eventually become legends, by the mid-'70s even they enjoyed only uneven commercial success.) The music on *Terminal Love* was also very precise. Peter used a drum machine, very rare at the time, as constant rhythmic presence, the record's heartbeat. He used a saxophone to mimic the sound of a dinosaur waking up from a long slumber; he played Coke bottles to capture the effect of Andean flutes; and he orchestrated one-man, three-part harmonica instrumentals. On top of it all were his witty lyrics and unusual voice, which he described to one interviewer with a typically ambiguous blend of candor, self-effacement, and arrogance: "Finally, of course, there's the sound of my voice: laughable at first, then seductive."

They finally found the tone they had been looking for in the toilet bowl in the studio bathroom. Peter crouched over the toilet like someone at the end of a bad night, his head halfway into the bowl, microphone in hand, singing his heart out.

LA, Universal Amphitheatre, 8:00 p.m.

The show had not even started, but thousands of fans at the Universal Amphitheatre were already cheering, ecstatic at having managed to get their hands on one of the year's hottest tickets. Fleetwood Mac was touring their self-titled breakthrough album to packed houses throughout the country, and the Universal was straining at capacity, beyond sold-out.

It was a safe bet that most in the amped-up audience had not heard of the opening act, Peter Ivers, or the album he was touring, *Terminal Love*. The album had been out for over a year, and it wasn't selling very well. Still, Peter had made a fan out of Mo Ostin, and Linda and Durrie had lobbied tirelessly to get him this gig touring with the label's most popular act. The prevailing thinking among Peter's friends about why the album had not caught fire was the same problem he had faced with Epic: promotion. Peter's music was hot but totally different from everything else out there. The label, at a loss for how to position it, had more or less thrown up its hands. It had been up to Peter's industry friends, and young label supporters like Charlie Haas, to come up with a strategy to lift him and his record out of the doldrums.

Enter Fleetwood Mac. The idea was simple: associate Peter with a commercial dynamo, and leapfrog the marketing problem by delivering him in person to tens of thousands of potential fans. Get the music in their ears, get Peter in their hearts, get the record in their hands. If there was a consensus on anything, it was that Peter knew how to communicate from the stage. Nearly everyone who had seen him perform—in the local gigs and parties he played in bands with Neidlinger, in living rooms, record label offices, and on the street—found him a seductive and electrifying stage presence. He and his friends often lamented that what had once seemed like a gift was turning into an albatross, his arduous and inefficient signature: winning fans over "one at a time." Opening for Fleetwood Mac would allow him to expand the circuit many thousands of times over.

Peter's supporters were optimistic but anxious. This tour made possible the mainstream infiltration he sought. It was also very likely his last real hope for achieving it.

Peter stood just offstage with the band, awaiting his cue. He could see Lucy, close to the front row, with the group of movie executives she had brought from work. Recently she had gotten what she considered her first "real job," reading freelance scripts for United Artists. Until then, aside from a temporary research job for Van Dyke Parks, the occasional publicity work Peter had helped her to get, and a stint writing and reading weather for a local news station's graveyard shift, Lucy had spent most of her time playing tennis, hanging out, and eating breakfast every day with Peter at Schwab's drugstore.

It was a youthful, hippie life, very Peter Pan and Wendy, and for Lucy that had been just fine.

Peter was the one with the Big Plans; she assumed she would eventually settle into a job in publishing or museums or some similar extension of her liberal arts degree. In the meantime, she had come to California at age twenty-two and was more than happy to spend her postgraduation years on an open-ended rock-and-roll adventure in LA.

More and more though, Peter had become focused—obsessed—with making music and making it big. Midconversation, he would pull a pad out of his pocket and jot down notes for a song. Even when they went to the beach, he would pack his electric piano in the trunk in case inspiration struck while he was sunbathing or surfing a wave. Lucy supported Peter's ambition, and the shift in focus didn't bring any noticeable change in his personality, his conviction that we were put on earth to roam freely and enjoy ourselves, or in his loving way with her. It did, however, leave her with substantially more time on her hands. And while Lucy enjoyed the social whirlwind Peter stirred up wherever he went, and often brought into their home, by nature she was a far more private person. With Peter less available for play dates, her focus turned toward her new job.

The job was happy to oblige. This was Hollywood, after all; there was no shortage of scripts to be read. Visitors during that time developed an impression of Lucy as the bookish girlfriend reading in bed late at night, under the covers, stacks of scripts piled up on the nightstand, while Peter and his musician friends jammed and rehearsed in the living room. On quieter nights he worked in his studio, hunched over his reel-to-reel, plugged into studio-quality headphones.

Peter and Lucy had been living in their own place in Laurel Canyon for about two years. It was sunny and green, bursting with bougainvilleas, a quiet refuge in the Hollywood Hills. Hillary Klein came for a housewarming visit soon after they moved in and was struck by Lucy's strong domestic imprint. She nurtured an extensive garden and filled the house with what must have been fifty plants.

Around the same time, Merle and Ricki came out for their first visit. In the car from the airport, Peter informed them that he was planning to have a party the following night. "Oh good, how nice," Merle said, and Lucy explained that Peter was not speaking off the cuff: he had sent out formal, hand-designed invitations to all his friends, letting them know that his mother was coming to town and a party was to be held in her honor for a select group of guests. In the refrigerator, she found stacks of champagne bottles. Impressed and flattered at the care and scope of the planning on her behalf, Merle asked what kind of hors d'oeuvres they intended to serve. Cheese and crackers? Crudités? Again it fell on Lucy to explain: "No, your son is having chocolate marshmallow cookies." And so it was. The guests drank champagne and munched on Peter's favorite dessert, and Merle was seated on a chair in the back of the room to receive official introductions.

Another visitor during Lucy and Peter's first year in Laurel Canyon was a stocky young Albanian American comic Doug knew from the *Lampoon*. About a year after launching, the magazine had begun making forays into radio, vinyl, and the stage. To translate their highly literary brand of satire into performance, they had brought in a crop of young comedians who not only shared the skewed *Lampoon* sensibility, but also could act it out in real time. John Belushi was admired for his radioactively intense stage presence and his over-the-top commitment to every persona he inhabited.

The first *Lampoon* stage outing, *National Lampoon Lemmings*, had been a breakout national success. The second effort, *The National Lampoon Stage Show*, was less successful, and over the editors' protests the performers had been let go. This freed Belushi up for his next gig. He had been hired by NBC as a cast member for a new sketch comedy show, drawing on the *Lampoon*'s spirit of ballsy satire (and on several of its former and current editors and actors), to air live on Saturday nights. Belushi crashed with Peter and Lucy in Laurel Canyon about a week before the pilot was scheduled to air.

Ensconced in her cozy Hollywood hideout, still essentially a "rock-and-roll old lady" (a popular designation at the time for rocker girlfriends, which she hated), Lucy quietly, diligently began a career at the bottom of the Hollywood food chain. She read her scripts late into the night and borrowed Peter's car to drive in her reports. She took the work seriously and soon was recognized by the studio executives as a hard worker with a sharp mind and a discerning eye. At every opportunity, she talked up her rocker boyfriend and was ecstatic at the opportunity to invite her bosses to what could very well be his breakout show. A number had taken her up on it. After all, they must have reasoned: if he was opening for Fleetwood Mac, how bad could it be?

She stood with the executives, waiting for Peter to be introduced. The emcee called his name, and he jogged out onto the stage—clad only in a diaper. The other bandmembers followed and launched into the first song. The audience was so primed that for the first minute or so their general enthusiasm carried over. Peter was manic onstage. He delivered his lyrics snarling and loud and jumped around frenetically. The crowd soon quieted down, unsure of what they were watching.

It was a bad-boy stage persona Peter had begun to cultivate only recently. Even his bandmates were at a loss. Paul Lenart and Alice de Buhr came from a straight-rock background and didn't understand the need for what seemed to them a lot of posturing. Why not just play the music and let the songs speak for themselves? It all seemed a little too Hollywood. Peter had pulled a similar stunt recently at the Palladium in Hollywood, opening for the New York Dolls. He'd come out in a diaper, with a squirt gun inside it filled with milk, covered with a rubber penis. He squirted the milk out onto the audience, which promptly booed him off the stage. At least with the Dolls crowd, Peter could be excused for expecting some punk-rock enthusiasm for his wild stage antics. It was a miscalculation, but at least there was some logic to it. And at that show Iggy Pop—pioneer of the stage dive, smearer of raw meat on his naked chest, public vomiter, roller around in shards of glass—had been backstage. He hung out with the band and lent some cred-by-association; Pop had been heckled offstage plenty of times early in his career. It helped. Being booed for outrageous stage behavior feels a lot less bad when Iggy, the original Wild Child, is there to tell you it's okay.

Still, it had to be asked: what was Peter thinking this time? Here, at the Universal Amphitheatre, there was no Iggy Pop, no punk rock crowd or cred, no room for such a miscalculation, and thus no real excuse. There was just Peter, outfitted in a diaper and a snarl; his mystified band; a huge stadium filled with eager if conventional fans; and the chance of a lifetime.

If the Dolls fans had been put off by Peter's diaper routine, the Fleetwood Mac fans were outraged. After a short grace period, they too began booing, and their vicious disapproval only grew louder and more insistent as Peter continued to jump around in his diaper and belt out his quirky lyrics.

Time warp space warp, rockin' in fury
Caught my darlin' Alpha Centauri

Circlin' systems searchin' aflurry
Streamlined gleamin' Alpha Centauri . . .

His bandmates, who took the heat with him, for him, onstage; his friends in the audience, who died a hundred deaths on his behalf; his supporters at Warner Bros., watching their efforts circle the drain; Merle, who would hear about it later from Peter himself, bewildered and crushed. There was an abundance of theories, but in the final analysis no one really had a clue what Peter had been thinking. Did he even really want rock star success? Some said yes, but only on his own uncompromisingly personal terms. Many friends believed it all went back to his father: he had to succeed in order to show Paul he had chosen a worthwhile path, but he had to do it without selling out, lest Paul's philosophy of compromise and deferring to the system be granted a back-door victory. By this thinking, the margin for what could constitute real success in Peter's eyes was so slim it was all but impossible. Paul was the demon who chased him down the rabbit hole of his own conflicted ambitions.

Some felt Peter's tendency for self-sabotage reflected a deeper ambivalence towards recognition and the demands it would bring. He had a pretty good life, after all, a life of leisure and art. He had no interest in touring or any of the other rigors of self-promotion. Then again, he did seem to crave recognition, to want desperately to be seen and heard, appreciated, applauded, and loved—and not only for his music, but for the creation he had worked on the longest and was undoubtedly his greatest work to date: Peter Ivers. When the interviewer for a promotional piece at Warner Bros. asked Peter if there was a specific persona behind his lyrics, his answer had been tellingly direct: "Yeah, me . . . I hope the listener will feel close to the persona, want to hug him, maybe sleep with him."

Some speculated that Peter had gone out in diapers at the Fleetwood Mac show naïvely expecting to win over the crowd by just being himself. Maybe the unequivocal acceptance he'd enjoyed from Merle growing up, and from a steady stream of friends and admirers in the meantime—whose constant refrain about Peter was that he didn't do things that were cool: what he did *became* cool—had led him to believe it was only a matter of time: all he had to do was keep doing his thing. Everyone, eventually, would come around.

Others thought that he only really cared about his personal guer-rilla theatre, that at his core he was a consummate artist, engaged first and always by his personal vision, disdainful of pandering and ulti-mately indifferent to audience response. In other words, that he sim-ply didn't give a fuck.

Unfortunately for Peter, as he looked out upon a hostile, booing audience of thousands, the two people who would have supported him no matter which of these theories was true were both thousands of miles away. Recently, Mayer's father had gotten sick, and Mayer had stepped in to run the family business. In a scenario worthy of a Tim Mayer production, Mayer himself was currently traveling up and down the Eastern Seaboard, hawking wholesale sporting-goods sup-plies to retail stores. He still managed to socialize among the literati in Manhattan and Martha's Vineyard. He and Doug Kenney moved to-gether—and drank, and, increasingly, did drugs together—in that world. The arrangement with the business would only be temporary, and in the meantime he still wrote plays and published poems. But it was a long way from the cover of *Time* magazine.

After his summer with Lucy and Peter, Doug had returned to the *Lampoon* for a few months, only to take off again for Martha's Vine-yard in the winter, determined to write *TACOS* and establish himself once and for all as the great American literary satirist of his time. After about six months, he returned with a manuscript. Upon reading it, his friend and *Lampoon* cofounder Henry Beard's only response was a slight but clear shake of the head. Doug threw the manuscript in the trash and never went back to it.

Subsequently, he returned to what came naturally. Along with a relatively recent addition to the *Lampoon* squad, newbie P. J. O'Rourke, he wrote and edited a full-length parody of that most time-honored American document: *The National Lampoon 1964 High School Year-book Parody*. Filled with nostalgia and bitterness, sexual perversity and scatological rage, pitch-perfect renditions of every familiar high school type, and photo spreads capturing the period and the personas in obsessive detail—with the *Yearbook Parody*, Doug found the voice that had eluded him in the novel.

Commercially, it was an instant success, selling more copies than any stand-alone book parody before or since and raking in millions for the *Lampoon*.

A few months before the parody was released, Doug had made a few million of his own. The deal he, Henry, and their other cofounder had structured with the *Lampoon*'s publisher upon its inception required that the publisher buy out their share after five years. In 1975, business was booming, and the buyout made the three young satirists very rich.

Kenney and Mayer had arrived at very different places in their lives, but they'd remained close, and both relied on the friendship. When Tim got a call that Doug was having a bona fide breakdown out on the Vineyard, he went out immediately and stayed with him until he was well.

Tonight, though, for Peter, there was no Tim and no Doug. Just thousands of Fleetwood Mac fans who did not think Peter was brilliant or even cute. Who, by the sound of their booing, seemed to want him strung up on a tree. Tonight, there was only one person among the throngs of the Universal Amphitheatre who knew the real Peter—and Lucy Fisher seemed prepared to take on the whole crowd. He certainly could not have asked for a fiercer, more fearless defender. Furious, she stood up on her chair and turned to her section of the audience—or, more accurately, turned on them. She waved her arms and started screaming, first at the crowd surrounding her and then at individual people unfortunate enough to be caught in her glare.

"Shut up! Shut up! Just listen! Listen! He's great!"

But the booing crowd drowned out her shouts. Then it drowned out Peter's singing. Eventually, it drowned out the band. They left the stage before completing their set.

==================================== *close-up:*

The '70s in Sunny Los Angeles

LINDA PERRY

"He was madly in love with Lucy, and she loved him. What else do you need? I'm not saying smooth sailing, or that he didn't have an eye for other women. But anything he did, to Lucy it was wonderful. How do you not love someone that thinks you're so wonderful?"

Every time you attack your heart, your heart will attack you . . .
—Peter Ivers, "Terminal Love" (<>) song #4

Terminal Love, Peter's Second Official Album

"I've got good instincts for old-fashioned sexual drama—you can always arouse someone if you're making them laugh while you do it."
—*Peter Ivers, Circular, July 29, 1974*

"Buell and I produced *Terminal Love* together. Buell is Buell Neidlinger, bass player of excellence, with a world reputation in classical, jazz, and rock circles. He's appeared with everybody from Billie Holiday to the London Symphony, everywhere from Newport to Carnegie Hall. He's played with Cecil Taylor, and most every other major jazz artist, and more recently, with dozens of rock luminaries."
—*Peter Ivers, Warner Bros. press kit interview, 1974*

Approaching Peter Ivers's first album *Terminal Love* (Warners), is not just a casual listening experience. The music compares to nothing else in rock. . . . Ivers commands enough lyrical swagger to make Bowie retire (again), Lou Reed worry, and Cole Porter move over . . .
—*James Spina, Women's Wear Daily, July 24, 1974*

JELLO BIAFRA

"*Terminal Love* came out and tried to make him more radio friendly. But you can't get away from his voice."

He sounds, in fact, like an androgynous eight-year-old traumatized by Mighty Mouse.

　　　—*Warner Bros. press release*

JELLO BIAFRA

"And his lyrics are pretty damn good too. Every once in a while I still think of situations I'm in, in my own life, and I think, Outer space is goddamn cold without you."

Time warp, space warp, rockin in fury,
Caught my darlin' Alpha Centauri
Circlin' systems searchin a flurry,
Streamlined, gleaming Alpha centauri . . .
Can't survive another day without you.
Outer space is goddamn cold without you.
　　—*"Alpha centauri" (<>) song #5*

"I think I fit right in as an heir to the American songwriting tradition of Gershwin, Berlin, et cetera, but, you know, more modern. I don't write genre songs. I'd rather stretch out and advance the form, in my playing and writing. I want to write a new kind of love song."

　　—*Peter Ivers, Warner Bros. interview, July 1974*

VAN DYKE PARKS

"I remember his meetings with Mo Ostin. A quote from Mo Ostin with Peter: 'Okay Mo, so what is great music?' Mo, without missing a beat: Great music— tonnage my boy, tonnage.' That's from Mo Ostin. Any idea that Warner Bros. had a moment to tolerate or condone or nurture anybody who didn't fit the stripe, whatever that was, was quickly out of the door. There was no Mister Nice Guy in any of this. There is no way around this. This is not happy face stuff."

"Other records that I think deliver this kind of complete and consistent sound-image are *Rubber Soul*, the first Dr. John *Gris-Gris*, and second Jimi Hendrix, *Axis: Bold as Love*, albums.

　　—*Peter Ivers*

BUELL NEIDLINGER

"He was trying to get a hit record. What else do people try to do? He thought he had one, but it was in the hands of the inept. That's spelled i-n-e-p-t."

CHARLIE HAAS (colleague, Editorial Director, Warner Bros. Records)

"Well, it was the mid-'70s, so punk hadn't really happened yet. It wasn't a terribly interesting time."

JELLO BIAFRA

"I hesitate to call Peter ahead of his time as much as I would call him outside of his time. *Terminal Love* is just so unique that you either get it or you don't. There wasn't the indie rock touring circuit that there is today, so the best they could have done with him was put him on the road with some Eagles wannabe, and hope that somebody would get it."

LUCY FISHER

"He honestly thought he was going to go to California and be a millionaire, and it looked like it was happening too. He really wanted to show up his dad and have his mother have a nice house. He wanted to prove that he could do it his way, but it also had to be the most complicated, hard, way."

> "My songs are like the flip side of normal songs . . . they talk about the part of experience that occurs after other songs end, or before they begin."
> —*Peter Ivers,* Circular, *July 29, 1974*

PAUL MICHAEL GLASER

"Well, you're talking about the '70s and we were getting our heads handed to us by Vietnam as a country, but things were also pretty gullible and pretty innocent compared to life today. So, you know, there was still a bit of romance attached to rebelling. It was a different time and people were more vulnerable and gullible. It was an era, a time of waking up."

VAN DYKE PARKS

"To be dropped by a label confers a special kind of character on a person. It brings a certain humility to a person that has been to the mountain, in terms of ego. You are an artist and then all of a sudden you are nothing. That puts a man in the kitchen with the ashes, groveling, who once was great."

Punk Comics

The young in recent years have seemed so angry, serious, self-absorbed, and just plain blue that one could scarcely guess that they had it in them to produce an uproariously funny spoof of the rock scene and its counterculture folk heroes. Nonetheless, *National Lampoon* staffers have done just that on the Off-Broadway stage, and with wicked precision.

— *"A Rock Musical Review,"* Time, *February 19, 1973*

HAROLD RAMIS

"I grew up in Chicago and ended up moving back to Chicago after college and started working as an editor. I started freelancing for a newspaper and got hired as an editor at *Playboy* magazine, I started doing workshops and got into Second City. Then I took time off, went to Europe, and they hired Belushi as a replacement for me. When I got back, John and I were in the company together, that's when we became friends with the Murray brothers. Gilda, Aykroyd, and John Candy were also there. So Belushi went off to do the *National Lampoon's Lemmings* show, which is the first stage performance. He brought a bunch of us to New York to work for the *Lampoon*, and we became a *Lampoon* show."

HOWARD CUTLER

"*The National Lampoon*, when it got successful, had a spinoff called *The National Lampoon Radio Hour*, which is what brought all those Second City people to New York. So most of those guys that eventually became *SNL*, came in through *The National Lampoon Radio Hour*, and that eventually led to *SNL*."

JUDY BELUSHI

"All those people came together. Then Lorne came in from Canada and Danny too. Michael O'Donoghue and Chevy were also there."

LINDA PERRY

"Everyone in that time, the brilliant ones like Van Dyke, and Peter, and Doug Kenney, it was all visual as well as music. Nobody else was really that visionary at that time."

case book *part 4*

DETECTIVE CLIFFORD SHEPARD
"Back in '83, they didn't know what DNA was. They were doing blood groups at the time. From what I see [of the evidence] that was booked, I mean, a lot of things were like credit cards and driver's license, and that wasn't going to help. If there had been a struggle, and the murderer would have been injured, then there would be a chance that there was something left behind."

* * *

DETECTIVE HANK PETROVSKY
"So you're putting this book together, interviewing these people, you are gone from the scene, whatever the evidence is, they either have no prints or some prints, identified or unidentified. It was a hard place to fingerprint anything. It's not like a house, it's a big old room with big tall ceilings. So we followed all the leads people gave us, whether we thought they were crazy or not."

DAVE ALVIN, musician, the Blasters
"Then after that came the rumors. All that kind of stuff. It was this it was that. It wasn't like one rumor that just sticks, there were just so many."

PAUL FLATTERY, colleague, video producer
"One theory was that he had, there was some group from San Francisco that he led on, or they thought he had led them on, towards thinking that he could get them a record deal, and something fell out on that."

BUDDY HELM, friend, drummer, bandmate
"It was a job somebody got paid to do. I thought that, of all the footage I had from *At Sunset* [a television talk show

Helm produced and Peter briefly hosted], I was so sure I had the killer on tape. I've limited it to three people, local scenesters involved with the USA *New Wave Theatre* cable show."

HOWARD SMITH

"The one thing I heard was that the people who lived down there felt that it was this heroin addict that suddenly disappeared. He was a fixture downtown that was around, and then all of a sudden wasn't there anymore. That was the street vibe."

PETER RAFELSON

"One of the more common theories is that he owed people money and they threatened him. So that might have been income instability showing through. He always cavalierly walked into dangerous situations. So, yes, certainly this man was probably in dangerous situations, and finally felt he could take some control of his [financial] destiny."

JEFF EYRICH, friend, bandmate

"There was all kinds of theories, Peter was involved with drugs somehow. But I don't know, other than smoke pot, it was all recreational, that was it. I didn't know anybody who was mad at Peter or had a grudge against him. The whole thing just never added up."

STUART CORNFELD

"And the cops, everyone they interviewed they asked about his sex life—"

JOHANNA WENT

"If it was a gay thing."

HILARY KLEIN

"Lucy told me that when the police were investigating, they found pictures that made it seem like Peter was gay, so they stopped investigating. Peter showed up with this guy once, a young film executive, and I was doing a lot of photography back then, and Peter said, 'You have to take our picture,' so Peter took him into the shower, and I photographed them together. And that was just so Peter, to find an odd place to be photographed, and they were totally dressed."

ANNE RAMIS

"I remember talking to Harry Shearer, and that he thought Peter was gay and some gay guy did it. He thought he was gay and that he flirted with somebody. I mean, he was a flirt; he flirted with everybody."

PETER RAFELSON

"I was told that there was some insane, seven-foot transvestite seen going up to his place late that night."

STEVE MARTIN

"Do you really think a transvestite would be able to sneak into his place without him knowing, or break into his place without him knowing it? And sneak up on him? Think about it for a minute. I mean, a tall transvestite? Okay, I'm a crazy tall transvestite, and I'm going to sneak into this building and I'm going to go to a place where someone is, kill them, and steal a cassette recorder."

LINDA PERRY

"The only thing they could figure out was that, because he knew such odd people, it could have been anyone from anywhere."

ROGER KOZAL (HIGH SCHOOL FRIEND)

"The only thing we would talk about was, since he was so open to finding new people, he picked up the wrong person."

HAROLD RAMIS

"Peter could not have been loved by more people, and was a creature of light."

DETECTIVE HANK PETROVSKY

"It's a tough case because there is no evidence. I don't think, if it was a burglar, that he intended to kill him, but then you would think, if he was sleeping, why disturb him, take something and leave? He didn't hear you come in, why would he hear you coming out? If it was a friend, there would have been an argument first. In that case, Peter Ivers would have been awake and gotten up, but that doesn't make sense either. I don't know, some cases never get solved."

HOWARD SMITH

The other thing, which was again just a vibe going around, was that the detectives thought they knew who did it but they didn't have enough evidence to make a case. It was from a pretty decent source. Didn't Lucy hire a personal detective? I think that's where I got it from. That the police actually had a pretty good idea of who they thought it was."

LUCY FISHER

"Merle tried to dissuade me from continuing the pursuit, fearing it would never be solved and worrying that my obsession would only harm me and harm my relationship with Doug [Wick, whom she was dating at the time]. But I couldn't stomach the idea of the killer still walking around free, and I was adamant that Peter deserved the dignity of justice, or at least a conclusion."

* * *

DETECTIVE CLIFFORD SHEPARD

"When we have nothing else to follow up on, you've analyzed everything you can, nobody else you can talk to, you've looked at all potential suspects. Generally our murder cases lay on the shelf for sixty-two days, and evidence usually gets destroyed long before that. Detectives aren't supposed to destroy things, but sometimes they do screw up and evidence gets destroyed."

chapter 6

The Lady in the Radiator

LA, Studio Session, 1975, 2:15 p.m.

Peter's hot new band—the Peter Peter Ivers Band—was rocking the studio, when suddenly Peter halted midverse. A delivery had arrived, and Peter bolted to the door to receive it. His bandmates and producer watched to see what could be so important to bring the session to such an abrupt halt. Peter held it up in two hands, displaying it like the Holy Grail. It was a head of iceberg lettuce. He lowered it to his mouth and chomped into it like an apple.

The sessions for the next album were coming along fine, though not without their hiccups. After the critical success and commercial disappointment of *Terminal Love*, followed by the Fleetwood Mac debacle, Mo Ostin had canceled a Terminal Love tour, leaving Peter, his players, and what was left of the album's prospects cut off at the knees. Still, Peter had one more record on his WB contract, and they had decided to try to give him a boost—and to try to give themselves one more shot at a return on their investment. Neidlinger, while still highly esteemed as a bassist, was rejected as a producer by the label. Instead, they assigned Peter a proven hit maker, keyboardist, producer, and solo artist Gary Wright.

Wright had nothing if not mainstream industry cred. In the late '60s his first band, the British rock group Spooky Tooth, in which he sang and played keyboard, had opened sell-out U.S. tours for Jimi Hendrix and the Rolling Stones. In the early '70s he became a producer and session musician, producing a Traffic record and playing keyboards on George Harrison's multiplatinum solo album *All Things*

Must Pass. In '74 Wright signed as a solo artist with Warner Bros., hitting gold, then platinum, then multiplatinum—with his first release, 1975's *The Dream Weaver*, whose title track held *Billboard*'s number 2 spot for three weeks.

For his own album, Wright had pioneered the first all-keyboard and synthesizer band, producing a sound very much in line with the slick, broad, orchestral rock that seemed to be resonating with audiences of the time—Supertramp, Yes, and so on. In pairing him with Peter, the label no doubt hoped to bridge the gap between Peter's quirky personal vision and what the listening public seemed ready to hear. Wright, while excited by the challenge also seemed to be the only person in the room baffled by Peter's lettuce-chomping break.

Some of Peter's friends questioned his decision to go along with Warner Bros.'s plan. For the most part, though, they held their tongues. Durrie Parks, who had become one of Peter's closest industry confidantes, could see how desperately he wanted to be successful and that even he, the eternal optimist, could see his window was closing. This kind of commercially motivated partnering at the heart of his creative enterprise, which even a year ago Peter might have rejected out of hand, had begun to seem at least partially attractive to him. Neidlinger, as always, was less diplomatic (and as always completely intolerant of artistic compromise). He took to referring to Peter's new collaborator as "Gary Wrong."

The WB executive who had solicited Wright to work on the project had described Peter as an eclectic, unusual artist, and when he played Wright some of Peter's songs the producer agreed. Indeed, the range of styles within each of his two previous albums was impressive; the development from one to the next was downright unusual. In *Knight of the Blue Communion*, Peter had taken his Roxbury and Harvard education and ground it into a fine powder using the rough edges of jazz, blues, and rock, mixing dark poetic lyrics (one critic had aptly called them "obliquely Dylanesque"), creamy jazz vocals, playful classical instrumentation, his own muscular blues harp, and rock beats at once driving and complex. It had a loose, improvisational feel, yet without ever seeming to falter or miss. It was what a progressive rock band might have sounded like playing in the court of a medieval French king. It was King Crimson meets Little Walter meets David Bowie meets Thelonious Monk.

Terminal Love, on the other hand, had clearly been attempting, at least, to be a pop album. The songs were shorter and followed standard variations on the verse-chorus-verse structure, for which Mayer had no use. It was more blues and blues-rock driven, leaving Peter's classical and jazz influence in the deep background. While less baroque than its predecessor, the album was still intensely thoughtful and layered, and Peter used all his top-caliber musician friends to great effect (Marty Krystall's howling saxophone is a high point). The songs themselves were diverse, ranging from hard rock, to blues, to Caribbean calypso, to a funky New Orleans sound, to what Peter referred to as "two of the sensual, raging, hot jungle songs I'm famous for." Peter's harp also got lots of play, both as an accent standing in for synthesizer flourishes and as warm, grounding presence in a musical and lyrical world filled with parody, irony, and absurdist flights. Peter's lyrics themselves, while no less literary or clever than Mayer's, were far less dark—whimsical and sensual, "crisply kinky" in one reviewer's words. Between the playful lyrics, and vocals another reviewer described as "florid wispiness," it was hard to escape the sense that Peter was addressing his audience with a wink, at least those sophisticated enough to be in on the joke. And while *Rolling Stone* had described *Terminal Love* (not unadmiringly) as an "uncomfortable album" populated by cynical, "bloodless characters," someone listening closely enough to the sci-fi allegory of "Alpha Centauri" might also pick up on the subtle poignancy of lines like, "Since you been out of town, the supply's all gone / You gotta come back with my energy pack intact."

A reviewer for *Women's Wear Daily* described the album as a whole as a "jagged blend of delicate frenzy," and Wright, meeting Peter in person, found more of the same: an intellectual, eccentric artist with wide-ranging tastes, who was also a very nice person. Wright was charmed. Working with Peter Ivers promised to be a fun, interesting project, and certainly different from anything he'd done before. With his production and arranging skills, Wright could infuse Peter's jagged frenzy with melodic clarity, rhythmic form, and the shot at mainstream accessibility Peter was looking for.

In the studio, however, the gap between the two artists' sensibilities began to show itself early on. Peter's intention may have been to let the Dream Weaver do his magic and make his record a hit. He may have believed Wright could get him past this period of obscurity and struggle, and in theory he may have been willing to compromise by allowing more commercial influences into his work. In practice, though, Peter knew exactly what he wanted. And knew he wanted things the way he wanted them.

Despite tensions in the studio, Peter maintained high hopes for the album. He had a great band, a famous producer, and Carly Simon singing with him on one track. (When an interviewer noted that this put him in the same boat as Mick Jagger, Peter shot back, "We get different mileage out of her, though—in my case I admit I'm so vain.") After producing the demo, he sent a copy to his lawyer Alan Siegel with a note saying, "I definitely think this demo is it. I am demo'd in all the brilliance of a silver anvil being beaten by 10,000 gold-dipped fireflies."

Indeed, by all accounts the sessions were hot. Peter's musicians, as always, delivered, and so did Wright. His arrangements added a new element of pianos and strings to round out some of Peter's edges without muting his alternative sound, unifying Peter's tunes with strong melodic lines and fleshing out the emotionality often hidden in his lyrics, thus pushing him to express it in his vocals as well. Indeed, perhaps not despite their creative tensions, but because of them, Peter and Wright had produced an album made up only of what mattered to them most. Everyone who heard the demo agreed that it was both highly original and commercially hot. Peter's buoyancy at the record's prospects seemed entirely well-founded.

LA, Yoga Studio, 8:00 a.m.

"Exhale."

Yogi Alan Finger instructed his students to release on a mantra with an oddly familiar ring. Peter, for one, recognized it right away—but not from yoga.

"OOOOOoooooooooooooooooyyyyyyyyyyyyyyyyyyyyyyyyyyyyyyyyyyy yyyyy."

In his yoga studio, Finger drew upon the spiritual resources of many religious traditions. A South African Jew who had been exposed to both yoga and Yiddish from a young age, he would often pepper his sessions with Jewish jokes.

"OOOoooooooooooooyyyyyyyyyyyyyyyyyVVVVVVvvvveeeeeeeeeeeee yyyyyyyyyyyy."

In 1976, yoga was virtually unknown in LA. The entire "scene" consisted of one or two obscure, sparsely populated studios. Finger's happened to be down the hill from Peter and Lucy's Laurel Canyon pad. Peter stumbled on to it almost by accident, but when he did it was like discovering a long-lost twin. Since his wrestling days, Peter had treated his body with disciplined care. In his performances, it was his most indispensable instrument. Soon after coming to LA Peter had taken up karate; he earned his first black belt within a year. While he continued to practice martial arts, in yoga he found an even more profound vehicle for unifying the physical and mental. And in Alan Finger he'd found a teacher from whom he felt he had much to learn.

Finger's expansive philosophy—yoga not merely as a physical discipline or even a spiritual practice, but an encompassing way of life— and his refusal to take himself too seriously made him the perfect mentor for Peter. The studio had a small back door that had been built for deliveries, and often Peter would arrive in the middle of class and crawl through the doorway reciting mantras.

Finger saw his role as helping Peter to refine and amplify his natural gifts. They began spending time together outside of the studio, on long walks around the city, immersed in conversations ranging from the physical to the metaphysical, the sublime to the ridiculous, often cracking each other up. Peter became close with Finger's family, adding them to his rounds of unannounced daily drop-ins. He also became closely bonded with the studio's other regulars. The group shared a strong sense of being on a journey together that few others at the time were even aware of, and trusted fully in Finger's steady spiritual compass.

Like Finger, Peter viewed spirituality as something that was practiced in the everyday—in his relationships with food, sex, art, in his professional decisions, and especially in his interactions with other people. Rochelle Robertson, one of Finger's disciples with whom Peter became friends, understood the goal of tantric yoga as learning to be completely present with whatever one is doing in his life, and Finger himself went a step further: to be able to love, and be joyous, for no reason at all. Finger and Robertson both saw Peter as preternaturally gifted in these regards. (His Harvard friend John Leone always carried with him the time Peter admonished him, "John, whenever you're about to be mean to someone, just remember everyone lives in pain.") When, as often happened, those who encountered him—from close friends to people he met only once or twice—would talk about coming away with an intense spiritual feeling and describe Peter himself as a heightened spiritual being, this is probably what they meant.

Peter brought his usual exuberance to yoga, talking up Finger to everyone he knew, insisting they stop by for a class. The change in him was readily apparent to his friends. He seemed even more vividly present, more focused on the moment. His own emotions seemed to become heightened, and he was even more open about expressing them. If he felt sad about something, he might stop in the middle of the street and start crying until the feeling passed. One friend commented that Peter lived his life like a woman giving birth without painkillers. Sometimes while in conversation, he would shift into a yoga pose and quietly say the mantra Finger had given to him to make his own:

Om-gatay-gatay-gatay-pom-gatee-parsalt-sum-gatee-oh-per-sam-gatee-udi-swah-ha.

In some people, such displays might seem childish or affected, but Peter went about his business with such matter-of-factness that it barely disrupted the conversational flow. When he did want to bring a conversation to a halt, he might demonstrate the various advanced nasal cleansing techniques Finger had taught him—inhaling saltwater, or running two cords into his nose, down the back of his throat and out his mouth, and pulling the two ends back and forth. He clearly relished the shock value as much as the spiritual value. Inspired by his example, many of Peter's friends started visiting the yoga studio, and a number, like Tim Hunter, became regulars. Over time the classes became extremely popular, and Finger had more students than he could take on. He made Peter a yogi and assigned him to teach the overflow.

Lucy was as impressed with Peter's yoga accomplishments as his other friends were. She did see them, though, in a somewhat more complicated light. To the outside world Peter appeared preternaturally calm, kind, balanced, gentle, playful, and enlightened—qualities nearly unheard of in an aspiring rock star negotiating LA's music industry. What the outside world missed was the intense self-control that made this stalwart calm possible, and moreover, the personal pathos driving the discipline: what Lucy referred to as Peter's "demons," namely his father's disapproving voice, always loud in Peter's head. She knew that Peter's intense drive to succeed, not only creatively but also financially, was born in large part out of a desire to win Paul's approval. A constant refrain, starting with his first record deal in Boston and continuing throughout the years in LA, was that his first act on making it big would be to send a $500,000 check to Paul, settling their lifelong dispute once and for all.

Lucy saw a side of Peter that few others saw—the boy who had lost one father to natural causes and another to rigid principles. She considered Paul nothing short of sadistic, and saw how Peter suffered from his constant belittlement and yet craved his acceptance. The discipline he applied to his yoga, his meditation, and his art was impressive, but it was also necessary, since it made it possible for him to sustain his distinct sense of clarity, purpose, mission, and self. He practiced not because he was peaceful, but because he was desperately in need of peace.

Hawaii, 8:30 a.m.

Lucy sat alone in the hotel breakfast room, staring down a very large plate of food. The chair across from her was empty. Behind her the buffet line buzzed with couples and families on vacation. Everyone was hungry, and breakfast came with the room. Meanwhile, Peter sat alone on the expansive beach, set in his yoga pose, facing the sea.

Lucy was understanding when Peter's dedication to his practice turned rigid and, at times, inconvenient. His daily morning yoga practice conflicted with the hotel breakfast. But while she appreciated his need to keep up with his practice, she also appreciated her own need not to waste good money. So Peter did his yoga, and Lucy went to breakfast alone every morning that they were in Hawaii.

Their stubbornness was in many ways a product of the optimism of youth. They had no immediate plans to get married, but they were happy. They had no plan other than to continue the blissful life they shared and grow old together. They didn't feel pressed to share breakfast on this trip because there would be many other breakfasts, many other trips. What were a few missed meals in the face of the long life they would obviously share?

Santa Monica, Nuart Theatre, circa 1977–78, Midnight

Doug Martin's friends were tired, but worse than that they were bored. What had started out as a gag and a favor for a friend—coming to the theatre every Friday at midnight, chanting the name of the movie as soon as the lead actor appeared onscreen until the rest of the crowd chanted along—was starting to feel like a job. A job that didn't pay.

"*Eraserhead, Eraserhead, Eraserhead, Eraserhead . . .*"

Well, for Doug Martin, it was a job. He worked in marketing for the company that owned the art theatre where his identical-twin brother Steve worked as a projectionist. The theatre had picked up *Eraserhead*—the dark, surreal, first film by a young David Lynch—for a Friday midnight slot. With the manic popularity of *The Rocky Horror Picture Show*, the midnight-movie trend had blossomed into a full-fledged craze. In the year since it had reinvented itself as an art house, the Nuart Theatre had held down the Saturday midnight slot with *Pink Flamingos*, John Waters's cult raunchfest—including scenes of public urination, mother-son fellatio, consumption of dog feces, and the infamous "chicken fuck"—whose success was measured by how many people threw up in the aisles of a given showing, and which, based on that measure, had been a consistent, raving success. Friday night had been given to *The Harder They Come*, Jimmy Cliff's reggae crime thriller whose breakout soundtrack had made it a midnight favorite nationwide. *Eraserhead,* with its dark themes and obscure plotline, lacked the ready hooks of those films and was going to be a gamble for the theatre.

Doug and Steve were LA's premier art film enthusiasts. Upstairs, in the comfortably cramped booth, Steve meticulously set the film reel into the old but reliable projector. Doug was down below, working a few different angles he'd come up with to get attention for the film. His first marketing decision was to write off the possibility of any woman ever coming to see it. He aimed the advertising at college men, with the message that the film was so unsettling that they should not, under any circumstances, bring their ladies. This generated some buzz among the fraternity crowds, and all the macho disclaimers—*you don't want to see this, baby, it's way too gross*—piqued their girl-friends' interest. Looking around the theatre he had already noticed young women trickling in to see what all the fuss was about. It had also been Doug's idea to capitalize on the audience-participation angle of midnight movie trend to build a base of devoted fans who would tell their friends. Lacking the flamboyance that characterized most other successful midnight films, *Eraserhead* did not make it easy. Every Friday Doug would show up with a couple friends, and the moment the main character with the title hairdo appeared on the screen, they would quietly start the chant.

"*Eraserhead, Eraserhead, Eraserhead, Eraserhead . . .*"

The film itself, with its bleak atmosphere and indecipherably personal artistic vision, would have been much better suited for the Nuart's weekly roster, were it not for the fact that its director, David Lynch, was only thirty-one years old and *Eraserhead* was a student film. The theatre specialized in themed double features from acknowledged greats—Kurosawa, Kubrick, Antonioni, and other foreign directors known only to the film community elite—classics that spent most of their time collecting dust in distributors' vaults.

Built as a neighborhood movie house on Santa Monica Boulevard in the '30s—before the 405 Freeway had scrambled the demographics of LA and caused the neighborhood to go largely to seed—the theatre had seen better days. Its five hundred seats were worn; the original, ornate marquee, though up and running, was permanently encased in grime. But the faded glory of the theatre and the neighborhood had an unintended positive effect. There were no restaurants, no nightlife, no reason to be there other than to see movies you couldn't see anywhere else. Almost by default, the Nuart had started to become that most sought-after thing, a *destination*—at least for a faithful following of people who cared about quality film. It helped that LA music was in something of an in-between period, with film—and increasingly, the experiments at audio-visual synthesis that were starting to get local play—taking up much of the cultural slack. Steve, who was in film school at the time, helped drive the momentum by helping to fix it up, over time installing a new screen, new sound system, and an impressive set of lenses. Between showings he played his favorite songs over the speakers, an eclectic mix of electronic, blues, German pop, punk, Van Dyke Parks and whatever else fit the film being shown. Doug had designed an illustrated monthly calendar that had brought a notable spike in attendance.

None of which made *Eraserhead* an obvious choice for the Friday night slot.

But marketing the film was a labor of love for Doug. A few years prior he had done some graphic design work for AFI and gotten to know some of the students and their work. He felt an instant kinship with this community. One day, hanging out on the campus, he had stumbled upon an outdoor patio that gave him a creepy feeling he could not quite place. It took him a moment to realize the patio was a film set. It took him another moment to realize whoever set this belonged to was making a very weird film. Which, in the vocabulary of unconventional film and music people at the time, was one of the highest compliments an artist could receive.

Lynch's travails in getting his AFI thesis made were well known in the underground film scene. The first cohorts had graduated in 1971. Tim Hunter, Lynch's classmate that first year, had already moved to Santa Cruz, taught film for four years at the university, returned to LA and begun making inroads in Hollywood. Unlike his classmates, though, all of whom had made shorts at AFI, Lynch was working on a feature-length film. Lacking the funds for such an extensive project, he had spent the lion's share of the '70s making the film in chunks, stopping when the money ran out and hustling to raise enough for the next scene. His dogged long-term commitment in the face of such a grueling stop-start process had earned him the respect of his peers. That the film got made at all was a minor miracle.

One of the first nights Steve projected it, only sixteen people showed up. One of them was Stuart Cornfeld, a budding producer who had recently assisted Mel Brooks on his Hitchrock parody *High Anxiety*. Cornfeld had run a summer camp with the Martin brothers and came on their recommendation. The lights went down; Doug Martin announced "Alright: *Eraserhead*"; and when the film ended eighty-nine minutes later, Cornfeld felt he was a different person—as if he had experienced a kind of cinematic rebirth.

It was only the first of many revelations the movie would inspire. When Doug Martin saw it that night, he had a strange feeling of recognition, and realized that this was the film onto whose set he had wandered several years before. He realized also that his initial intuition had been correct: this was indeed a very weird, and very great, film.

Steve, who had watched the movie through the projector window up in his booth, was hit perhaps hardest of all. The movie haunted him. Its strange musical set piece was particularly evocative: A character known only as "The Lady in the Radiator"—a platinum blonde in a shiny '50s-era dress with strange, mufflery protrusions emanating from her cheeks—sings a song consisting mainly of five words repeated slowly and sweetly, to beautiful and incredibly unsettling effect.

In Heaven, everything is fine
In Heaven, everything is fine
In Heaven, everything is fine
You've got your good things, and I've got mine.

In Heaven, everything is fine
In Heaven, everything is fine
In Heaven, everything is fine
You've got your good things, and you've got mine.
In Heaven, everything is fine.

Steve watched the film every Friday night for months, and once the general, pervasive creepiness of the Lady in the Radiator began to pass, he realized something else about the song was nagging at him. The voice sounded so familiar, and it didn't belong to the actress with the shiny dress and fuzzy cheeks. Scanning the credits, he saw Peter's name, and it finally clicked into place. Doug had been given *Terminal Love* as a present a couple of years back, and when the brothers listened to it together their reaction was similar to Doug's walking onto the *Eraserhead* patio at AFI: *Wow, this is very weird.* It was quirky, smart, literate, and funny. What's more, Peter was a monster on the harp and he had the formidable Buell Neidlinger backing him up on bass.

Steve had been sure to buy Peter's self-titled follow-up album as soon as it came out. He was one of only a handful of people to make that purchase. Despite Wright's slick production, a guest appearance by Carly Simon, and critical support upon release ("Ivers's irony," quoth *Rolling Stone*, "bitter and unpredictable, is vicious but worth watching"; while the *Soho Weekly News* called it "decent rock and roll that grows to very decent to joyously indecent through tongue-in-cheek humor that's plunked in lyric and tune"), the album died on the table, failing to find a popular pulse. Warner Bros., having fulfilled its two-record obligation, dropped Peter from the label. Had WB's marketing department figured out a way to reach the few thousand others who shared the Martin brothers' taste for independent-sounding music, Peter may have had a chance at achieving with his record what Lynch did with his film. One hopeful critic predicted as much, citing the "clever lyrics and a strong musical feel which should be enough for Ivers to build a devoted cult following." Lynch himself, after all, believed enough in their shared sensibility to charge Peter with writing and singing the number that would become the film's centerpiece.

In 1977, though, America had spent much of the preceding decade in an explosive renaissance of artistic filmmaking and was far more primed to accept something strange and offbeat emanating from movie projectors than from their record players or eight-track cassettes. By the time *Eraserhead* hit the Nuart, Cassavetes, Scorsese, Coppola, Altman, Bogdanovich, and Bob Rafelson had each made several major films noted for their idiosyncratic storylines, counter-cultural themes, and intense, often startlingly realistic portrayals of sex and violence, training filmgoers to expect to be unsettled as well as entertained in the theatre.

Still, unlike *Pink Flamingos* and many of the other midnight films, *Eraserhead* was not an instant smash. Nor was it a flop; each week, a few more curious souls filled the seats. But for the Martin brothers, for whom the film had become something equivalent to a new religion, the buildup was painstakingly slow. Stuart Cornfeld, their fellow devotee, drummed up buzz with a convert's zeal, dragging as many of his Hollywood exec comrades as he could to make the midnight pilgrimage. And Doug Martin corralled his friends, week in, week out, to be ringers and start up the chant he hoped and prayed would catch on.

The first couple of times had been fun. But by now, a little over a month into the film's run, his friends had found other things to do. Doug was the only one left. Tonight he was going to have to start a chant of one, a demoralizing task. At five minutes to midnight, Doug sat in the theatre anxiously brainstorming other ways to get the word out when this particular campaign sputtered out.

Out on the sidewalk in front of the theatre, Steve paced and waited for last-minute patrons. He checked his watch one more time, then turned and walked back into the lobby. It was close enough. He was anxious to get the night moving, and not particularly looking forward to another 2:30 a.m. closing time.

Then, through the glass doors, he noticed some guys hanging out in front of the theatre, wearing what looked like matching homemade T-shirts. Handstitched into each shirt was the word "DEVO"—not like a fan shirt, Steve observed. Like a costume. He stuck his head out the door and asked the obvious question. "Are you in Devo?"

"I am Devo," was the answer he received.

Steve knew about Devo, the concept band that satirized consumerist conformity with intentionally monotonous synth-driven music and bizarre stage personas outfitted in identical, industrial-themed costumes. The guys he met outside the Nuart in the homemade Devo T-shirts were just strange enough to be telling the truth. They were also intelligent, unpretentious, and friendly in a Midwestern kind of way, definitely not from LA. They had seen *Eraserhead* and walked over thinking maybe they would come see it again. Steve invited them in.

Steve killed the lights. Doug stood up, "Alright everyone: *Eraserhead.*" The screen lit up, the projector started cranking the reel. Henry, the antihero played by the actor Jack Nance, made his entrance onscreen. Doug took a deep breath. But before he could utter a sound, he was overwhelmed by a collective rumble. Unprompted by him, the rest of the audience had begun to chant.

"Eraserhead, Eraserhead, Eraserhead . . ."

He looked around and began to recognize some of the faces, people who had been there for previous showings. They knew the chant, and they knew the cue. Lynch's AFI art film had officially become a midnight movie.

"ERASERHEAD, ERASERHEAD, ERASERHEAD, ERASER-HEAD, ERASERHEAD, ERASERHEAD . . ."

All Doug had to do was join in.

LA, Bob's Big Boy, 1977, Noon

The meeting would be at Bob's Big Boy—that was the only nonnegotiable term. Among the qualities that Peter and David Lynch shared, both were extreme creatures of habit. When it came to food, this reliance on routine went even further. Peter had Duke's, then Schwab's; for Lynch there was only Bob's Big Boy, his daily chocolate shake (aka the "Silver Goblet"), and a cup of coffee. Devo had expressed interest in playing "In Heaven" in concert, so Steve Martin had set up a meeting between Lynch and the band.

The person who had answered "I am Devo" that night at the Nuart was Jerry Casale, who had formed the group with fellow Akronite and Kent State art student Mark Mothersbaugh in 1974. It had started as a very art-schooly concept, a visual representation of an idea born of comic books and marathon pot-smoking brainstorms. In one of the comic books, the word *devolution* is used to describe a mad scientist who, seeing the opposite of true progress and evolution in the world around him, starts turning people into freak mutant animals. The scientist's plight resonated with Casale and Mothersbaugh, who looked around Akron—and America—and saw their fellow citizens regressing, getting dumber, turning off their critical faculties, and falling prey to a surfeit of disinformation that led to a kind of passive, bovine mentality. De-evolution. Devolution. Devo.

Whenever Casale and Mothersbaugh got together they would toss the idea around, try to advance and envision it: what would devolution look like? Eventually the problem extended from the visual to the musical: What would Devo music sound like? They tried to come up with the most powerful, harsh, primal sound possible—industrial-sounding synthesizers over rigid, repressive, mechanical beats—and to hold a song there for as long as possible, longer than was comfortable, stripped down, without making the expected changes. The music was full of big ideas, and they tried to let the ideas, rather than arbitrary musical conventions, define the structure of each song.

The same ideas gave rise to their stage personas and the identical, workmanlike costumes (usually with some futuristic accent and processed hairdo) in which they performed. Their performances were often confrontational, playing the same monotonous licks for up to a half hour and repeating their slogan—"Are we not men? We are Devo!"—until the audience became hostile, screaming and attacking the stage.

A year before meeting Steve Martin, Devo had had its big break. Its short film, *The Truth About De-Evolution*, won a prize at the Ann Arbor Film Festival, bringing it to the attention of David Bowie and Iggy Pop. Their support led to a recording contract with Warner Bros. The band's first album, produced by Brian Eno, was slated to come out the following year.

The nexus of Devo, the Martin brothers, David Lynch, and Peter Ivers was nothing short of a match made—it had to be said—in heaven. The band worshiped Lynch and his film, which shared elements of associative visual collage they were using in their own video work. They felt a special kinship with Peter's song, which struck them almost as a variation on the kind of eerie falsetto they were writing for Mothersbaugh's Booji Boy character, a stunted overgrown boy in an orange nuclear suit. The Martins started hanging out with Casale and going to Devo shows. Someone had the idea for the band to play "In Heaven" in concert. Doug Martin seized on it as a potential marketing campaign. Steve said he would run the idea by Lynch and gave him a call.

"Hey, Devo wants to meet you," he said.

Lynch, who was living reclusively on some property near AFI, responded, "Who's that?"

Initially, the meeting was just going to involve the Martin brothers, Devo, and Lynch. But Stuart Cornfeld showed up unexpectedly, announcing that this was a meeting he was not going to miss. Lynch arrived with a friend no one recognized, dressed unassumingly in a T-shirt, cargo pants, and canvas army boots. From their easy rapport, they seemed to Steve like old college buddies. Lynch introduced his friend as Peter Ivers, and Steve lit up, telling Peter how much he loved *Terminal Love*. Peter seemed a little surprised. "Did you set this up?" he asked. Steve confirmed that he had. "Okay," Peter said, letting it hang there awkwardly.

Peter was feeling confident, maybe even a little cocky. *Eraserhead* was getting people's attention, and he had just done a whole new score for cult mogul Roger Corman. *Grand Theft Auto* was an extended car chase, a love story, a light comedy, and beloved child actor Ron

Howard's directorial debut. Peter got the job through his friend Toby Rafelson and viewed it as another chance to flex his musical muscles, work with some of his favorite session guys, and (always top on his mind) help them get paid. His bandmates described the *Grand Theft* sessions as "Classic Peter Ivers": fifteen to twenty musicians in the studio playing live, exotic instruments, Van Dyke Parks on keys, limited rehearsals, and no cues, everything just being created spontaneously and hanging together almost miraculously by an intricate web of invisible threads. The editor, Joe Dante, had been impressed with how well it turned out, much better than the music that typically appeared in low-budget films. Usually they just threw together whatever they could find and tried to keep it as innocuous as possible. This time, Dante wanted to turn it up. He was one of many who saw that Peter easily could have made a nice, lucrative career out of scoring films. Many who had worked on Corman's scores had followed that route and become major Hollywood composers. Peter wasn't biting, though, and Dante got the feeling he was just doing this job because it was something he had never done before.

Devo arrived at Bob's Big Boy, and with everyone assembled, synapses began to fire. Peter and Lynch were clearly excited (and more than a little surprised) at the groundswell of interest *Eraserhead* had begun to generate in LA—thanks in large part to Doug and Steve's creativity and dedication. In Devo they recognized fellow travelers and were flattered by the band's request. The band, for their part, were thrilled to meet Lynch and Peter and giddy about the prospect of playing "In Heaven" on tour. The question of permission was a no-brainer, granted by the song's writers without hesitation. There was little talk of business.

Jerry Casale's impression of Peter as a kindred spirit was instantly confirmed. He saw him as an electric bundle of manic mental energy: a kind of new wave shaman, a trickster, an imp. Back in Akron, Mothersbaugh had used a baby mask to create the alter ego he called Booji Boy (pronounced "Boogie Boy"), and Casale became a character they called the Chinaman. They would go out to restaurants and stores in character, playing it straight for shock value and real-life situation comedy. This was art for art's sake; it had nothing to do with a career. No cameras rolled as they sat in middle American diners and deadpanned to the waitress that Booji Boy needed all his food chopped up in a blender because he had a hole where his mouth should have been. Like Devo, Peter was always testing people, always playing, performing his one-man guerrilla theatre for whomever happened to be there. Had they met in Akron, Peter undoubtedly would have been part of Devo. Lucky for Peter, Casale thought, he wasn't in Akron.

But he would be with them, at least in spirit, from now on: Devo would bring Peter's song with them on tour, making it a staple of their live act. Whenever possible, Peter would come to the shows and cheer them on.

As lunch wound down, Casale asked Peter to transcribe the song. Among his friends, Peter was known for his crisp, meticulous handwriting, especially when writing out music. He would crouch over the page, with the concentration of a second-grader taking his first handwriting test. Peter grabbed a napkin from the booth at Bob's Big Boy, and, temporarily shutting out everything else in the room, wrote out the chords and the words to "In Heaven." He handed the napkin to Jerry as Lynch polished off his coffee and drew a last, long slurpy sip of his Silver Goblet.

Laurel Canyon, Home of Lucy and Peter, 1977, Noon

> *I saw you Alice and I lost control,*
> *Of my heart and my mouth and my senses.*
> *I want you, Alice,*
> *And if you hadn't been cold*
> *I wouldn't have killed all my chances . . .*
> "I'm Sorry Alice," Peter Ivers (<>) song #6

The woman outside Peter and Lucy's house was beside herself, huffing and puffing and pounding on the door. As soon as Lucy opened the door, the woman started shouting, "That song! That goddamn song!"

Though she didn't live particularly close to them, it had sounded as if an entire band was camped out on her lawn, blasting music into her home, the same song again and again—Alice this, Alice that—all goddamn day! She had been up and down the canyon for hours trying to locate its source. Finally, she managed to isolate it to Peter and Lucy's place. She had a few choice feelings to share.

"I hate that stupid Alice song! You've been playing it for five hours!"

Among its many charms—unassuming natural beauty, a friendly bohemian artist scene—Laurel Canyon (being a canyon) was known for its strong, unpredictable echoes.

Peter had been rehearsing the same song ("I'm Sorry Alice") for five hours. He was reworking, and he had to get it exactly right. Everything he had achieved could be traced back to his superhuman focus, his high threshold for repetition. When he was working, everything else went on mute, the world around him receded, and time ceased to exist.

Which is not to say he begrudged this woman the interruption. To the contrary, he welcomed it as a kind of found art, another scene in his theatre of the everyday.

"Can you wait here for a sec?" he asked her. He disappeared into his studio.

Lucy took it all in stride. She smiled and introduced herself. "I'm Jill," the woman said, trying to maintain her indignation. Lucy tried to make small talk as they waited for Peter to return.

Peter returned with a video camera in his hand. In 1977, the devices were relatively new and rare. They were used mainly by visual artists, who considered video the next frontier, and in performance art.

Peter had encountered video by way of a chance meeting at an art exhibition with a woman named Nancy Drew. When he walked in the door, Drew saw a lightning bolt. Dressed all in white, with longish hair, he looked like a vision. She understood immediately that this was going to be an important person in her life, and Peter seemed to have been struck by the same feeling. He followed her around the exhibit, and as soon as they started talking, there was an instant bond. He told Drew he thought they had met previously, but she thought that was just because they both were small people (Drew was 5'2") who understood each other like a brother and sister. He reminded her of Baryshnikov, a small, sexy man with incredible natural charisma, the kind of person you would walk across the street just to look at. It was the only time in her life Drew had felt such an instant connection to another human being.

At the time she met Peter, Nancy Drew was running an organization she'd founded called Some Serious Business. The organization produced "art performances," importing New York's late-'70s performance art to LA when few people west of Alphabet City had even heard the term. The artists she worked with had begun to use the new medium of video in interesting, experimental ways. While Peter had been exposed to the audio-visual experimentation of his AFI friends like Howard Smith, and the stuff Van Dyke and Durrie were doing at Warner Bros., the video–performance art nexus was a new animal altogether. The music-film work being done was for the most part a form of montage, editing together existing footage. It rarely involved the creation of new performances with visual palettes and storylines of their own. (One notable exception, familiar to Peter, was Devo, whose art school background and theoretical bent put them far ahead of the curve.)

By the time Peter met Nancy Drew he had been honing his stage-craft for years. His antics and energy imbued his performance with a dramatic quality that to Nancy suggested development for the stage. The songs themselves were also extremely vivid, and many lent themselves to visual representation. Drew, a maven in the field, was not familiar with anyone in the experimental video—performance art world who created song-inspired theatre for video. To her, it seemed to be what Peter was groping towards without knowing the medium existed. To Nancy, Peter was not just a musician. He was a performance artist.

Drew introduced him to everyone she knew in the field, and Peter soon became a fixture, his transition to video seamless. Enlisting the help of film-savvy friends like Doug Martin and Howard Smith, corralling his bandmates into costumes and onto sets, he started making theatrical videos based on his songs, which generated art-world buzz.

Nancy loved to watch Peter rifle through her closet to see if there was anything provocative enough to use in an act. It cracked her up. They were roughly the same size.

Drew became the curator of the Long Beach Museum of Art, and began to buy airtime to put video art on broadcast TV. Paying $1,500 for a 30-second slot, she would air experimental pieces by serious artists like commercials between shows. Peter became one part of that group, the first person she knew to produce and televise something that did not yet have a name, but might accurately have been described as "music video." Without knowing or intending it, he became a pioneer of the movement to bring video art into people's living rooms.

Some of Peter's friends observed that "performance artist" just put a fancy label on something he'd been doing informally for most of his life—creating spontaneous theatre out of everyday experience. Video just gave him another prop with which to tweak that experience and document it.

Peter turned on his camera and pointed it at Jill, asking her, "Could you please say all that again?"

Jill was still angry. Now she also seemed confused.

"It's art," Peter explained, smiling triumphantly. So she said it all again.

"Okay, great," Peter said. "Thank you. Now, I'm going to take on your role. I'm going to say your part." He turned the camera on himself and gave his best imitation of her tirade.

He turned the camera back on Jill.

"Now it's your turn," he said. "You do my part."

They held the conversation for a while in reverse. By the end of it, Jill had made a compelling case for why she should be able to rehearse her music. Peter, of course, would not stand for it. Lucy watched and smiled. With Peter, you never knew what was going to happen. You knew it was coming, you knew *something* was coming. And yet somehow it was always a surprise.

==*close-up:*

Dream Weavers and Eraserheads

What does Gary Wright do when he's not receiving gold album awards, working on the follow-up to "The Dream Weaver," or touring his organ off? In the past few months, he's been putting his extra time to excellent use: producing a long-awaited new album by one of Warners' classiest acts: Peter Ivers.
—Rolling Stone, *July 1, 1976*

Peter Ivers vs. *Peter Ivers:* The Third Album

Dear Alan,

I just realized what a careful rearrangement of the letters in your name could lead to. I was knocked out by the news from Warners, but I will try to reserve unbridled enthusiasm for the moment when the full scope of the deal is revealed . . .

The sound of the record has to be the sound of a completely unique world, in the way that can be found on the 1st Dr. John record, Sgt. Pepper, the 2nd Jimi Hendrix, and to a lesser extent on the Sly Stone's records and the newer work of Stevie Wonder. I intend to sell a lot of records and attention to detail is the key. Details take time!

Thank Lenore for her special brand of ribald efficiency.
Peter Ivers

GARY WRIGHT
"The songs had catchy little titles and they were fun; it was fun working with him."

You used to be Stevie Wonder, I was the Magnavox,
You pushed and pulled me through hard times and rising costs.
You used to be Gene Vincent, I was the echo machine.
Tape delayed sweetheart, we vibrated rock and roll dreams.
"You Used to Be Stevie Wonder" (<>) song #7

He was criticized for being abstract in "You Used to Be Stevie Wonder," Ivers said, but explained he was only trying to show "how our life is reflected in the rock and roll artifacts around us. Ivers might not be right for everybody's taste, but he is a refreshing performer on today's musical scene. Wright's production is glossy enough to make Ivers's occasional starkness commercially viable.

  —Tom Von Malder, Chicago Herald, *September 3, 1976*

RICHARD GREENE
"Well, that was a mismatch of aesthetics. A really commercial kind of guy trying to jive with Peter Ivers? That was the record company trying to soften Peter's edges."

DURRIE PARKS
"I think at that point, there was a part of Peter where [working with a mainstream producer like Wright] would sound attractive to him, because I think he desperately wanted to be successful."

JELLO BIAFRA
"Clearly they were trying to market him more as a straight singer-songwriter and hope for the best. I mean, you can't take the Ivers out of the Peter."

In Ivers's songs, rock and roll is a slippery symbol, something to be both honored and made fun of. Sometimes, he seems to be contrasting the idealistic vision of Sixties rock with the dull realities of its aging dependents.

  —Rolling Stone, *October 7, 1976*

Peter Ivers lingers long after you've played the record. I find myself using Ivers's words and sprinkling his sentiments throughout my daily conversations to cope with a spectrum of particulars from kissing to dancing. Peter loves the former, has trouble downing the intricate new steps of the latter, and left his girlfriend lonely on many nights while crafting this record. Her loss is our gain.

  —James Spina, Women's Wear Daily

GARY WRIGHT

"He probably would have been better in more of the '80s, in the more quirky kind of stuff, like the B-52's and those kind of bands. It was just kind of before his time for the stuff he was doing."

> Ivers is a talented writer with a very different vocal sound and a remarkable skilled style on the harmonica to boot . . . should be enough for Ivers to build a devoted cult following.
> —Philadelphia, *September 14–September 21,*

The New Wave of Film: The Story of Eraserhead

> From the moment of his arrival, Ivers was a fixture on the Los Angeles cultural scene. He was one of the few links between its underground art community and its above ground entertainment establishment.
> —*Michael London*, Los Angeles Times, *March 27, 1983*

STEVE MARTIN

"In the early '70s, it was music that ruled the city, and then film was taking over, and film became the hip means of expression, the same way that film in many ways was supplanted, or is being supplanted by the internet. Mainstream Hollywood then was taken over by independent films, which then became mainstream Hollywood."

LUCY FISHER

"Well, it took them three or four years to make the movie because most of the AFI movies were shorts, but his was a long movie, and cost a lot more. He hired Peter early, but by the time he recorded 'In Heaven,' it was towards the end of it. I just remember Lynch was living in a barn near AFI or something, some property."

DAVID LYNCH

"It might have been 1974. I was using [bluesman] Fats Waller in my film *Eraserhead*, and I had written lyrics for a song called 'In Heaven,' and I needed the music for that, and I needed a girl to sing that. So I ended up at Peter Ivers's house with my friend Alan Splet, and lo and behold, he saw a [Fats Waller] album, and he thought the album was out of print and completely rare, but Peter had all the Fats Waller stuff, and we were very impressed with that. I had all these tapes Alan had saved, but now here was the album, Peter had the album. He had loved Fats Waller from a long time ago, and I knew I had gone to the right guy. So I gave Peter the lyrics, and I apologized for how simple the lyrics were, and he said, 'No no,' and he went to work. And when I went there the next time, he sang the song to me, right in front of me, and he had done the organ in the spirit of Fats Waller. He sat on the couch and sang the thing in a falsetto voice, and it was a done deal. He gave it to me and I walked out."

DOUG MARTIN

"Peter's was a really weird vocal track, a really odd recording of that song. On one hand, it was beautiful and, on the other hand, it was really creepy, and because of that it was beautiful. It was sweet as blue cotton candy."

VAN DYKE PARKS

"I loved what he did with that score, because in a way, he used an old saw that could still cut the wood. It is not how big the gun, but how good the shots. He had that sensibility where he knew how to use what he had very effectively."

STEVE MARTIN

"We started showing *Eraserhead* and getting this interesting crowd of very smart people coming to see it. People would leave scratching their heads, like what was that? They seemed sort of freaked out, mostly about the baby. No, let me correct that: entirely about the baby."

> Terrifying Vortex: Lynch comes amazingly close to the logic of dreams and nightmares, in which successive layers of reality seem to dissolve, sucking you into a terrifying vortex . . . The movie clearly deals with an apocalypse, but the apocalypse is not external, not political or technological. It is internal, the ultimate corruption of matter itself throughout the universe.
>
> —*Jack Knoll*, Newsweek, *September 11, 1978*

CHARLES THOMPSON, Musician, the Pixies, Frank Black

"There weren't a lot of kids at Amherst doing the midnight movie thing, it wasn't enough of a punk rock place for that . . . but I was learning about art films in a class, and then probably read about [*Eraserhead*] more in the music, punk rock press, or discussion in the media, and heard about this David Lynch guy."

DOUG MARTIN

"[*Eraserhead*] is A dream of dark and troubling things, [quoting Lynch] but the plot is straightforward. A printer knocks up a girl and he meets her parents, everything that could go wrong goes wrong. It's a nightmare with a freak baby."

STUART CORNFELD

"I was born again over David and that film. I thought it was the greatest movie I had ever seen."

JERRY CASALE

"We had met Peter and we had met the Martins and Lucy and David Lynch, and it was just a new life, changed our world."

DOUG MARTIN

"[Devo] wore *Eraserhead* T-shirts. That helped promote the film."

JERRY CASALE

"In '79, on the whole tour, we played it every night. Booji Boy came out, we played it on little wasp synthesizers, and he sang 'In Heaven.' "

CHARLES THOMPSON

"I was really impressed with the movie, I liked the movie a lot, but the song jumps out as the theme song. It's like, in a film that is just filled with industrial spooky sound scape and sort of chaos of space, you know, it's filled with that kind of sound, and finally there's some music that jumps out in a real way. It's almost a nod to a musical when it gets to the scene, and the music becomes dark and ironic. If you were going to point to a light comedic scene, if you can call it that, in the film, that might be the most light, and the most kind of, entertainment."

DAVID LYNCH

"It opened in New York at the Cinema Village, and then it went on to play in seventeen cities for some time. I think it may have played up to four years in theatres, so it was the midnight circuit that made *Eraserhead* . . ."

Nirvana Cuba: The Unfinished Album

I'm a little hot dog on the grill,
Your love is hot, but that's the thrill,
I'm happy on the grill.
It's been said that God's dead,
And it's lucky for us he died,
'Cause if he saw the mess that we made
He wouldn't let a soul survive.
"He'd burn the world with fire till everything was still,
But I'd be . . . happy on the grill . . .
—"Happy on the Grill," Nirvana Cuba (<>) Song #8

STEVE MARTIN
"So in 1979, Peter had this band called Ivers Divers. It was the band that could play *Nirvana Cuba*. It seems that it was getting more clear that Peter wasn't going to fit into this sort of new wave folk pop bullshit that was really taking over. It didn't seem like he was working that hard to fit into a square, traditional role in the entertainment world, other than being Peter Ivers, the musician-genius."

ROCHELLE ROBERTSON (colleague, friend)
"*Nirvana Cuba* was really interesting. The most remarkable song or songs that I remember were about love in the Middle East. I don't know how to explain any of his shows. It was performance art, we played different characters. We had choreography."

MARK STUMPF
"His was not a mainstream muse."

LUCY FISHER
"He wasn't self-destructive; he just didn't want to make it easy on himself. He wanted to do each thing in a way that he had never done before. And it wasn't just him being defiant, when he sat down to do it, it would be different from the way everyone else did it. He wanted to prove that he could do it his way, but it also had to be the most complicated hard way."

DOUG MARTIN

"The thread that held all of Peter's projects together was Peter. Some had a more stripped-down sound, some had a more linear quality to the performance where it was more consistent. When Peter Ivers was with a group of professional musicians, the result was always something where you were left with, I can't classify what I just heard, but it sounded great. It had references to the best of what he liked, and then some things not normally referenced he would tie in and sew up with harmonica. It was difficult to compare when really the only thread was often Peter."

case book *part 5*

DAVID CHARBONNEAU, private detective hired by Lucy
Fisher
"Just prior to Peter and all of this going on, you did have
somebody in a Hollywood way try to assassinate the president
of the United States, Ronald Reagan. They shot him because
of something Jodie Foster said through a movie, right? So
this stuff was happening. Instead of just the typical, we're
going to hire off-duty cops to be your bodyguards. [Gavin]
De Becker [Hollywood security guru] had it wired. He would
sell to producers, directors, the studios, et cetera, and
say, You know, we need to be smarter about this. There is
a lot of money invested in these people and they are important people and good artists, everyone had one or two
people close to them."

LUCY FISHER
"When I couldn't make any progress with the police, my boss
at Warner Communications, Steve Ross, asked one of his
lawyers, Mickey Rudin, who had also been Frank Sinatra's
lawyer, to look in on the case. But [there was no making
up] for botched initial evidence. So through Jane Fonda,
my close friend Paula Weinstein secured the name of a private detective for me and I hired David Charbonneau to
restart the hunt."

STEVE MARTIN
"He must have felt overwhelmed, there was a lot of pressure and not a lot to go on, especially with the, 'Oh this
must have something to do with *New Wave Theatre*, or the
punk scene.' He was a Hollywood detective, a pro, nice
enough guy."

DAVID CHARBONNEAU
"I got the call from Jane Fonda directly. She said, Would
you be interested in helping out some friends of mine in

the movie business? They are concerned that the police aren't doing much and the case was basically cold and they're frustrated. And I said sure. [I met with] Lucy Fisher, Paula Weinstein, and Peter's mother. They gave me as much background as they could. His life and what world he was in."

LUCY FISHER

"It was five weeks after the death by then."

DAVID CHARBONNEAU

"I got lists of people from Paula and Fisher. I talked to the cops first; they didn't have much. I asked them what their theory was and they didn't have a clue. They said it could be somebody close to him, or somebody he just brought into his house that night, or a burglar that came out of the blue. I asked them about working theories, who has an alibi and who doesn't. I never got a good sense that they had followed up strongly on alibis."

STEVE MARTIN

"You are talking about captains of industry and the people who run the movie business, run the music business, run the publishing world, you know. Highly accomplished, extremely well-educated people."

DAVID CHARBONNEAU

"I sat down with Harold Ramis. I wanted his impressions. I remember being real blunt with him and asking him if he had an alibi. He said yes and I checked it with the cops the next day. And none of us thought he did it.

"Speaking with Anne I could tell, next to Peter's mom and Lucy, she was wrecked."

ANNE RAMIS

"I remember [that day] Harold and I went over there to talk to the police, they wanted some information. And I remember we went back and picked up Violet from school and we told her. And she said, 'No more Vitamin Pink [a rock musical written and staged by Peter, in which Violet performed]?' I felt really bad. I mean, I felt bad about other things. It was scarier because of the rain. It was raining the whole day in a haunting way.'"

DAVID CHARBONNEAU

"I could tell, just in the way they talked about how unique he was. Everybody had a different take on Peter, and all of them considered him a friend, a confidante even. So here are these Hollywood people, powerful people, and I got the sense that those people wished he'd go a little more mainstream with them because they saw him as someone that could bring a lot to the table for them in terms of artistic expression. Then at the same time I knew he was in the alternative, punk world. So right from the beginning, I knew it was going to be a multilayered, onion-peeling process of even trying to understand this guy's world. And I thought, *This is going to be hard.*"

chapter 7

Our Paris in the '20s

Laurel Canyon, Home of Lucy and Peter, 1977, Late Afternoon

Lucy was crying, and she knew Peter could hear her. He was only in the next room. But he was working on his music, and so she also knew that she could cry all night, all week, all year, and until he was done, she might as well be crying in outer space. It wasn't cruelty exactly. It was discipline. It was how Peter accomplished everything he'd accomplished, and the only way he knew how to get anything done. When Peter was working, the world around him receded until all he could hear were the thoughts in his head, the music he played, and the ideas and feelings he struggled with and played with and shaped into art. Lucy knew all this. She kept crying anyway. She cried because it was Sunday, and tomorrow morning she was to start her new job—her first "real studio job"—at MGM. Somehow, since she began reading scripts as a freelancer for United Artists, four years had passed. Two of them she had spent at UA, another two as a low-level story editor at Samuel Goldwyn Jr. Productions. During this dues-paying period she had worked diligently and exhibited strong instincts for recognizing the qualities of good film. She had also garnered the respect and friendship of an impressive array of industry executives. The crackling intelligence, generosity of spirit, earthy self-possession, and rock-and-roll edge that had made her the most popular waitress at the Signet—and made Peter the envy of many of his friends (and hers)—had buoyed her in this new world as well and landed her on the radar of Hollywood's elite. MGM hired her as executive in charge of creative affairs. She was twenty-nine years old. And at the moment, she felt she would do anything to get out of having to show up for her first day of work.

MGM was widely acknowledged as the worst studio in Hollywood. Its glory days long past, it had missed out altogether on the artist-driven renaissance that was infusing new life into American film. With its parent company channeling resources elsewhere, the studio's output had slowed to a crawl.

The truth was that Lucy was not even sure she wanted a studio job. Thus far, all her work had been about the writers and their scripts. She was allied with the artists, playing a role in the creative process. This fit with her background, her sense of herself and what she had always imagined she would do: play some role in supporting the arts. Becoming an executive, stepping over to the other side, felt a lot like selling out. (And, adding insult to injury, the pay wasn't even that great. If she was going to sell out, she might as well be well compensated.)

Siding with the artists also dovetailed nicely with the life she and Peter shared, and which she cherished. Laurel Canyon in the '70s had something of Greenwich Village in the '60s, or Paris in the '20s: a sense that you were part of a family of artists overflowing with creativity and new ideas, collaborating with and supporting each other, making exciting work. Over the years Peter and Lucy's Laurel Canyon pad had become a bustling hub of work, play, and refuge for this community, in part because she had made their house irresistibly cozy. Their living room had a couch along the back wall that faced a big picture window overlooking the canyon. A large balcony stretched out from the window, where you could sit outside and enjoy the sunshine and the bucolic view sheltered from the distraction of otherwise pervasive city lights. Looking out from the balcony, all you could see were pretty canyon hillsides dotted with small houses on streets with names like Wonderland Avenue and Happy Lane. Van Dyke Parks lived on the latter, Neidlinger lived nearby on Laurel Pass, and there was always music ricocheting off the canyon walls. The porch was where Lucy often read her scripts, with the near-constant backdrop of Peter's music emanating from down the short hallway hung with quilted, patterned fabric.

At the end of the hall were two bedrooms, one of which served as Peter's office. Peter kept the room clean and stark as an ashram, with all his recording equipment packed under the bed. Opposite the office was Peter and Lucy's bedroom, which faced a little back patio Lucy had filled with flowers and plants. Something was always in bloom, and Lucy and Peter often sat out there. Half of what they had was bought secondhand; the other half was homemade. Peter had made a wooden frame for their bed. A piece of foam Lucy found became their mattress. She quilted the pillow covers herself.

If Lucy was the nurturing, domestic anchor of their Laurel Canyon home, Peter was its social director. With his ever-growing network of artist-collaborator-friends, there was a constant influx of guests. Peter's schedule in those days was simple: sit in the studio all day writing songs, with people stopping by periodically to listen, collaborate, rehearse, give feedback, and hang out.

The first time Steve Martin visited Peter and Lucy in Laurel Canyon, he didn't want to leave, ever. He couldn't explain it; it was just a cool vibe. There were bookcases full of all the books you wanted to read. There was Peter with his recording equipment, there was Lucy with her scripts. He found them both so smart and beautiful and funny and welcoming and warm, the low-key hipster power couple happy to share their home. Peter brought Steve and Doug into his world, introducing them around to his friends, many of whom also happened to be their heroes. He always referred to the Martin brothers as his "collaborators," to their abiding gratitude and delight. When he introduced them to Van Dyke Parks in this way, they only barely managed to hold it together. Each knew what the other was thinking: *Holy shit. That's Van Dyke Parks.*

Another precocious young artist Peter mentored was Peter Rafelson, son of Toby and Bob. When Peter met Toby (through Durrie Parks and Linda Perry, back in his Tropicana year), Rafelson was twelve. Many Sundays his mother would load him and his little sister in the car, pick up her friend, and take everyone out to breakfast. The young Rafelson didn't know what to make of this kid-sized adult who spoke to him and his sister no differently than he spoke to their mom. He often looked at Peter and thought, *How silly: a grown-up acting like a kid.* Who seemed to have a kid's heart, who would regularly do things like roll up into a ball and hide in the car, and, when everyone came back and settled in, pop up and surprise them. He was like a leprechaun. Rafelson had a hard time working out exactly what Peter's relationship with his mom was all about. (Peter was constantly surrounded by the wives of Hollywood. Rumors ran rampant, but for some reason, since it was Peter, no one seemed to mind.)

In his teen years, Rafelson got involved in music, and Peter played with him and introduced him to his friends. Rafelson was no stranger to the world of artists, having grown up in a Hollywood hub of his own. The Rafelson home was a gathering place and way station for the '70s film industry who's who. But in that context he was always "the son of," the kid, whereas Peter treated him as a peer. He introduced him as a fellow musician and invited him to hang out in Laurel Canyon, to sit in on jam sessions with all his musician friends, and sometimes perform with him in his bands.

Tim Hunter also lived in Laurel Canyon in those days, and was a frequent guest. He adored Peter and loved to hear whatever he was working on. After Peter played, they would sit on the couch, talk about it, and discuss whatever projects they had in the works, often over a joint or two. (Since his Harvard days Peter had relaxed his anti-drug stance to allow for one exception.) These visits would be proceeded by a meal at Schwab's, where Peter ordered, every time, the hot turkey sandwich with gravy.

Lucy's friend Elisabeth Glaser was another Laurel Canyon regular. When she and her husband Paul were in the market for a new place, they stayed with Peter and Lucy. Peter and Paul, an actor who had done some guest spots on shows like *The Waltons* and *Kojak*, became fast friends. One night several months after the Glasers had found their own place, Lucy felt they hadn't seen each other in too long and called to invite them out to a movie. Elisabeth seemed shocked by the suggestion, though Lucy couldn't fathom why. Somewhat exasperated, Elisabeth explained that if Paul showed his face in public they would all be mobbed. Lucy still didn't understand. It emerged that since they last spoke, Paul had landed the lead on a new cop show called *Starsky & Hutch*. The show was a runaway hit, and Paul Michael Glaser was now the most famous lawman-heartthrob in the country. Peter and Lucy, who didn't have a TV, had no idea. They did go out with the reluctant Glasers that night, and sure enough, they were mobbed.

Laurel Canyon, Home of Lucy and Peter, Later That Afternoon

Still weepy imagining what it was she would be getting herself into at MGM, Lucy busied herself with things around the house. She could hear Peter rustling in his office. She recognized the sound and knew it meant that in an hour their house would be filled with musicians and music. It was one of her favorite things about their Laurel Canyon life. But thinking about it made her upset all over again. Was she selling out, going corporate? Could she still live a Laurel Canyon life with an "executive"-titled job? (If there was one thing she never thought she would be, it was an executive.)

There was nothing she valued more than the life she and Peter had. Was she giving all this up? And if so, for *what*?

Peter kneeled down and carefully pulled out a large electric piano from the snug hollow below his desk. It was the first act of one of his favorite rituals: transforming his home into a fully functioning recording studio and rehearsal space. There was something almost magical about how much he had packed away in there; to the naked eye, his office seemed ascetically bare. His friends would watch in awe as from every crack and crevice he produced a new piece of studio-grade equipment. Howard Smith found the process so captivating he captured it on film and used it as the basis of a music video for one of Peter's songs. After scooting the keyboard down the short hallway into the sunny living room, he returned to his office and came back with an armful of microphone stands. He set up the stands, returned to the workroom, and from a gap between two desks conjured up a reel-to-reel recorder. He rolled it slowly out into the open living room and took stock of his handiwork, considering what other equipment the day's session would require.

Roderick Falconer, a singer-songwriter Peter had met soon after arriving in LA, was another frequent guest and close friend. Peter had played harp on his first album. For Falconer, having a network of smart and capable peers—available around the clock to constructively respond to your work, assess and react, and help you see it more clearly—was a precious commodity. Peter was a magnet for this kind of collaboration. Once, Falconer was hanging out with Peter and Lucy in Laurel Canyon, playing some of his new songs. When he finished, Peter said, "They want fucking hits—and you'll give them the hits!"

Since being dropped from Warner Bros., in addition to his regular gigs with Neidlinger's bands, Peter had started forming a new band of his own and working on a new album, which brought a whole new deluge of music and musicians. He reconnected with Marty Krystall, the sax player on *Terminal Love*, who came over often to rehearse, hang out, and play duets with Peter. Jeff Eyrich, the bass player on both *Peter Peter Ivers* and the *Grand Theft Auto* soundtrack, had met Peter at Alan Finger's yoga studio. Eyrich wasn't interested in yoga, but he thought it would be a good place to pick up girls. The plan had proven foolproof: he'd gotten a date with Rochelle Robertson, Peter's yoga comrade and sometime vocalist, who he had brought in to sing on the new record he was working on. Robertson told Eyrich he and Peter would hit it off, and Eyrich, who lived nearby, showed up at an impromptu jam session in the Laurel Canyon living room. Robertson was right: Eyrich found Peter to be a strange, interesting character, musically and personally. The feeling was mutual. Many jam sessions and rehearsals ensued.

Peter set all the microphones onto their stands and hooked them up to their cords. He did the same with the recorder and keyboard. The transformation from living room to home recording studio was complete. He surveyed his handiwork and dropped into a yoga position, waiting for the others to show.

Lucy and Peter also hosted a steady stream of out-of-town relatives and friends. On the floor in the corner of the living room was a mattress Lucy had covered and pillowed and fixed up as a couch. John Belushi had curled up there on his visit a few weeks before debuting on *Saturday Night Live,* and over the years Tim and Doug had each spent many nights on it as well.

In fact, by the time Lucy got the job at MGM, Doug had become an increasingly regular guest. After striking gold with the *1964 High School Yearbook Parody* one year and becoming a millionaire with the *Lampoon* payout the next, he had become restless and somewhat aimless, angling for a new challenge. Technically still employed by the *Lampoon,* his contributions dwindled and finally sputtered out. For over a year he floated around New York, hanging out with the *SNL* crowd, driving around in the new Porsche he'd paid for in cash, dropping extravagant tips at exclusive restaurants. He tried his hand at acting, hired a painter to have his portrait made. He bought his parents two houses and two cars. At Tim's thirtieth birthday party, Tim introduced Doug to an old friend who had been part of the Harvard theatre heyday and was now a successful stage and television actress. Since his first marriage had ended not long after the ambivalent "I do," Doug was a free agent in his personal life as well. It was a setup, and it worked: Doug and Kathryn Walker became inseparable. So he had a girlfriend. Now all he needed was something to do.

Fortunately for Doug, the *Lampoon* itself was in more or less the same boat. Since its founding, the magazine had made its name as the national source for smart, raw, taboo-smashing satire, and the national home for brilliant misfits to convert their twisted insights into bankable skills. By 1975 it had amassed a stable of the country's most formidable literary-comic minds. Early attempts at expanding the brand into comic performance had been largely—in some cases wildly—successful. They had also brought a new crop of comic actors under the *Lampoon* banner, raucous talents who channeled the magazine's ethos into over-the-top performances for radio and stage. Rivaling the writers for mad eccentricity and in some cases outright menace, these included then little knowns with names like Chevy Chase, John Belushi, Christopher Guest, Gilda Radner, Brian Doyle Murray and his brother Bill, Joe Flaherty, and Harold Ramis.

Then, in 1975, the *Lampoon*'s publisher made a historic misstep. Presented with the opportunity to create a *Lampoon*-based TV show for NBC, he demurred. Soon after, the network premiered *Saturday Night Live*, raiding the *Lampoon*'s talent pool and eclipsing its reputation in ninety minutes flat. Michael O'Donoghue, a *Lampoon* editor considered a genius on par with Doug, became the show's head writer. Chase, Belushi, Radner, and eventually Bill Murray all signed on as well.

With Doug casting around for a new project and the magazine deflated, desperate to rehabilitate its good bad name, both arrived at the same conclusion: time to go to the movies. Doug was paired with Ramis and tasked with writing a *National Lampoon* movie. After bouncing around some concepts, like doing a high school movie in the spirit of the *Yearbook Parody*, they settled on a comedy based on frat-house rivalry. They brought on a *Lampoon* editor who had written some fraternity-based pieces, and together created a script. From the start, they had Belushi in mind for the lead, and the movie was named in keeping with the energy they felt he brought to the screen: *Animal*

House. John Landis, a young director who had recently made the cult sketch-comedy film *Kentucky Fried Movie*, was signed on to direct.

Doug's nascent film career brought him out to the West Coast more frequently, and he stopped over at Laurel Canyon whenever possible. It was one of the few places in his life that really felt like a home. Over the years, Doug had become close friends with John and Judy Belushi, and their place was his New York City home-away-from-home—even though it was the same city in which his real home could also be found. He referred to them as his "East Coast Peter and Lucy," and to Peter and Lucy as his "West Coast Judy and John."

This was the life Peter and Lucy had created together, the life Lucy would have done anything to protect. They weren't hippies anymore and they weren't kids, but they weren't grown-ups exactly, either. They were Laurel Canyon people. They had a nice little garden and kitchen, a room to make music in, and a couch to put friends on. They were in love. What could she possibly want to change?

Peter's music buddies were showing up to practice. The stuff he was working on was for an album he had titled *Nirvana Cuba*. So far it was getting a great response. To Steve Martin, it felt like so much more than an album. It told a complete story, and was filled with visual hooks. It was more like the soundtrack to a play or film, which was exactly what Peter had in mind. In line with his training in theatre, his work in film, and his current experimentation with video, the end product of *Nirvana Cuba* was going to be not just a series of songs but a performance: acted, directed, staged, and filmed.

The musicians assembled in the living room, tuning and adjusting their amps. Peter cued them, and they started to play. And as they played, as if on cue, Lucy started crying again.

Because it was Sunday, and Lucy loved her life. And on Monday she was going to start a new one.

LA, MGM, the Next Day, Early Morning

Luckily, Doug and Tim were in town that weekend, and they helped Lucy move into her new MGM office. Peter was noticeably absent. As was often the case, he was busy working.

As they arrived, lugging boxes, the person Lucy had been hired to replace was walking out. He looked her over and said, "Why on earth are you taking this dead-end job?" Doug and Tim looked at each other and pretended not to hear; they set the boxes down in what was to be her new office.

It was a variation on the question she had asked Doug the first time she met him, when he was engaged to a woman of whom he spoke badly and did not seem particularly interested in being around. Lucy could not understand why someone would follow through on a decision so clearly destined to turn out badly. But then, Doug was a tortured soul to begin with; he probably figured, How much worse can it get? Lucy was satisfied with almost every aspect of her Laurel Canyon life. What was *her* excuse? However different the circumstances, her answer now was the same as Doug's had been back then.

"I have no idea."

LA, Doug Kenney's Home, 1978, 11:00 p.m.

Steve Martin made his way through the dense crowd at Doug Kenney's luxurious bachelor pad, trying to keep his head down, half in shock. He could not believe he had been invited to this party and was terrified of saying the wrong thing—of saying *anything*, to anyone— certain a single sentence would give him away as the impostor he was and have him summarily shown the door. So he kept his mouth shut and his eyes wide open, observing in person the faces he only knew from movie screens. Steve was much younger than the rest of the guests, and at what it would be an understatement to call a very different place in his career. The invitation, of course, had come from Peter.

After a while, elated and still slightly spooked, Steve decided he had absorbed all he could for one night and went to the bedroom where the coats had been thrown. There he found Chevy Chase sprawled out on the bed, perched impossibly atop the coat pile, chatting up a girl. He was not about to ask Chevy Chase to get up so he could find his coat. Trapped, he returned to the party.

Gradually, his fear of being discovered as a nonsuperstar and kicked out subsided. It struck him how warm and good-natured everyone was, enjoying their success but not flaunting it. They just seemed to be having a good time.

In a corner, Peter and Doug huddled together like brothers at a family reunion, half-giddy just to be living in the same city again.

There was much to be giddy about, and much to report on both sides. Doug's presence in Hollywood was a joyful boon to his and Peter's friendship. In the past year he had become one of the most celebrated and influential figures in American entertainment. The next chapter was his to write, and as always he looked to his best friend for guidance and support.

Doug had moved out to Hollywood shortly after *National Lampoon's Animal House* debuted as the number-one movie in America. It held the spot for three months, became the highest-grossing film comedy of all time, and put John Belushi on the cover of *Newsweek*. It also touched off a revolution in Hollywood. With its theme of smart-ass misfits triumphing over the establishment straights, the movie seemed intended as a kind of manifesto, a call to arms for disgruntled eccentrics everywhere to say exactly what was on their minds. This message struck a resounding chord across late-'70s America. The result was not only a commercial sensation but a kind of self-fulfilling prophecy for its creators. Kenny, Ramis, Belushi, Landis—they *were* the smart-ass misfits they created and portrayed. As Doug told an interviewer for *Time* magazine shortly after the film's release: "The *Harvard Lampoon* was my Animal House." With millions of young Americans laughing their asses off and shelling out hard cash, the establishment straights in Hollywood had no choice but to hand over the keys to the vault and throw open the studio gates.

Doug and Ramis led the charge. They moved to LA, *Animal House* cohort in tow, sparking a shift in America's center-of-comedy. Everyone wanted to be the one to write, produce, and direct the next *Animal House*. Doug, of course, was the prettiest girl at the ball, bombarded with offers and top executives' calls and invitations to meet.

Peter and Lucy were glad to see Doug, if not exactly happy, at least more at ease with all the opportunities that continued to open up to him. LA was their town, and in a flurry of jam sessions and Hollywood parties like the one that night, their friends became Doug's friends; Doug's friends became their friends; the friends became friends; and the City of Angels was suddenly an exponentially more fun place to be. That Peter was still essentially a struggling musician and Doug a multimillionaire did not seem to register on anyone's radar. Doug's high regard for him and Peter's own high-voltage presence made him a favorite with the *Lampoon* crowd.

Harold Ramis in particular loved Peter, and the two struck up an instant friendship. Ramis appreciated the literary quality of Peter, Doug, and Lucy's epic friendship, and he loved that Peter could be smart and extremely funny without being mean. This was a welcome relief from the relentless hostile irony that had become much of the *Lampoon* crowd's stock-in-trade. This generosity of spirit stood in stark contrast with the incessant needy angling that in Hollywood was taken for granted as part of the game. Peter was clearly on his own trip and had no interest in exploiting anyone to get anywhere, a purity of motive all the more refreshing for being so rare. In a town where everyone else was networking, to his new friend Harold, Peter just seemed to be living.

Ramis was particularly impressed by Peter's spiritual discipline and physical poise, his accomplishments in yoga and martial arts. His wife, Anne, was into yoga, and he told her she had to meet this guy, Doug's best friend, he was a yoga master, they would get along great. She invited him over to do yoga, and when they finished she introduced him to their baby girl. Peter took out his harmonica and began to serenade Violet Ramis, who could not yet speak but squealed her toddler's delight. Anne went out and bought her a harmonica, and hung it on a chain around her neck. From then on, when Violet wanted to express herself, she put it to her mouth and played. As his friendship with the Ramises grew, Peter was often at the house, and he and Violet spent lots of time together communicating in their secret language. The harp had become her mother tongue. Violet Ramis may have been Peter's first musical protégé, but she was far from the last.

Notwithstanding their breakout success and sudden wealth, the *Lampoon* comics still saw themselves as outsiders; more than anything, it was this self-image that united and defined them. They were also, on the whole, highly educated, intelligent people who loved playing with words and ideas. They mingled easily with the musicians and artists of Laurel Canyon. Doug's literary temperament and aversion to authority made him a natural fit with people like Durrie and Van Dyke Parks, who recognized what he was doing not just as entertainment but as iconoclastic literary art—a recognition Doug had been looking for all his life. Working in different media, they were all striving for essentially the same thing.

Of all the comics, Belushi took to Laurel Canyon with particular zeal. A true music fiend and positively an animal for the blues, he was in heaven as Peter led him around and introduced him to the wide variety of offerings. The first time Durrie Parks saw the two of them together was at a jam session in the LA home of a Chicago bluesman Belushi knew. Belushi's next movie was going to be a feature-length comedy about the blues, and this friend was signed on to play keys. For Durrie, whose whole life was music, the evening was explosive, a fireworks display. She was surprised to find Belushi to be polite, at times self-effacing, nothing at all like the manic overbearing persona he was known for. This scene was repeated frequently, often at Peter and Lucy's place, with Belushi on drums, Peter on harp, and shifting configurations of the usual crowd on everything else.

Steve Martin wandered around Doug's vast, lavish house, examining it as the party around him wound down. Most of the people he knew, like Peter and Lucy, had groovy apartments they rented on the cheap and fixed up with arts and crafts. But this was an honest-to-God grown-up house. Though he wasn't sure why, this seemed to Steve an important moment in his life, and he marked it in his mind.

Peter and Doug were still huddled in the corner, talking animatedly, cracking each other up. Steve felt bad interrupting, but now he really did have to go. He approached Doug, and thanked him for having him in his home. A part of him still felt self-conscious for being there, like he'd come on a forged passport.

Doug took his hand, gave him a big smile, and said, "Thank you for coming."

Doug Kenney was a good-looking guy, women seemed to dig him, but in that moment Steve understood his true appeal. It was his face: such a warm, sweet, open face. A face that showed everything, that did not know how to lie. *What a nice guy*, Martin thought.

"Really, thank you," Doug said. He meant it.

LA, 20th Century Fox, 1979

Paula Weinstein was at a loss for words—which, for a high-level movie executive, was saying something. Rendering talkative people speechless was one of Peter's great talents, and it was one of the qualities Weinstein loved about him. Since Lucy started at 20th Century Fox, he had become a familiar face around the studio. He would often pop into her office to deliver some funny, irreverent quip: zinger insights that punched holes into the obvious and everyday and often left you feeling both slightly elated and slightly unnerved. In short, she thought he was delicious.

Today, Peter presented Weinstein with a wrapped gift. She unwrapped it immediately, knowing that coming from Peter it could be virtually anything. It was a vibrator. Paula looked up at Peter. He could not stop smiling. "Since you're between boyfriends," he explained, grinning even more proudly than before.

Weinstein had brought Lucy to 20th Century Fox after only six months at MGM, a merciful reprieve from a job that was every bit the professional purgatory she'd been led to expect. 20th Century Fox was just the opposite: the most prestigious and exciting studio in Hollywood. Shortly after Lucy arrived, a popular magazine had published an article about Hollywood's "baby moguls," the young, hungry executives who were taking over. Weinstein had insisted that Lucy be part of the article, which included a prominent group photo. Her reputation skyrocketed. She became known as a formidable force in the business. Shortly thereafter, a group of 20th Century Fox execs left the studio to form their own company. Lucy rose from the lowest to the highest vice president virtually overnight.

With her new job came long hours. She enjoyed the work, especially the camaraderie among the other young female executives like Weinstein. It was the first time in the industry's history that so many women occupied such influential positions, with real power to decide what films should get made. She and Peter saw less and less of each other, but he was proud of her achievement and happy to see her happy. Busy with his own projects, he was also glad to have the house to himself. Both probably noticed, at some level, that a distance was growing between them. Peter's work obsession, which only grew more intense as time passed, was partly a natural expression of his creative mind. Lucy could see that it was also an expression of his frustration and disappointment at not having made it after ten years of projects he felt certain would hit. This humiliation only emboldened the demons that goaded him; he had to push harder to keep a step ahead of them. His bright outlook began to show signs of wear; at times a dark edge crept into his mood. He did more yoga, meditated longer, and practiced harder at martial arts.

Lucy knew he was a genius and believed that one of his many endeavors was bound to take off. Still, his frustration brought a heaviness into their home, which at times could be hard to live with. In her more honest moments, she had to admit that his inability to convert his talent into even a modest, consistent career was frustrating for her as well. And, while it was never spoken about overtly, the fact that Lucy was making real money now while Peter could not or would not land a regular paying gig, could not have been good for their relationship. When they came out west together, she was the college girl and he was the rocker with the record deal. Now she was the one financing both their lifestyle and his rock-star dreams.

It wasn't just the money. Lucy was now at the center of an exciting industry, doing creative work with creative people. She had the power to orchestrate collaboration—always Peter's specialty—with all the resources of a big studio behind her.

Doug Kenney was completing his follow-up to *Animal House*, a country club farce with Chevy Chase and Bill Murray, with Ramis directing. Doug had a production company, and after feeling compromised and burned by his studio he sought refuge with ever-protective Big Sis. Lucy now had the backing to give him what he was always looking for: a home. She signed his company to 20th Century Fox to develop a number of scripts. She brought Tim Mayer out to write one of them with their old Harvard friend John Leone.

While their relationship grew increasingly complicated, two constants kept Peter and Lucy afloat: Peter's faith in the work he was doing, and their deep love. Despite the career gap that had opened between them, Peter was always himself, always working, always passionate and magnetic. Everyone who met them noticed the special connection they shared, the mutual respect and adoration. Steve Martin often went out with them, and one scene always stuck in his mind. They were at a rock concert, with a crowd of hundreds jumping and dancing around them. In the middle of it all were Peter and Lucy, holding each other, dancing close. They weren't dancing to the music; it seemed to Steve they were barely aware of the music or the crowd. They were slow-dancing.

Steve thought, *That is a couple in love.*

Florida, Rolling Hills Golf Course, 1979

Tim Mayer was looking for Peter. Really, though, he was looking for someone to play with. Actually, he was looking for something, anything, to do.

Mayer found himself in possibly the farthest place imaginable from his natural habitat: the Rolling Hills Golf Club in Davies, Florida (a *suburb* of Fort Lauderdale). To Mark Stumpf, a friend of Doug's from the *Harvard Lampoon* who was also visiting him on the *Caddyshack* set, Mayer seemed aimless, uncomfortable, out of place. Since graduating, he had continued to write and produce plays, small shows for regional theatre and a few well-received pieces for public television. He had an aristocrat's disdain for pop culture, and many of Doug's show business friends who met Mayer got the sense that he felt he was slumming.

Stumpf also noticed that Doug seemed remote and distracted. He was not happy with how the movie was going. Throughout the *Caddyshack* shoot, Doug lumbered around in a self-medicated haze. In this, at least, he was not alone. Much of the cast, with the notable exception of veteran actor Ted Knight, spent their nights and days consuming substances in an unbroken stream. The difference was that Doug was not taking drugs to party; he was taking them just to get by.

Still, when it was time to start shooting, he would watch the actors, and between nodding off somehow manage to punch up their lines and improvise new ones, and at times entire monologues and scenes—all in the pitch-perfect dialogue and deadpan absurdity that had made him one of the country's most successful comic writers. It was almost as if humor, for Doug, was something unconscious: even with his brain saturated with drugs, what came out when he spoke were comic gems. For Doug, work was the easy part of life. It was everything else that was the problem.

Tim was no stranger to any of this. While they were both on the East Coast, they spent plenty of time together in New York and on Martha's Vineyard, abusing the good life and taking turns saving each other when the abuse turned on them.

But this was different, Doug was working and Tim had no real reason to be there. So he wandered the clubhouse, then some of the

Peter Ivers promo shot, 1980.

Peter (center) on his high school prom committee, 1964.

Peter and Tim Mayer, 1969.

Peter in his studio in Laurel Canyon, 1974.

Peter with Devo at the Santa
Monica Civic Center, July 1979.

Peter with John Cale at the
Whisky a Go Go, March 1980.

Peter in Jerusalem with
Lucy Fisher's family, 1978.

Doug Kenney on *New Wave Theatre*, June 17, 1980.
Copyright New Wave Theatre/ Night Flight

Left to right: Tim Mayer, Doug Kenney, Peter, Lucy Fisher, and Harold Ramis, 1978.

Peter and David Lynch (left) on *New Wave Theatre*, March 12, 1980.
Copyright New Wave Theatre/ Night Flight

Peter with Jello Biafra of the Dead Kennedys on *New Wave Theatre*, January 21, 1981.
Copyright New Wave Theatre/ Night Flight

Peter doing his opening monologue on *New Wave Theatre*.
Copyright New Wave Theatre/ Night Flight

Peter with Fear: Lee Ving, Derf Scratch, and Philo Cramer, September 21, 1982. Copyright New Wave Theatre/Night Flight

Left to right: Roderick Taylor, Peter, Lucy Fisher, Jody Uttal, and an unknown woman, 1979.

John Belushi with The Dead Boys: Jimmy Zero, Johnny Blitz, Cheetah Chrome, and Stiv Bators, 1978.

Peter and the
New Wave Theatre
regulars, 1981.

Peter and Tequila Mockingbird on *New Wave Theatre* with Vitamin Pink, 1982.

Harold Ramis and daughter Violet.
Courtesy of Michael Dare—www.dareland.com

David Jove at *New Wave Theatre*.
Courtesy of Michael Dare—www.dareland.com

Peter with *New Wave Theatre* regulars.
Courtesy of Michael Dare—www.dareland.com

John Belushi on the set of *The Blues Brothers*.
Courtesy of Michael Dare—www.dareland.com

Penelope Spheeris at *New Wave Theatre*.
Courtesy of Michael Dare—www.dareland.com

Judy and Jim Belushi.
Courtesy of Michael Dare—www.dareland.com

Peter on *New Wave Theatre*, 1982.

Peter and Anthony Keidis on *New Wave Theatre*, pre–Red Hot Chili Peppers, June 24, 1980. Copyright New Wave Theatre/Night Flight

Jello Biafra performing with the Dead Kennedys on *New Wave Theatre*, **January 21, 1981.** Copyright New Wave Theatre/Night Flight

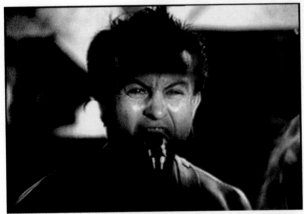

Lee Ving performing with Fear on *New Wave Theatre*, **September 21, 1982.** Copyright New Wave Theatre/ Night Flight

Robert Roll as Chris Genkel on *New Wave Theatre*, **1981.** Copyright New Wave Theatre/Night Flight

Peter with Ghost Host Elvira on *New Wave Theatre*, March 9, 1982.
Copyright New Wave Theatre/ Night Flight

Peter with Ghost Host Michael O'Donahue on *New Wave Theatre*, February 23, 1982.
Copyright New Wave Theatre/ Night Flight

Peter with Ghost Host Beverly D'Angelo on *New Wave Theatre*, January 26, 1982. Copyright New Wave Theatre/Night Flight

Zachary and Peter on
New Wave Theatre, **1982.**
Copyright New Wave Theatre/
Night Flight

Poster for Peter Ivers's
Vitamin Pink Fantasy Revue, **June 8 and 9, 1982, Lingerie Club, Los Angeles, California.**

Peter interviewing Fear
on *New Wave Theatre*,
September 21, 1982.
Copyright New Wave Theatre/
Night Flight

New Wave Theatre flyer, 1982.

Peter and Lucy at their Laurel Canyon home, 1974.

hills and greens, asking if anyone had seen Peter. Peter had brought his grandfather to the set, but no one seemed to have seen either of them. Tim walked some of the more remote courses. Though he continued to work, and was still recognized in his circle as a top-notch writer and dramatist, Tim, much like Peter, had failed to find his niche. His circle included Carly Simon, Joni Mitchell, and James Taylor, with whom he sometimes collaborated. But his close friends, especially those who knew him from the Agassiz days, could not help but wonder why he had avoided the obvious and not made a run at Broadway. Even if he could not turn Harvard theatre into his American theatrical revolution, he certainly had a brilliant future in the upper echelons of the national stage. Some hesitancy had prevented him from pursuing what everyone who knew him believed to be his destiny.

After walking for some time, Tim was ready to give up when he heard some human sounds coming from the next hill. Atop the green, he found a group of people he recognized as the film crew—techies and assistants and grips. They seemed to be moving in rough concert with one another, bending and sitting and striking strange poses. He got closer, and finally found the source of all the strangeness. It was the only explanation, and of course made perfect sense. He was an idiot for not realizing it sooner.

He found Peter.

Specifically, he found Peter leading the crew of *Caddyshack* in a vigorous session of yoga on the eighteenth hole of the Rolling Hills Golf Club.

LA, Public Access Theta Channel Three, 1980, 10:00 p.m.

If you were a bored suburban teenager in the vicinity of Los Angeles in mid-1980—bored for good reason, because for as long as you'd known it your city had been a cultural wasteland, devoid of music that had anything to say to you, or even (unless you happened to catch word of a cool midnight scene at an art house in a remote, run-down neighborhood, which your parents' would let you near over their dead bodies) movies you wanted to see—you might have heard about a new show on one of the new "public access" stations to be found on previously unused notches of your television dial.

You might have heard that this show featured local LA bands

playing music you'd never heard because radios didn't play it: angry, loud, subversive music about stuff you cared about by young people with tattoos and freaky costumes and wild hair, who seemed truly not to give a fuck what anyone said or thought—music that people were calling punk and new wave. The show had a weird host with weird clothes who introduced the bands and then asked them weird questions that had nothing to do with the music (*Is there hope for the planet? Do you believe in God? What is the meaning of life?*). Sometimes the bands got pissed off, sometimes they insulted the host, or threatened him, or put their hands on him, and you couldn't tell if it was staged or real, but it was definitely cool and fun to watch. Between the bands there were little segments, fake commercials, and other weird surreal comedy bits, usually mocking the corporate mainstream. Sometimes there were *really* weird segments, something the host called "performance art." The host opened and closed every episode with philosophical raps about politics and consciousness and art, and this new movement he called new wave, which was not just the music but a whole way of looking at the world, of being creative and independent and questioning everything.

You may have heard about the show and watched it and realized you had never seen anything like it before. Then you may have started tuning in religiously every Sunday night at 10:00 to Theta Channel Three. You may have started to see this *New Wave Theatre* as a kind of lifeline.

One of those Sunday nights in mid-1980, between bands, you may have caught the following segment:

Close-up on host, early-thirties, boyish good looks, dressed in jaunty sequined cowboy ensemble, staring earnestly into the camera, holding microphone to his lips. Over live, anticipatory drumbeat he introduces a short segment between the punk and new wave bands that form the show's core.

"The producer has been begging me to bring a freak on the show, and I finally got one. The man with the biggest mouth in the world: Ghost Host Doug."

He turns, and the camera pans to reveal a tall, good-looking man, same age as the host, thinning blond hair and round wire-rimmed glasses, dapper in a suit. As the shot closes in, something about the eyes themselves comes into focus, something lost and disarming and sweet. He looks awkward

about being on camera but also eager to perform. The host holds the micro-
phone to this Ghost Host's face:

"Okay—do it."

The guest hooks an index finger into the corner of one cheek and raises a
fist to his face. Staring into the camera, he yanks the cheek and starts forcing
the fist into his mouth. He pushes it in until the knuckles are flush with his
lips.

The host says, "That's new wave!" and makes an emphatic percussive
sound effect into the microphone.

A few people laugh and clap offscreen as the guest scuttles offstage.
Close in again on the face of the host, who stares into the camera and intro-
duces the next band with an androgynous snarl and a high-pitched yelp,
before turning and making his way off the stage in a slinky dance.

The band kicks in, no buildup, hard and loud and fast from the start.

At the beginning of the show, a young, fresh-faced kid in a tuxedo
delivered a grand, '50s variety-show introduction for the host in
the funny clothes: *"Ladies and Gentlemen, welcome to New Wave*
Theatre. And now, your talented host, Peter Ivers!" But you would
not have known that the Ghost Host with the fist-sized mouth was
Doug Kenney, founder of the *National Lampoon*, writer of *Animal*
House and *Caddyshack*—according to many critics, one of the found-
ers of modern comedy—and that the host in the funny clothes was a
Harvard wunderkind with as many records as all the bands on the
show put together.

Peter had always been the one to discover, throw himself into, and
turn his friends on to the coolest, most interesting music scenes. In the
two years since *Animal House* had prompted a mass migration of unruly New York comics to LA, a new scene had begun to bubble up
from the LA music underground. The early stages of punk rock, which
in the early to mid-'70s had stormed New York and London, had in
large part passed Hollywood by. While bands like the Germs, the
Weirdos, Black Flag, the Circle Jerks, and X sparked varying degrees
of cult devotion in Southern CA, the sound as a whole, and the attitude and aesthetic that came with it, did not really begin to catch on
until the late '70s, when the tectonic rumblings of two of punk's most
potent second-wave manifestations began to crack the town's placid
facade.

LA punk and new wave emerged around a handful of clubs in un-glamorous parts of town. Their numbers steadily grew. By 1980 there were seven clubs, each with three shows a night of three different bands, seven days a week. Unlike New York City, LA had a reputation as a town that slept plenty but, suddenly it boasted a twenty-four-hour scene. The Zero Zero, owned by Wayzatta de Camerone of the Braniacs, exhibited underground art during the day and became a music club at 1:00 a.m. Five dollars gained you all-night entrance and unlimited beer.

Peter's involvement with LA punk came through a source both unlikely and, given his penchant for turning self-proclaimed messianic visionaries into colleagues and friends, par for the course. David Jove was, if nothing else, a character: an acid guru cokehead with a fierce creative streak; a devoted father and gun freak; a snake-oil huckster and video prophet with intuitive mastery of camerawork and editing; a new world order cosmic hippie and paranoid narcissist and dedi-cated recent patron of punk and new wave. Compared alternately to Charles Manson, Hunter S. Thompson, and Jesus, David Jove inspired equal amounts of love and devotion, fear and loathing, wonder and begrudging respect among the circle of disciples and adversaries that seemed always to swirl around him.

Originally from Canada, where he supposedly grew up as a child actor before becoming a folk songwriter, musician, and occasional Shakespearean actor, by the late-'60s Jove had already gained a repu-tation as a kind of extreme prankster and late-night, all-around "good-time guy." Some of the good times apparently ran him afoul of Canadian authorities, who pursued him on a host of federal drug-, weapons-, and according to some, assault-related charges. (One of many stories circulating at the time had him wanted for spiking the Canadian water supply with a vat of LSD.) Jove fled to New York on a false passport, landed himself in a Greenwich Village mental hospital to escape deportation, broke out of the mental hospital, and eventu-ally made his way to Europe. A virtuosic party crasher with a mile-a-minute rap and uncanny ability to cop the collective vibe—assisted by an ability to supply large quantities of quality LSD—he gained close access to both the Beatles and the Rolling Stones. Jove claimed to have been the one to turn John Lennon on to acid, and corroborating ac-counts placed him at the scene, as both supplier and informant, of the infamous Redlands bust that earned jail sentences for Mick Jagger and Keith Richards (though Richard's conviction was overruled and neither ultimately served time). The "Acid King David Schneiderman" (one of Jove's many aliases) had walked away from the bust with a briefcase full of illegal drugs, skipped the country, and was never seen or heard from again. Many of the party goers had reportedly continued looking for him.

After London, Jove (which was itself known to be an alias; articles at the time reported his real name as David Jordan or David Schneiderman) had traveled around the world, always writing and recording music and taking notes in his journal. He was, one friend often thought, "the star of his own movie": a dedicated self-chronicler and myth maker obsessed with his place in the world and the transformative impact he felt destined to exert upon it. Based on his charisma, formidable smarts, and sometimes penetrating cultural insight, many of those who met him did not find this self-estimation altogether far-fetched. In a sense, what was most interesting about Jove were not the stories he told about himself—few of which could be externally corroborated, if only because of where and when they'd taken place—but the fact that to many people, the better they got to know him, the more plausible the stories came to seem.

By the mid-'70s Jove had determined to stop running and settle into a life "underground." To hide out, he chose the heavily Jewish Fairfax neighborhood of LA, next to the famous Canter's Deli, where you could get a corned-beef sandwich at all hours of the night. One of the first people he sought out in Hollywood was Ed Ochs, a writer with a high-level editorial position at *Billboard* magazine. Ochs knew of Jove from his Canadian songwriter days, and found credible the stories of his British adventures with the Beatles and Rolling Stones. Even Jove's claim that he cowrote some of John Lennon's lyrics and coined the term "instant karma" for the song of that name, while unprovable, was not something Ochs would have put past him. He had never met a faster talker, and with his own eyes had watched Jove charm his way into exclusive circles, distributing drugs and philosophy, a pied piper of LSD.

Ochs knew Jove was on the run from the law and had no illusions about his emotional stability or moral core. On many occasions he watched Jove, a knife and gun fetishist, blow holes in the walls and ceilings of his apartment with various shotguns. (Asked if anyone was living upstairs, Jove would offhandedly answer, "Don't know.") Still, Ochs found him to be a serious thinker, dazzling wordsmith, profound lover of music, and often inspired creative soul. The two men shared many common interests, had long, lively conversations, and became fast friends. Ochs saw Jove as an aggressive original on the order of Hunter S. Thompson, always high on something, always selling some new project or idea, always flirting with madness and genius. The kind of person it was always interesting to have around, who you liked to hang out with if not necessarily invite into your home.

Around 1980, Jove had become bored, and that was bad news for Ed Ochs. Ochs would pick up the phone in the morning and hear Jove's voice on the line: "How're you doing?" "Fine." "Look out the window." And there would be Jove, his van parked in Ochs's driveway, making the call from some kind of newfangled portable phone. Jove could be all-consuming. Most of the people he knew worked for him in some official or unofficial capacity; but Ed Ochs already had a good job. In order for him to retain his autonomy and not get swallowed up in Jove's trip, he needed to find his friend a hobby, and fast.

He suggested Jove buy a video camera—the kind of toy that lent itself to obsessive, consuming use. Jove wanted to know what he would do with it. A music aficionado plugged in to the emerging underground new wave, Ochs knew this trend was largely undocumented. He told Jove to go around to the clubs and capture the movement: hundreds of bands with no deals and no demos, who needed video to get themselves seen. It was a rough crowd, where drug- and booze-fueled suburban teen angst played out not only in ink, piercings, and leather but in regular outbursts of physical violence. If Ochs knew anyone who could penetrate such a scene, it was David Jove, and by filming it he felt confident Jove could secure video deals with record companies.

Jove took his advice, though this did not exactly achieve Ochs's goal of getting his friend off his back. Jove went into the clubs and shot hundreds of hours of videos of bands unknown except within their small, tight-knit circles. He called Ochs to come look at the footage.

Ochs was surprised by what he saw—in fact, he was bowled over. It wasn't only the music. Jove had a strange, intuitive handheld camera style that maintained visual coherence even while constantly moving. In the meantime, Jove had also bought editing equipment, and at this too he proved a kind of compulsive savant. He edited for hours, cut scenes into their smallest, quickest bits, a cut per second, sometimes splicing in random images so quickly you could not be sure what you had seen (his favorite was the star-filled sky)—all in rhythmic and thematic sympathy with the music.

Ochs was duly impressed, but Jove was looking for more than accolades. He wanted to know what to do with it. Ochs responded by informing him about another emerging trend. Regulations on the new phenomenon of cable television required that certain channels be made available for public access. For a nominal fee ($15 per half-hour segment), anyone could reserve airtime. Ochs told Jove to turn his footage into a television show. He could call it something like *New Wave Theatre*.

Jove caught fire for the idea. Ochs was happy to see him channeling his manic energy into something productive. Moreover, Jove disappeared into the work. Ochs wouldn't hear from him for weeks—a wonderful thing. Then he'd get a call: "Come over, I want to show you something." Eventually Jove decided they would need something to open and close the show with, so together they composed monologues—mad manifestos combining politics, metaphysics, sociology, and sex. But who would deliver them? Jove had some acting experience, but because of his sketchy background he refused to put himself on the air. Ochs recorded the first opening and closing monologues himself. But he was uncomfortable in front of the camera, and, besides, the whole idea of the project had been to put distance between them. So Jove went out in search of a host.

He wanted someone who could hold his own with the aggressive punks, someone unafraid of putting on a show. He also wanted someone with name recognition and connections. The problem was that in LA, Jove had kept a low public profile. If he had any currency and legitimacy in Hollywood, it was for one reason and one reason only: he had married a good woman. Lotus Weinstock was a beloved figure in the entertainment industry. A matriarch of the female stand-up comedy scene with a strong personal and professional reputation of her own, her storied relationship with Lenny Bruce (the couple was engaged when Bruce died of a morphine overdose in 1966) had given

Weinstock a kind of royalty status in Hollywood. She and Jove had a child together—Lily, over whom they both unabashedly doted—and while they kept separate homes, they also seemed to have a loving, respectful marriage, and often socialized among Lotus's friends. It was through a connection to Lotus that Jove became acquainted with Peter Ivers, at one of the many parties sprinkled over the Hollywood workweek.

The appeal to Peter of a character like David Jove—fiercely independent and contemptuous of convention, highly verbal and spiritually inclined, a cultural visionary with cultish appeal; precisely the kind of person who would piss his father off—was not hard to understand. Though domineering and not infrequently enraged, Jove was at heart a collaborator who required a community of formidable personalities and talents with whom to refine and actualize his ideas. Peter lived for collaboration, and Jove's interests—video, music, and comedy—made a perfect intersection with his own.

Jove asked Peter to host *New Wave Theatre* the day before the first episode was scheduled to tape. He explained the show's concept, its underlying philosophy, the meaning and significance of the underground scene. Peter shot back with his own analysis, igniting a verbal sparring match that lasted for hours. Peter himself had spent much of the last three years contemplating the power of video, and the future of artistic movements that would be rendered more potent and palatable through the accessible platform. He was also keenly in search of his "next move," and very clear about what that move needed to help him accomplish: sending his father a bag of money; becoming a star. Peter showed up the next day to host the show.

Though musically he had little in common with punk and new wave—whose appeal lay precisely in its accessibility, the ability of any angry adolescent to pick up an instrument and start a band—Peter's affinity with its attitude is easy to grasp. Having spent the last ten years scrabbling as a self-made artist, he was no stranger to punk's DIY (do-it-yourself) ethic. In some ways (as some of his friends would observe), Peter was an LA punk before it had a name.

The main difference was that what Peter did with subtlety, sensuality, and a smirk, punk did by shouting "Fuck you" to a country that had gorged on its own smug self-indulgence, and "Wake up" to a music industry that for the better part of the decade had given that self-indulgence a soundtrack. The marginalization of independent voices was something Peter knew about firsthand, and in the LA underground he found thousands of young people creating their own venues to speak and be heard. The high shock quotient that was central to punk's aesthetic didn't hurt. He had, after all, been wearing diapers onstage when some of these bands were barely out of diapers in real life.

New Wave Theatre offered Peter the opportunity to combine his interests in independent music, experimental video, and performance art. It also offered the opportunity to get his face on TV.

Peter's music friends hadn't gotten it when he initially started playing with his own punk persona. Musical purists, they cared far less about spectacle and attitude than fine composition and a good, sweaty jam. They didn't get it now either. They still played with Peter, but for the most part steered clear of *New Wave Theatre*.

His *Lampoon* friends were another story. Relishing spectacle, particularly subversive spectacle, they were regular visitors to the *NWT* set and occasional cameo-making Ghost Hosts. Some liked the music more than others, but they all loved the primal unfettered wildness of it all and the sneering middle finger to America. The punks were the ultimate misfits, taunting polite society by holding up a fun-house mirror to its rhetoric of freedom and openness, overturning every rock to expose the intolerance and hypocrisy seething maggotlike underneath. The same stale American verities the comics attacked by making people laugh, the punks poured gasoline on and set a match to with distorted guitars and screaming lead singers.

In the universe envisioned by the *Lampoon* there were two kinds of people: slobs and snobs. Belushi's Bluto and Bill Murray's gopher-hunting caddy went up against the cheerleaders, the preps, and the rich politicians, employing an arsenal of absurdity and gross disdain of social norms. Fear, Angry Samoans, Dead Kennedys, and 45 Grave went up against everyone in much the same way except in place of laughter they wanted people to jump up and down and cheer on the apocalypse. In the presence of angry outsiders bent on telling the truth even if it meant destroying everything around them—including themselves—people like Doug Kenney, Michael O'Donoghue, John Belushi, and Harold Ramis felt right at home, if not with the music, at least with the message.

Perhaps even more than the rest of them, this was something Kenney desperately needed—to feel a part of something countercultural, uncorrupted by commerce. Though he had managed to find a voice and a medium that spoke to the masses, sold like crazy, and made him rich, Doug was, at his core, an artist. He felt *Caddyshack* had been stolen from him, and thus didn't give a damn how well it was doing at the box office. Needling producers had insinuated their influence into nearly ever aspect of production: hijacked the editing, added new scenes (many starring a mechanical gopher he had not written and stridently opposed), marred his vision, and stolen his film. Unlike at the *Lampoon*, where he worked in solitude and always had final say, in Hollywood he could only sit back and watch as his creation was ground up and gnashed through machinations he had no power to stop. That after *Caddyshack*'s release, he continued to be hailed as a genius and courted by studios only deepened Doug's cynicism, convincing him that Hollywood was a place filled with idiots and sycophants. Despair drove him to seek further comfort in cocaine. He kept a large open sugar bowl piled high with the white powder perched on the mantle of his lonely, extravagant Hollywood pad.

Within the space of two years, Doug had gone from being the new king of Hollywood to being a jittery, angry, addled shell. Shortly before *Caddyshack* was released, Dough and Peter attended a screening of the disaster farce *Airplane!* Peter had written a funny folk song parody for the film, sung by a stewardess playing an acoustic guitar. Usually one of Peter's biggest cheerleaders, Doug spent most of the movie convincing himself that the film he was watching far surpassed his own spoiled film, that as a result of losing creative control over his work his time in the spotlight had expired. By the end of *Airplane!* Dough was so defeated that he barely remembered to congratulate Peter on his song.

Doug had come to rely on Peter more than ever during this time. For him, as for others in their crowd who had made it commercially, Peter represented uncompromising integrity at all costs. (And it had cost him plenty.) Doug felt that Peter was one of only a few people in the world—and hands down the only one currently residing in LA—he could really talk to and who would understand. But perhaps more important than both of those things was that Peter was the only person in Hollywood who, when you mentioned Evelyn Waugh, would respond with something other than a blank stare. Doug would take pulling thirty-second absurdist gags with Peter as a *New Wave Theatre* Ghost Host over all the studio meetings in the world.

If you were a bored LA teenager, chances are you would not have known about Doug Kenney and his disgust with Hollywood and his reliance on his best friend Peter to keep him grounded in the underground. But, watching them goof around on New Wave Theatre, you might have felt that your world just got a little more interesting. You might have heard about it from your friends, and told your friends who hadn't heard about it yet, and on Sunday night at 10:00 you might have turned on the television and flipped the cable box to Theta Channel Three. The next day at school, you might have talked about the cool new bands, and what they looked like, and the funny fake-commercials and the bizarre host with his flamboyant clothes and philosophical questions and psychedelic raps. For the first time you can remember since caring about such things, you might have felt there was something going on in the culture that you could relate to, that seemed to care about relating to *you*. You might have been excited and grateful, or at least just a little less bored.

Close-up on host, dressed in red shirt and large, glittery silver-sequined vest.

"Call for service," he says, and a waiter's arm enters from the left: mustard uniform, towel-draped wrist, a plastic glass of wine in the open palm. Pan out to find the arm attached to a tall, good-looking man, same age as the host, with thinning blond hair and round wire-rimmed glasses.

"You look like a successful guy," Peter says. "What does success mean to you?"

Close-up on the waiter's face, his wild bugged-out eyes that may or may not be part of the character.

"Success," Doug Kenney says, "means never having to say, 'you're welcome.'"

•

LA, Studio Screening Room, 1979, 12:00 p.m.

Francis Ford Coppola sat in a private Hollywood screening room, waiting for the film to start. Next to him sat Lucy Fisher, the new head of his recently formed Zoetrope Studio. If she was anxiously anticipating Coppola's reaction to the film—she had brought it to him in the hope of signing its talented young director to the studio—Lucy did not let on. The renegade genius and his top executive seemed to have a natural rapport and spoke closely as the rest of the small, select audience took their seats. Next to Lucy sat Peter. Among circles in Hollywood, this increasingly is how Peter was becoming known: as Lucy Fisher's boyfriend. The lights went down, the projector clicked and filled the screen with the opening scene of *The Elephant Man*, David Lynch's second film.

The suggestion to sign Lynch to Zoetrope was a signal to Coppola of the kind of talent Lucy was capable of bringing to the studio and intended to foster under its name. She thought Zoetrope would be the perfect home to nurture the brilliant, twisted vision of someone like David Lynch. Lucy knew Lynch through Peter, and the film itself had come about largely through the efforts of Stuart Cornfeld, another Peter connection. (Peter and Cornfeld had met at the Bob's Big Boy meeting and remained friendly.) Since his "rebirth" that fateful night at the Nuart, Cornfeld had become Lynch's number-one advocate in Hollywood. Ascending the executive ranks, he was trying to help his cinematic hero get his second original screenplay produced when a colleague handed him the *Elephant Man* script. Cornfeld knew instantly that the film belonged to Lynch. He called his old mentor Mel Brooks to ask if his production company would take it on. Brooks wanted to see what Lynch could do, so Cornfeld arranged a screening of *Eraserhead*. At the end of the screening, Brooks supposedly walked out of the theater and into the lobby where Lynch was standing and said, "You're either a fucking madman or a genius, I can't tell which." Banking on the latter, he signed his company to produce. Lynch created a masterpiece, which Lucy now used to convince Coppola that the director should be part of his new team.

All the connections to the film had come through Peter. Yet he was the odd man out. This painful irony was not lost on Steve Martin. Seated directly behind Peter, Lucy, and Coppola in the small screening room, Steve seethed on Peter's behalf. Or at least, part of him seethed. The other part was doing back flips about his new job. Lucy had hired Steve to work with her at Zoetrope. He was assistant director of creative development at the hippest movie studio in town. Things that previously only happened in his film school fantasies now happened in his office. One day George Lucas came in. Steve was such a big fan of Lucas that he not only loved *THX 1138* and *American Graffiti*, but also knew that Lucas was a camera operator on the Maysles brothers' Rolling Stones documentary *Gimme Shelter*. Steve shook his hero's hand and was struck by how tiny it was. From then on he noticed Lucas always kept his hands in his pockets and wondered if that was why. In other words, Steve Martin was in heaven.

At the moment, though, he was also torn. Peter was cool under pressure, but Martin could only imagine how he must be feeling. Then, as the opening credits rolled, Coppola reached his arm around the back of Lucy's chair. It didn't strike Steve as inappropriate or flirtatious, more of a fatherly kind of gesture. But as the movie progressed, he had a hard time keeping his attention fully on the screen. He watched as Coppola would periodically pull Lucy towards him and make a comment in her ear. She was the only person in the room he seemed interested in talking to. The dynamic was clearly professional, with no trace of flirtation on either side. But there was also an unavoidable intimacy to their quiet communication, to the life and the world that they shared. They were powerful people making powerful decisions, together, and the intensity of their connection was undeniable. There was also the sheer fact of Coppola: a famous, influential, wealthy older man, universally recognized for his brilliance. He had achieved artistic and commercial success on his own terms—everything to which Peter aspired and at which he had thus far failed. Coppola was living Peter's dream, and now Lucy was living it with him.

Martin knew his friend must be dying a thousand deaths. Part of him wanted Peter to stand up and say, "Get your fucking hands off my girlfriend!"

There were rumors. People falsely assumed Lucy was sleeping with Coppola and took the liberty of spreading it as fact. This annoyed Lucy, but it was the least of her concerns. The reality was far less tawdry, and far more painful for all involved.

A few weeks before the screening, Coppola had literally gotten down on his knees. On a sidewalk in San Francisco, he had lowered himself to the ground and begged her to take the job. After two years at 20th Century Fox, she had become a well-known and highly desired commodity in the industry. She went to fancy parties, got invited to the Oscars, was written up in *Time* magazine. Coppola found her through a mutual friend, invited her to San Francisco, and dropped to his knees. He did not mince words.

"Please run my studio."

Lucy had some real doubts about working for Coppola, who was reputed to have gone crazy during the shooting of *Apocalypse Now*. She countered that she was underqualified for the job—or at least, underexperienced. Coppola would not hear it.

"What's the worst that could happen? I'll go bankrupt and you'll learn more about making movies that any other studio exec!"

What's the worst that could happen? For Lucy, it was hardly a rhetorical question. All was not well in Laurel Canyon. It was true that Lucy and Peter's relationship had been idling for a while. But when Lucy signed on at Zoetrope, the slow encroaching distance between them grew. Unspoken resentments and disappointments gradually hollowed out what had been holding them together. Both busy with work most of the day, they made less time for each other. They remained affectionate and spoke often on the phone, but it became clear they were living not one shared life, but two parallel lives. They became like old friends who happened to share a house.

The problem went much deeper than discrepancies in income and success, which they had already shown they could weather. It went all the way down to one of the central tenets of their relationship which, on some level, Lucy understood went something like this: Peter was an artist and had to do things his own inimitable way. Lucy loved that about him and supported everything he did; someday it would turn out to be whatever it was meant to be, and meanwhile, it was great.

But the two biggest developments in each of their lives were making this agreement less and less sustainable. For one thing, Lucy despised *New Wave Theatre*. The music was so unmusical, the scene so unpleasant. While still and always Peter's biggest fan—she remained mesmerized every time he picked up the harmonica and never stopped being in the emotional grip of his music and songs—she hated that he was subverting his own work to be, as she saw it, a mouthpiece for David Jove. She understood the value of Peter's using the show to hone his live-camera performance skills, but she also felt that the overweening creepiness of Jove and his milieu outweighed any potential benefit. It was not only beneath Peter's dignity and talent; it felt dangerous in ways Lucy could not fully explain. She knew that Peter always had a soft spot for the underappreciated, for the angry, for the dangerous. Lucy was always the straight man of their duo and had always enjoyed the subterranean worlds and characters he exposed her to. But going to blues clubs in sketchy neighborhoods to see Muddy Waters was one thing. *New Wave Theatre* was no Muddy Waters. She didn't even want to use the bathrooms at *New Wave Theatre*. She felt unsafe there. It was the first time in their relationship that she could not relate to Peter's choices, the first thing she was not thrilled to watch him do. When Peter showed up to the tapings, she was rarely there to cheer him on.

In the past, she had never questioned his judgment. It wasn't only that she thought he was brilliant. In their division of labor, he was the artist, she the adoring fan. Even when Lucy was at 20th Century Fox, climbing the ranks and enjoying her work, she never thought it was cool in the way Peter was cool. The connection to him and his world helped assuage her ambivalence about becoming part of the establishment.

At Zoetrope, all of that changed. The studio was precisely the kind of community Peter was always cultivating, of which he was always at the heart. It was the successful, establishment version of Peter's dream: a bunch of artists having their place to be nutty, creative geniuses and get paid. Coppola was the towering figure at the heart of it, and Coppola was undisputedly cool. At the same time that Lucy was feeling disenchanted by Peter's vision, through her own hard work she had earned a place of prominence in a world she did deeply connect to, and the opportunity to sit and learn at another visionary's knee. The satisfaction and excitement she once depended on Peter for now came through of her own work. Not only did she get to work with celebrated German transplant director Wim Wenders, but she found herself in the position of having to *fire* him. (In fact, it was one of the first tasks Coppola gave her.) She no longer relied on Peter as her source for quirky artists, her supplier of cool. She was buying into someone else's dream—a dream that had come true—and this, more than the money or success, proved to be the biggest problem of all.

Though Peter never said it, Lucy understood how hard it was for him to see her become engrossed in someone else's enterprise while he was struggling to stay afloat. She also understood how hard it was for him to watch her hire his friends and bring them into her enterprise.

Of course, she was only doing what he would have done had he been in her position—what, in fact, he did do when given the chance. As she always had, Lucy talked Peter up to her new boss, and after spending some time with him, Coppola came to appreciate and respect who and what Peter was. He asked him for a list of the best musicians in town, a roster of people to use for his movies. Peter responded with a manifesto outlining the talents and singing the praises of all his friends, a who's who of the Laurel Canyon world. Given the opportunity to impress upon Coppola who should be at the musical vanguard of independent film, he eschewed self-promotion to advertise all his favorite collaborators, from Van Dyke Parks and Buell Neidlinger to Devo and Barbara Smith.

However well-meaning, Coppola's gesture was cold comfort, and in many ways brought the essential point home. Coppola had the money to buy a studio; Peter could barely pay rent. Neither Peter nor Lucy fully comprehended the toll these forces were taking on their relationship; they still loved each other and did not want to acknowledge that something could be going so wrong. No words were exchanged; there was never a fight. They just continued to drift into their separate schedules and worlds, as the distance between them hardened.

Peter wasn't the only one feeling jilted by Lucy's new life. If his spiritual practice and natural poise allowed him to repress his resentment for Coppola, the twin furies of cocaine and despair goaded Doug Kenney to shout his from every rooftop. One night he reputedly drove over to the studio and screamed at a security guard, demanding to be let in so he could show Coppola how a movie ought to be made.

Of course, his gripe was really with Lucy. Before starting at Zoetrope, she had signed Doug's production company to 20th Century Fox. Their friendship had been his reason for striking the deal. She was going to help him build a Hollywood-proof studio that would encourage creativity and grant him total control. Not only had she left Doug, but he felt she had left to do the exact same thing for someone else. Coppola, after all, was living Doug's dream even more than Peter's. By virtue of sheer artistic vision, persistence, and will, he had triumphed over the asshole execs, emerging with his artistic dignity intact from the same Hollywood that, in the space of a single film, had taken a chunk out of Doug's soul. There were no mechanical gophers

in *The Godfather* or *Apocalypse Now*. Lucy was supposed to protect Doug and help him get his integrity and career back on track. Instead he felt Big Sis had abandoned him for a more glamorous family headed by the all-time coolest Dad.

Peter was experimenting with video and performance art in the punk–new wave underground. Lucy was running a think tank for the cinematic elite. The situation was clearly not sustainable, and neither of them was going to change direction anytime soon. On her first day at Zoetrope, Lucy was dazzled by the quality of the studio and the caliber of the people in the room. She felt honored just to be considered one of them. Coppola took her to her bungalow, where she found a box of pearls sitting on the desk and a note that read, *"I look forward to our collaboration."* The same day, when he saw the car she drove to work—a red Rabbit—Coppola told her it wasn't fitting for the position she now held. On the spot, he gave her a vintage 1954 baby blue hardtop convertible that happened to be sitting in his garage. Lucy thought it was the most beautiful car ever made, but she protested, "I could never drive that. I'll get into an accident."

She was not being coy. She truly was terrified to get behind the wheel. But Coppola had given her the keys, and she was not about to give them back. At the end of her first day at work, Lucy slid into the new car. For a while she just sat there, thinking. Peter had a brown, somewhat beat-up Fiat convertible that he zoomed around town in. Almost comically small, the car became one of his signatures: tough little Peter in his tough little car.

What would Peter think when she pulled up to Laurel Canyon in this little number? How would it make him feel? Lucy had a good idea.

She sat in the car a while longer, then turned the key and drove home.

Newtown, Connecticut, Village Cemetery, September 8, 1980

"WELCOME, KENNEY MOURNERS!"

The sign at the motel entrance, visible from the side of the road, had been devised by some of Doug's best friends. It had Doug's tone, his influence, all over it: a corny American artifact, pumped with a blast of deadpan American optimism and tweaked to convey the dark-

est, most unwelcome American truth. It was a tribute. Unfortunately, it was not a joke.

Peter, Mayer, and Lucy walked together up the hill, past the duck pond, towards the provincial church cemetery. Doug's friends and family were assembling at the gravesite, a crowd of about four hundred that included Chevy Chase, Bill and Brian Doyle Murray, Michael O'Donoghue, Michael O'Keefe, Chris Hart, Harold and Anne Ramis, and Mark Stumpf. They huddled in small groups, groping for words to capture the significance of what had been lost: "tortured angel," "golden boy," "completely compelling mess." The funniest people in the country were standing in one place, and no one could think of anything funny to say.

Kathryn Walker was there. She and Doug had been together since Tim introduced them at his birthday party three years before. They had the kind of intense, stormy connection common among highly accomplished people with formidable talents and insecurities to match. Lucy lamented that one of Doug's talents seemed to be choosing disapproving women. Peter thought Walker was self-absorbed and unkind to Doug; they did not get along. As the Kenney mourners took their places around Doug's open grave, Peter joined a small group that included Walker and Anne Ramis. "No one will ever know how close we were," Walker said between tears. After a respectful silence, Peter answered, "Why should they?"

Doug's casket was suspended over a hole in the ground. Chevy Chase stepped to the head of the grave and began to speak. Chase was the closest to Doug of all his Hollywood friends. To those who knew Doug well, it was clear that he idolized Chevy and saw him as a smoother, more confident, better-looking version of himself. Chase emulated Doug as well, and they enjoyed each other's company immensely. For Doug, Chevy was also someone with whom he could indulge freely in the fast life, let his demons run wild, racing their sports cars through the Hollywood Hills and doing lots and lots of drugs.

Though obviously shaken, Chase tried to lighten the mood with humor, something facetious about Doug having the capacity to be mean. It was almost as if he thought if he delivered some stinging barbs, Doug would have no choice but to sit up from his coffin and fire a few back. By some present, his words were taken badly. A certain tension between Doug's Harvard friends and his Hollywood

friends—the feeling among the former that the latter created the life-style that killed him and thus bore some responsibility for his death—began to choke the air.

There were plenty of recriminations to go around. It was Chase who had taken Doug to Hawaii to unwind after his dramatic post-*Caddyshack* deterioration. It was clear that Doug had developed a morbid obsession over his feeling that the film was a horrific flop. Lucy had called him regularly from Martha's Vineyard, where she and Peter were spending some vacation time, as she put it, "watching Tim drink." She tried to cheer him up with random good news about the film, but nothing seemed to get through. After almost a month, Chevy went back to LA, which some of Doug's friends construed as abandonment. For a few days, no one thought anything of the fact that Doug could not be reached. They were used to his disappearing act by now. A few days later, his body was discovered between some boulders at the base of the Hanapepe lookout, thirty feet below a cliff on the island of Kauai.

Most of the people there were asking themselves if there was something more they could have done.

Peter's thoughts were elsewhere. In his pocket he carried a piece of paper with a Hindi mantra given to him by Alan Finger. It was supposed to help free the soul and urge it on to its proper destination. Translated from the Hindi, it went:

Release your higher mind
beyond the beyond.
Beyond the beyond
into the beyond.

Peter repeated the mantra. He tried to concentrate on helping Doug move smoothly from this life into the next.

Tim Mayer stepped up next to eulogize Doug, issuing what some perceived as a corrective to Chase's unfortunate (albeit grief-stricken) choice of words.

Peter (as he recorded later that day in a notebook he titled "death notes") focused his thoughts: "Joyous in heart, joy and high feelings send him on his way. Sympathy sorrow and your own shock hold him back. Death isn't gloomy, only sorrow of living. Death enlightening."

As Tim concluded, Peter took his suit jacket off and wrapped it around his waist like a little boy. The ropes suspending Doug's coffin began lowering it into the ground.

A sudden sound filled the air, and a few people looked up, startled—was that a note, a chord? It was music. Peter stood over the scar of turned-up earth as his best friend was lowered into it and eulogized him in the language he knew best. He sent Doug Kenny into heaven with an angry blues version of a song called "Beautiful Dreamer." Without saying a word, he expressed what everyone on the hilltop by the duck pond was feeling. They stood silent, listening and crying.

Peter blew a last snarling chord, hurled his harp into the grave, and fell to his knees and screamed.

—————————————————————————close-up:

Harvard in Hollywood
The New Wave of Comedy

"Guys like Doug Kenney were the first rock stars of comedy."
  —*Richard Roeper*

Eight years ago, three newly graduated *Harvard Lampoon* editors had
a wild and crazy idea: Why not start the first modern national humor
magazine for American adults? . . . This week the magazine's first
film venture, a college satire titled *National Lampoon's Animal House*,
opens in 600 theatres nationwide. Bolstered by good reviews and star,
John Belushi, the movie is already playing to smash business in New
York City and should return a hefty profit on its modest $2.7-million
production cost.
  —*"The Lampoon Goes Hollywood,"* Time, *August 14, 1978*

Animal House: The Slobs vs. the Snobs

MICHAEL SHAMBERG, producer
"They were the first wave of Harvard guys to come out here. You had Tim the
playwright, Doug the *National Lampoon*, Peter the musician. Trying to take
over Hollywood."

HAROLD RAMIS
"Lucy Fisher, Peter, and Doug were great friends, they were like the Three
Musketeers. Their relationship had a very literary quality to it because they
were so smart, attractive, and successful in their own ways."

LINDA PERRY
"It was like, I don't know, during the Impressionist era in France. Artists that
respected each other and hung out together. It was a lot of fun."

MICHAEL SHAMBERG
"Paris in the '20s, Harvard in Hollywood."

WALLIS NICITA, casting director, producer
"It happened very briefly, and [Peter] was very central to it. Peter was such an intellectual provocateur in doing things that nobody else had been doing yet. He was a safe place to go creatively because you knew it was going to be about something other than grosses."

MICHAEL SHAMBERG
"[Peter] was a very positive energy, and he wanted to succeed. He wanted to succeed commercially for his talent, that whole group of people did. They thought they'd come out here and take it by storm."

JOHN LANDIS
"*Animal House*. That is how I met Danny [Aykroyd] and John [Belushi] and Peter, because Peter was friends with John and Doug."

DAN AYKROYD
"On my first meeting with John Belushi at Second City Theatre in Toronto where he performed in our set, and then later that night as we listened to music, I was surprised that as a Chicago denizen, he wasn't much of a blues fan. It was about two in the morning at my 505 after-hours, juke-joint, night-club. My affection for the man was instant."

JOHN LANDIS
"John had a large appetite. First of all, he was not stupid; John was a very smart guy. He liked playing in the blue-collar game. He was smart like a bull. He used to say 'strong like tractor, smart like bull.' We pretty much came to the conclusion together, that he was a cross between Harpo Marx and the Cookie Monster. Both of them had large appetites, and both of them were sweet and destructive."

WALLIS NICITA
"When they all started *Saturday Night Live*, they worshiped Doug Kenney. I mean, he was their god."

Caddyshack

MICHAEL O'KEEFE

"The sensibility [of *Caddyshack*] was that sort of slobs versus snobs thing, and that's a lot of what *Animal House* was about. I think they were trying to step into a different arena [from the frat world of *Animal House*], which was the country club, and tell a similar story."

MICHAEL SHAMBERG

"What is interesting for me is a time where the commercial system actually had a place for people like that. You have to look at the trajectory of everybody's ambition. These guys that came from Harvard, they wanted conventional success with an unconventional viewpoint, and for whatever reason the system promoted that at that point in time. So there was always this duality with Peter and Doug and these guys, which was really creative. They had these really great ideas and wanted to make it. What the Harvard guys did was that they came out here, and were the first wave to infiltrate and reinvigorate Hollywood."

MARK CANTON

"We were all in Fort Lauderdale in an ugly motel with a golf course and a lot of stoned people. Whatever stories you've heard are true, absolute chaos and mayhem, just like the movie. It was funny and fabulous, but there were a lot of tortured souls. And Peter was just there trying to do yoga and meditation. Kenney was there, stressed and disappearing."

MICHAEL O'KEEFE

"Everybody had their own light and dark side. The side we all know about is the part that is more public or funny in terms of success, but all those guys had to come to terms with success. They were antiestablishment and saw themselves as outsiders that were suddenly pulled into the mainstream, and that causes a lot of confusion for them. That was certainly what was troubling Doug."

MARK CANTON

"Doug Kenney was a freak. He was a genius writer. He was entrepreneurial. He didn't feel *Caddyshack* would live up to *Animal House*, and here's the irony: it has made me a cultural hero wherever I go."

"We were the generation that discovered that alienation is funny. We found that if you take an existentialist, add a hot Camaro, a skateboard, and a lot of dope, you have a working, vital existentialist who can get a job at the *National Lampoon*."
—*Doug Kenney,* Time, *August 14, 1978*

Zoetrope

FRANCIS FORD COPPOLA (Filmmaker)
"I always thought Peter was like Archimedes, trying to lift the world with a lever. . . ."

PAULA WEINSTEIN
"It was a special time in the business because, like it was in America, a lot of people came out of the '60s and we were all a version of radicals, so we brought that sensibility here and things opened up for us."

DEB NEWMYER, producer, Lucy's cousin
"It was a crazy time. Jeffrey [Katzenberg] had hair, [mogul] Don Simpson had holes in his shoes. People reinvent a family system. Paula is pretty much family, and Lucy is family, so that's what you do in this town. It doesn't exist unless you create it, and I know Peter was part of that, too."

STEVE MARTIN
"Around '79, I think, that's when I was taking stuff around and trying to get people interested in *Nirvana Cuba*, which was really a Broadway musical."

BUELL NEIDLINGER
"So [Peter] was having [professional] rejection, and meanwhile, his girlfriend was ascending into movie business heaven. She ran Zoetrope Studios."

ROD TAYLOR, friend, collaborator
"The truth is, there is a path to success for an executive. There is no path for an artist. An artist is out there with a prayer and a smile, and then they stop smiling back."

LUCY FISHER

"So as Peter was feeling more disappointed, I was a part of all this creativity on a grand scale. The only reason I and David Lynch were there was because Peter was there, but I was trying to tell Francis we should sign David, look isn't he great. So my role was merging Peter's friends with stuff, but Peter wasn't part of it."

STEVE MARTIN

"I don't remember how Peter got involved with Jove, but I must have started work at Zoetrope at this point. Either I was asked to, or was told that Peter was going to do this TV show, and Lucy wanted me to go see what was up with it. So I went to the first show and I saw what was going on."

The New Wave of Music

City Punk, Surf Punk, New Existentialist—anything new can usually find its way onto *New Wave Theatre* as long as it's dressed like a virus from outer space.
—*Patrick Goldstein,* Los Angeles Times

STEVE MARTIN

"LA was a fun place, and it wasn't as congested as it is now. Clubs were opening up, people were making music and listening to music, and not just high-powered bands. Some of the most exciting music were unknown bands, in the same way that Seattle took off later. LA was more new wave than punk, although the California version of punk was emerging, very different from the London version of punk. It was also referred to as hardcore, like Black Flag and the Germs."

DERF SCRATCH, musician, Fear

"I guess back then everybody considered bad music as punk rock. The engineer kept stopping the tape when we were recording albums, especially when Philo was doing his solo, and I had to walk in there and say no, he wants that mistake there, he wants it to sound like that. He said, but, no, you can't do that, but now it's accepted. That's what we were up against."

JELLO BIAFRA

"The Dead Kennedys helped to bury the '70s and did our part to burn down Hotel California. They call it old-school punk, but there wasn't any school, we blew up the school. It was all wide open and free form. The whole kissy-ass star system went out the door."

DAVE ALVIN, musician, the Blasters

"What sort of happened out here in the early '80s was the absorption or the defining of punk rock by some of the bands that came out of Orange County and the beach areas. There was Black Flag in Redondo, but yeah, they became punk rock to the point that there were all these kids in the audience. They wanted it punk, fast, and loud."

SPIT STIX, musician, Fear

"Music television wasn't born yet, *New Wave Theatre* was it if you had cable TV and you looked forward to some ray of hope that music was still alive. *New Wave Theatre* was a musical digest of what was going on in the underground. That was the most vibrant thing happening in music. *New Wave Theatre* offered something raw and uncut; it wasn't all homogenized yet. It just represented something I wanted to be a part of, so it seemed to me that getting on it was sort of a milestone."

> "People around the country will know what a real punk show is like," Jove asserted, "instead of getting it off a *20/20* segment."
> —L.A. Weekly, *May 14–20, 1982*

The New Wave of Theatre

> Los Angeles—It's around 10:00 o'clock on a Sunday night. Nothing going on. What the hell, you turn on the tube. . . . On the air for nine months now, *New Wave Theatre* has bombarded as many as 90,000 residences once a week with its unique format of music, interviews with new wave bands, performance pieces, . . . comedy spots, and monologues on the meaning of it all.
> —*Melodie Bryant,* "New Wave Theatre: *High Low-Tech TV*"

> The best thing on television.
> —*Jay Levin,* L.A. Weekly

ED OCHS

"It was a predecessor to MTV. Through *Billboard* I had relationships with the MTV people, and the timeline is more than coincidental. Peter was the first host really, Peter was the host of *New Wave Theatre* and deserves all the credit. To the MTV thing, I would say look what came before MTV and see what might have been rather than the commercial effort that MTV put on and wiped out the whole marketplace really."

STUART SHAPIRO, creator and Producer of *Night Flight*

"MTV should have dreamed all along that they wanted to be *New Wave Theatre*."

New Wave Theatre's dynamic approach has not been lost on either TV viewers or on industry representatives from other music shows— *Hollywood Heartbeat, America's Top Ten,* and *American Bandstand*— have all been spied snooping around the tapings.

—*Melodie Bryant*

THE IVERS PLAN
BY PETER IVERS
(UNPUBLISHED), 1979

... by next year more people will have seen *I Love Lucy* than have been alive on the planet; and space invaders has permanently changed human destiny. The plan is to create, develop, and produce high-quality mass-marketable video and audio works from low-budget underground sources à la Joe Papp and to translate and package these works for "overground" consumers. To take the "off broadway"/"off Hollywood" of film and video and market its high energy, raw-talent artists in new video forms designed for all possible outlets—cable, broadcast, pay or satellite, interplanetary cassette, and when possible, theatrical release ... Let us pray, brothers and sisters, for peace; a large piece.

LUCY FISHER

"He was interested in television as a medium, and I think his stuff was a precursor to MTV, and the *Nirvana Cuba* thing and *Vitamin Pink* were all versions of trying to do some hip musical thing that was going to be filmed or taped."

NANCY DREW

"It had never been done. And next to Andy Warhol's show, it was the most popular cable show. He and Peter were two of the most popular people. [Warhol] was still in the Factory, and he did something on cable in the early days, and Peter and Andy were the pioneers."

What Is a New Wave Theatre?

KEN YAS, colleague and friend of David Jove

"*New Wave Theatre*'s innovation was that it recreated the variety show on television. It was a punk *American Idol* meets *The Ed Sullivan Show*. It was like Ed Sullivan on acid meets *American Idol* on cocaine. It was all handheld video, and it was edited out of sequence. Stuff was shot three or four weeks apart and edited together as if it were shot on the same night. It was most innovative in the way the show was structured, a wild-ass variation on the theme of the variety shows with pretty much no rules. It was Ultimate Fighting Reality television. Like a talent show in the octagon. There were fights and beer throwing. It was a scene, a party."

ROBERT ROLL, aka Chris Ghenkel, *New Wave Theatre* performer

"This was the music version of *Saturday Night Live.* The introduction of anarchy into sketch comedy was a new unfolding of an ancient form, and like every artistic undertaking, music is sitting around in a circle and beating on skins, raising your voice, and these guys were doing it."

STEVE MARTIN

"In 1980, *New Wave Theatre* was like what YouTube is now. You could get on and do your thing, and nobody was going to put you down. Peter never said, 'Wow, you really stink.' He would just ask, 'Why are you doing this? What do you think?' "

MALCOLM LEO

"It was so ahead of its time and so brilliant. If you were to put a pedigree on some of the people that went through there, and in the mid-'70s LA took over the music scene, and when punk hit, people embraced it for better or worse. And then the groundswell of people had its own momentum, and Peter made that happen."

TEQUILA MOCKINGBIRD, friend, music promoter, vocalist
"Peter knew nothing about new wave, but he loved music. [Jove] chose Peter because his friends were like, the Ramises and he had all the hookups. David had nothing, so he hitched himself to the star."

> "I play a character, I try to tease everybody, but still stay supportive."
> —*Peter Ivers, Home Video, 1982*

STUART CORNFELD
"What I thought was interesting was that it was the last period of music that people went into not expecting to make money off of. Nobody's expectation was to make money."

> Los Angeles—*New Wave Theatre*, a shoestring video operation with basically a one-person staff a year ago, has grown into a four-camera, thirty-person operation being shot at Leon Russell's Paradise studios here. Also, the program is just seen on local Theta cable hookup. Earlier this month, New York's TelePrompter and Manhattan Cable began carrying the music show and negotiations are under way for outlets in Boston, Chicago, and perhaps even a network situation with NBC-TV as a monthly alternative for *Saturday Night Live*.
> —*Cary Darling, "Video Won't Swim in the Mainstream: 'New Wave Theatre' Cable Show Exposes Rock in Major Markets"*

The Fallen Musketeer

STUART CORNFELD
"Doug was the real thing, beyond anybody else. Doug really changed comedy. It was like really smart people doing really bad taste, funny stuff. In his own way, he was as important to white people as Richard Pryor was to African Americans. It was liberating."

MICHAEL O'KEEFE
"There was this sort of urban myth spreading back then that music was going to be a revolution in America, we all thought that being in the movie industry, we were going to change everything and that the world was going to change. There was this sort of wave people rode in the '60s and '70s people were still

surfing on. Nothing could have been further from the truth. What was coming was the '80s."

BOATY BOATWRIGHT, friend, talent agent
"The brilliant intelligence and intellect, that craziness, [Peter and Doug] nurtured each other. Oh, there was no way those two guys could have gone to school together and not become friends. They were each other's best fans. I remember Peter would talk to me and glow about Doug and vice versa."

MERLE IVERS
"Peter was very distressed about Doug. It's hard to understand why anybody does themselves in like that. I think today it is so prevalent because kids aren't brought up to cope. When I asked Peter if I was too strict with him, his answer to me was, 'Mom, absolutely not. If you hadn't been the way you were, I wouldn't have had the perseverance I've had these last twelve years.' To stick with his music when he was out making it."

MICHAEL O'KEEFE
"[Doug] was finding out that making movies in the studio system was not going to be like running the *Harvard Lampoon*."

LUCY FISHER
"Doug, he always felt pain. He was incredibly attractive, looked all-American and perfect Harvard, but he had these demons always. Not always, sometimes he was just fun loving, but he was out of tune with his own life and his own self."

MICHAEL O'KEEFE
"I remember seeing this documentary footage of Abbie Hoffman in the '60s, probably in Chicago, a low-grade video and he was saying something insane to the camera like, send us the drugs, send us the guns, and we'll take care of the revolution. That's kind of what everyone was thinking somehow. That just because we were feeling rebellious there was going to be a revolution. And there wasn't."

case book *part 6*

DETECTIVE CLIFFORD SHEPARD
"You've got to go to each case to see who did what. Sometimes they miss something, or they didn't get to interview certain witnesses that you could maybe find later."

* * *

DAVID CHARBONNEAU
"It was a series then of every night, sometimes multiple times a night, of meeting people after work, meeting people during work, and just going through, mostly at people's houses where people lived. I remember feeling like, Why are all these people connected? Some of these people were in show business, some of them weren't. Some of them may have been the kids of show business people, I couldn't tell, but everybody was on the scene, West LA. The more I peeled, the more I knew there was to peel. It just kind of depended on who you talked to, and it was almost like you were speaking about different people."

PETER RAFELSON
"Most people who knew Peter only knew him in the context of that particular lifestyle they knew him in. The whole town was dazed and confused."

STEVE MARTIN
"There was rampant speculation about what happened, who might have done it, who must have known about it, and there was a significant amount of finger pointing."

ED OCHS
"Some people blamed it on *New Wave Theatre*, some people blamed it on David Jove. Some people said David even did

it. But of course, that's ridiculous. When Peter died, David was bereft. I mean, he was devastated."

DETECTIVE HANK PETROVSKY
"Jove wasn't even a suspect. He was a 'person of interest' because of what other people told us about him, so we interviewed him. I can't remember what he said, but whatever he said didn't lead to suspicion, and even if it did, there was no connection. There were no fingerprints, readable ones anyway. There was nothing we had that was substantial enough to say anything about this guy."

DOUG KNOTT, colleague, lawyer, poet
"We were led to believe, and this may or may not be true, that David got immediately close to the investigative detectives."

KEN YAS
"I think it was a senior detective at the time on the case. David must have charmed him."

PETER RAFELSON
"[David] went out of his way almost suspiciously to get involved in the investigation and try to take on the role of investigator."

MICHAEL DARE, writer, performer, photographer, "Captain Preemo"
"I would sit with David and try to figure out who might have done it. The primary suspects were all people who had appeared on the show and were obviously violent."

TEQUILA MOCKINGBIRD
"All the more dark death-rock people that just didn't like Peter at all because Peter was just so light and airy. They were being thwarted by this little guy because he wore pink. They didn't get it. I think they'd get it now. They didn't

get it then because they were so into being dark and that was their image."

MICHAEL DARE
"The main one was the Mentors' El Duce."

JANET CUNNINGHAM
"El Duce had a persona, it was what happened when he got drunk. He got crazy."

STUART CORNFELD
"Nobody in those scenes was so serious about anything that they would just kill someone."

JOHANNA WENT, friend, performance artist
"I don't think that anyone hated him enough to care to do that."

ANNE RAMIS
"[Johanna Went] was in the local paper with worms all over her face. She had extraordinary shows, and he would go to them all. Even when [Went and Peter] stopped being boyfriend and girlfriend, he would always go to her shows. They were amazing spectacles of hand puppets and big masks, really oversized stuff. She was a big deal with, I guess you'd call it the underground, or punk scene."

DAVID CHARBONNEAU
"I talked to [Went] for not very long. I said, 'I'm swimming in a big wide ocean here, and my arms are getting tired. Was there anything going on between you two?' She said, 'Why should I deal with you, you're just being provocative, I just want to get on with my life.' So she walked away and that was the last time I saw her."

ED OCHS
"David believed that Peter did a bad drug deal and it came back to haunt him. He had his ideas of who did it, that there

was an Ecstasy deal and [Peter] owed twenty-five thousand dollars and didn't pay it back in time, so it was just a hit."

STEVE MARTIN
"There was so much insane finger-pointing going on, and guess who was leading a lot of it? David Jove. A horrible aspect of it was the realization that the misdirection was covering his ass. If you want to keep somebody from thinking clearly, you make them angry."

JANET CUNNINGHAM, punk rock casting agent
"People started talking about Peter and David, and people started thinking David Jove did it. It wasn't common knowledge, but common rumor, common speculation, that the only person that had a reason to kill Peter Ivers was David Jove."

HAROLD RAMIS
"As I grew to know David [Jove] a little better, it just accumulated, all the clues and evidence just made me think he was capable of anything. I couldn't say with certainty that he'd done anything, but of all the people I knew, he was the one person I couldn't rule out."

JIM TUCKER
"He didn't come up at first [in the police investigation]. But then later he became a suspect."

DAVID CHARBONNEAU
"I met with him early, the first night after that initial round. I met him with Rafelson first, we went over to his house. I just remember being like, Where are we going? I remember it being really dark, really unconventional-looking housing. Every window was covered. I remember Rafelson saying that we had to do this a certain way because everyone's upset, and no one is more paranoid about this than David. So we go to the door, he gives some kind of se-

cret knock, he lets us in. He had a lot of studio recording equipment there. Rafelson excuses himself and says he'll come back in an hour or so, and I just went through the same old questions with David and got the feeling right from the beginning that he was amused. This was almost funny to him. There was definitely a whimsical side to him."

ANNE RAMIS

"It's just that he was so creepy about it all. He used to have this jacket that Peter wore a lot, like a pink sequined jacket. I think it was hung up on the wall. And he had the bloody blankets that the police found [at the crime scene]. He kept those things at his house."

HAROLD RAMIS

"The Barbie heads in the window, and the steel door with the bar, and the firearms hung by the door. Quite a trip. He's kind of a magical, Nietzchian self-empowered dark lord, it's about making your own rules and your own reality. When you heard all of this from David, you were like, Ooh, what is he capable of?"

MICHAEL DARE

"David was an extremely violent person. I could imagine a situation in which it happened accidentally, but I couldn't imagine him deliberately doing it. I never saw any motive, but did he have the means? Yeah. Did he have the opportunity? Yeah. Was he nuts? Yeah."

RICHARD GREENE

"He had that anger thing. He could get angry and you were afraid."

PAUL FLATTERY, music video director

"I don't know, I think David was such an old hippie, I don't know that he would have had that in him. I mean, the guy, yeah, he carried guns and all that. But it was all posturing, you know?"

ZATAR, scenester, owned rock club the Pyramid
"Dave loved Peter. Dave would do anything for Peter. They were brothers. There are no ifs, ands, or buts. I mean, think about it: he's one of the people that were out there trying to right the wrong with the cops."

DAVID CHARBONNEAU
"David was just throwing out theories and ideas left, right, and center. He was just sick, twisted, and dark from the get-go, which is why everyone naturally wants to finger him there."

> Peter's sort of gradual departure from his Harvard scene into the "underground," his breakup with Lucy, and finally his move downtown were all attributed by many of his friends to the influence of *New Wave Theatre*. Though not publicly admitted, many were angry and jealous of the continuing effect *NWT* (i.e.: ME) was having on him. On the other hand, his success with *NWT* gave him an ever-growing stature on the music scene. A stature many bands resented.
> —*David Jove, draft letter to an editor of*
> L.A. Weekly

DERF SCRATCH, bassist, Fear
"Everybody thought it was David Jove. I got to know David well enough to know he didn't do it. He loved the notoriety and his success. He wanted so much to be accepted and popular, that he even increased people talking about him being the suspect."

TODD HOMER, musician, Angry Samoans
"He *wanted* to make people think that he did it."

DERF SCRATCH
"I used to laugh at him when he'd try to convince me that he could have. He'd get pissed off and point his .22 at me."

As sweet a guy as he was, there were many who resented him and the show, the general word on the
street was that *NWT* had killed him. Those radical
punks, the angry kids, and god knows what other
weirdness that lay amongst the punks had been at
least inadvertently responsible (i.e.: ME again).
Well, this is really real. I have talked to many
of his friends, my friends who though not cutting
me off have kept me at arm's length. OK, to be expected.
　　—David Jove, draft letter to an editor of
　　L.A. Weekly

HOWARD SMITH, friend, film editor
"A lot of people thought he was a bad influence on Peter,
[people] who really couldn't stand David Jove and hated
what Peter was doing. I think that Peter wasn't part of
that music scene directly, but he respected those people. It was absolutely true that a lot of Peter's friends
were horrified by all of that. I can remember a number
of people making statements and calling each other absolutely thinking that it was David Jove. To me, I couldn't
see it."

HUDSON MARQUEZ
"People in the scene were split on the whole thing. I
searched my mind to make sure, but David's not the guy that
would do this kind of thing. He would shoot somebody five
times. But he would never do this."

DAVID CHARBONNEAU
"I remember him saying, 'I don't have an alibi for that
night,' and 'The cops are stupid, aren't they?' And all
that. I was like, okay, there's a game being played here,
and he's playing me, and probably playing everyone else at
the same time, and he's obviously relishing part of it. I
told him, 'I heard people say Peter was getting a little

estranged from you.' And he said, 'No, no, we have our rough spots.' "

PETER RAFELSON

"He's such an obvious, easy target because of the fact that he was such a strange and aggressive person, and people would like to think it was that simple. I have a feeling that Peter was probably involved with some darker shit, not too far from David, but the heinous side of this speaks to something more psychopathic. Although David was incredibly intense, he wasn't psychopathic."

DAVID CHARBONNEAU

"I was getting burned out, I could feel it. I went back to one of the original two detectives. I said, 'I need stuff from you guys, you need to cooperate with me too.' He said that they didn't put a high priority on it, that they were on to other, bigger fish."

DETECTIVE HANK PETROVSKY

"Even if we thought [Jove] could have done it, you can't force him to tell you he did it. There was a lack of physical evidence. How can you connect anybody to the crime when nobody saw anything?"

DAVID CHARBONNEAU

"I do not believe it was a break-in. I do not believe it was just someone off the street that Peter brought in because he was a nice guy that night and fell asleep trusting them. I'm not buying it."

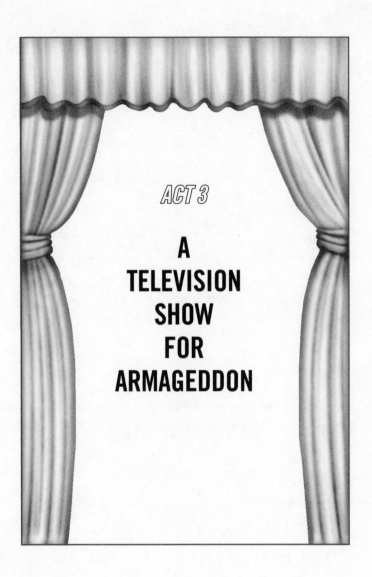

ACT 3

A
TELEVISION
SHOW
FOR
ARMAGEDDON

chapter 8

The Four Laws of Spermodynamics

In the '60s it was tune in and drop out, in the '80s it's let's freak
out and drop dead.
—*Peter, New Wave Theatre monologue*

Boston, Harvard, March 1981

Matina Horner picked up the phone to find her colleague in a state of
shrill agitation. "I've got Peter Ivers and Tim Mayer under my desk
smoking marijuana. What do I do?"

Horner could understand the marijuana. Lots of people smoked
pot. But how many grown men, established artists, Harvard grads,
played fort under the desk of Radcliffe College's director of the office
of the arts? She asked the arts director, Myra Mayman, to clarify. Were
they actually, literally under the table? They were.

In her tenure as Radcliffe president, Matina Horner had never
dealt with such a situation. She told Myra as much, adding that she
only hoped security and/or the cops didn't stop by. She would be there
as soon as she could.

Peter and Tim were back at their alma mater as distinguished
guests: dual recipients of the first annual Radcliffe College Visiting
Artist Fellowship. The fellowship's centerpiece was the commission-
ing of an original play, written and directed by Tim and scored by
Peter. For the two old friends, the timing could not have been better. A
few months after Doug's death, Peter and Lucy had separated, with
Lucy moving into Coppola's unoccupied LA "bachelor pad" and Peter
staying behind in Laurel Canyon. They still spoke daily, but they were
no longer a couple, and the separation hit Tim as well: for the past
twelve years, Peter and Lucy had been the closest thing he had to a
nuclear family. Still reeling from this double dose of loss—and from a
decade of personal and artistic struggles—the two remaining muske-

teers fell eagerly into the embrace of their alma mater. The vital collaboration that came easily and played to both of their strengths, in the setting where both had known their greatest growth and success, was the best comfort either could have hoped for.

In typical Mayer-Ivers fashion and top Mayer-Ivers form, the play itself seemed to channel all that complex pathos—the nostalgia for lost youth, and the unavoidable optimism that youth inspires—into a moving and provocative dramatic jaunt. An adaptation of one of the great coming-of-age tales, *Aladdin in Three Acts* seemed to sum up the spirit that had brought the three muskeeters together and kept them so close ever since. In a reflective, admiring review, *Crimson* writer David Edelstein described the play as a "wise and innocent paean to adolescence, that "state of grace" before the mask has been cemented to one's face, when one's body contains the universe and one's possibilities are similarly boundless . . ."

The play could be seen as both a tribute to Doug and a renewal of the pact between Peter and Mayer to reclaim the creative joyfulness that had brought them all together in the first place.

While Matina Horner may not have been privy to all the biographical subtleties behind *Aladdin*, she could hardly miss the very direct paean to adolescence giggling through a cloud of pot smoke under her colleague's desk. A lively woman who relished creative discourse with creative people, Horner was not particularly shocked or offended by the breach of protocol. She did worry, though, that she might have a practical problem on her hands. That evening she had scheduled a fundraising dinner for the Radcliffe arts program. The guest list was a roster of wealthy patrons. It also included Merle and Paul Ivers. Peter had agreed to play his harp at the dinner; his performance was to anchor the event. Now, in addition to refusing to come out from under the table, he was refusing to come to the dinner. Here Horner had to draw the line.

"Peter, come out from under that table."

"If I were to come, I could only perform in my diaper," Peter protested. "You wouldn't want me to do that in front of all those classy art people."

"You can wear whatever you want to wear," Horner shot back. "Wear a diaper, a black-tie suit, whatever. I just want you to play the harmonica."

"I can't, I can't. I need my diaper."

"I *told* you to wear the diaper. If that's what it takes, then go home and put your diaper on."

In her many conversations with Peter prior to that day, Horner had gotten the sense he was putting on a big act—that he liked to be controversial and startle people in order to put them off-guard, watch them, and figure them out. Horner saw a boy locked in conflict with authority: always on guard against his father's disappointment, crossing all the lines and daring you to disapprove. He was bright-eyed but wounded, collecting the friends he thought he could trust and taking the offensive against any who might judge him. Horner liked Peter and felt miscast as an embodiment of the dreaded authority. She did not shock easily, and the act quickly grew tiresome. She wanted to let him know he was aiming at the wrong target, and at a certain point she called him to the carpet.

"Listen, I'm a Greek, you're a Greek scholar. We're coming from the same place, we know all the same sources. Nobody's going to shock anybody here."

Peter, who always had a thing for strong women, was wooed. From that moment a mutual respect developed between them. Still, when Peter left the arts office to get his diaper for the benefit, she had no idea whether or not he would return. She caught him as he walked out the door.

"Between you and me, you cannot let me down. You are the only attraction for this night."

Matina Horner might have felt a little better had she been at Peter's *New Wave Theatre* taping a few days before. At least she might have realized that he was an equal-opportunity provocateur. If Peter was impatient with authority, it wasn't only of the ivory-tower variety—he had an equally low tolerance for the anti-intellectual orthodoxies that governed much of LA punk and new wave. He and Jove respected the punks' combative, antiestablishment attitude, but not the lack of self-reflection that often seemed a point of pride. They saw it as their task to poke and prod the *New Wave Theatre* bands (most of whom were teenagers) into seeing themselves as artists: to articulate principles, translate attitude into message and mission, and consciously locate themselves within a movement of like-minded agitators.

Peter himself was the foil. Decked out in an ever-revolving wardrobe of sequined jackets and leopard wraps, shower caps and feathered headbands, flower-print dresses and Spandex pants; speaking in a vaguely effeminate, hipster patter rife with new-agey insights and hippie ideals—everything about Peter's *New Wave Theatre* persona was designed to dig at the punks' own assumptions about what was cool (hypermasculinity, homophobia, nihilism, violence, an emphatic rejection of flamboyance); to piss them off, to make them talk and make them think.

While the entire show was essentially a staging area for Jove and Peter's guerrilla theatre, the vehicle they chose for direct confrontation was a new take on an old form: the band interview. Following each set, Peter would approach the bandleader in full regalia and, in an unnerving deadpan, pepper him or her relentlessly with Big Questions. Usually unanswerable, at times incomprehensible, and often vaguely insulting, the questions became the bane of many bands' existence. Though questions varied, one, Peter and Jove's favorite, became a constant, at least in part because it seemed most effective in pissing off the punks. *What is the meaning of life?*

"Stay gay all the way!" Such had been the answer of Lee Ving, lead singer of Fear, on the night of the taping before Peter boarded his flight to Boston. Ving, an imposing stage presence and outspoken homophobe who exuded violence even when standing perfectly still, answered only after some stalking and prodding by Peter. Fear was a *New Wave Theatre* regular, and it was known that Ving hated these questions almost as much as he hated Peter's gender-bending persona as host. Sometimes he turned away and ignored Peter, sometimes he threatened violence; once the entire band attacked Peter onstage. One of the things that made Peter so effective in his role was that his powerful build and physical confidence gave him an unnervingly impassive quality, a fearlessness which to the casual observer might have seemed suicidal. Neither the home viewers, nor the punks themselves, knew how well Peter could take care of himself if he had to. Watching the show, one often felt he was on the verge of being pummeled, and, bizarrely, did not seem to notice or care—all of which made for riveting, suspenseful television. In the face of characters like Lee Ving, he did not seem the least bit intimidated. He seemed amused. Which pissed off people like Lee Ving even more.

But not that particular night. That night, seeming satisfied with his answer, Ving switched into a more playful mood. Peter, in a samurai dress and orange fright wig, responded, "Well, then you've succeeded." As a follow-up, he asked Lee Ving if God exists.

"Yes. God exists but he is gay. He lives with a jaguar on Santa Monica Boulevard." He added, "So you're a fag, heh heh?"

This did seem to take Peter a little off-guard. He was still relatively new at the hosting job; though unafraid, he was not yet totally limber on his feet. He gave Ving a funny look and responded matter-of-factly, "No, I'm not."

"This is going to be the best part of our sequence here, this talk part," said an unusually jovial Ving.

If Matina Horner would have taken some comfort knowing Peter provoked the punks as well as the establishment, she would have been downright proud to watch him stand up for his alma mater with another band that night. The lead singer of Showdog, Ego Craig, performed "Fight Back or Die" in a beat-up Harvard T-shirt wrapped with loose speaker wire. At the song's conclusion, Peter approached him in the pink sequined dinner jacket and cowboy tie. "You're wearing a Harvard T-shirt," Peter observed. "That's my alma mater—and yet you appear to be a total moron. How do you explain that?"

Now that he was actually at Harvard, Peter had turned his sights on the target at hand. When he left Horner's office in search of his diaper, he had seemed so on-edge that she did not know if she would ever see him again. Later that night, at the fundraiser, she waited anxiously for some sign of him.

But he showed up all smiles in a black-tie suit, his only nod to new wave a shiny pink tie. He approached Matina Horner and gave her a big hug.

"Does the tie upset you?" he asked, sheepish, not wanting to get her in trouble with the patrons. For Horner, whose best-case had been Peter showing up to perform in a diaper, the tie was a welcome reprieve.

Paul Ivers, though, started the evening upset, and the tie only upset him more. Paul had never forgiven Peter for betraying him by snubbing the family business, for wasting his money and dashing his dreams to pursue the bohemian artist life. Over the years, his wounded rage had hardened into a thick scab of bitterness and distance. While Merle and her son were regularly in touch, Paul and Peter rarely spoke and for years had been effectively estranged.

Tonight, Paul felt that as long as Peter was here with these important people, he could at least dress normally. His anger was so palpable that even Matina Horner, a total stranger, could feel it seething off him.

By the end of the night, though, something seemed to happen. Peter's harp performance had been met with a stirring round of applause. The consensus was clear: he blew everyone's mind. Suddenly he was the talk of the room, with some of the wealthiest people in Boston falling over each other to congratulate and thank him. This left Paul in something of a quandary. Many of the people he respected most in the world—the people he would have liked his son to become—were showering Peter with admiration and praise. Matina Horner noticed that as the evening wore on, Paul's hostility and displeasure seemed to soften.

By the end of the night, he was positively enjoying himself. And he seemed to be looking at Peter, the prodigal son in whose return he had long ago lost hope, with something like respect.

Harvard University, Currier House
Senior Common Room, 8:00 p.m.

Peter stood at a lectern before a room of about twenty rapt Harvard undergrads. Outfitted in academic tweed and armed with lecture notes and a program of videotaped commercials, film excerpts, and music and television clips, the presentation was his fulfillment of the Visiting Artist Fellowship's final clause. His subject was "The New Wave Movement in Music, Television, and Film."

Peter was there to supply the students with firsthand dispatches from an underground world they knew only by its faint echoes and ripples, dissipated to the point of irrelevancy by the time it reached them. In a sense, this was his ideal audience: impressionable youth hungry for a taste of something substantial and raw, yet intellectual enough that Peter did not have to dumb himself down.

He let loose with both barrels, quoting freely from Cicero, Dead Kennedys, and Devo in support of his insights. He explicated his function as *New Wave Theatre*'s host bluntly: "I have to interview these punkers and rockers on the meaning of life—and part of my job is to be the object of scorn."

It was a job Peter certainly owned, and often seemed to enjoy. Still, absorbing all that negativity could also be wearying. At the end of the day, Peter identified with punk and new wave, seeing himself as a kind of movement elder. (*Terminal Love*, he told one interviewer, "completely foreshadowed new wave.") Yet he was so effective and convincing in his persona as host that most of the bands really *did* hold him in some form of contempt. When he called Ego Craig (of the Harvard T-shirt) a moron, Showdog's hulking drummer, who had been hovering in the background, stepped up to Peter and said, "That's a funny little outfit you're wearing." There was no trace of funny in his tone. He fingered Peter's cowboy tie menacingly and asked him, "You want to play with us sometime?" It didn't sound like he was talking about music.

The punks did not know about Peter's albums, they did not know he had played with many of their musical heroes or that those musicians held him in the highest regard. Had they known about his relationship with Little Walter and Muddy Waters; or that he often sat in on harmonica with John Cale of the Velvet Underground; or that Devo had played his song at every show of their '79 tour—perhaps they may have treated him differently. In fact, most of the *NWT* bands did not even know he was a musician. They just thought of him as a faggy poser with a TV show they would happily use if it could help them get seen.

Which is why he had been so heartened when, at the recent *New Wave Theatre* taping, a teenage punk had broken away from his band and made a beeline for Peter. Instead of the studied indifference or smarm Peter was accustomed to confronting, this kid seemed wide-eyed, almost nervous to meet him. Skipping introductions, he explained that he had been a huge fan since *Terminal Love*. In fact, Peter had been the one to inspire him to become a singer and start his own band. In high school, he had been relentlessly teased about his unique, nasal-sounding voice. Listening to Peter's vocals, the way he used his own thin, high-pitched sound to his advantage, bending certain words and notes with a kind of sultry Mae West inflection, showed the kid that having a weird voice could be an asset as long as you fully owned it. Since he already had a weird voice, he would make it as annoying, and unforgettable, as possible.

Peter seemed genuinely touched to meet someone in the punk scene who knew his music and liked it. The kid thought he sensed some sadness beneath Peter's appreciation—the sadness perhaps of being taken for granted, or of being weird in a different, less cool way than other, "cooler" people were being weird. Peter thanked him for his gracious words, and as he turned back to his band, Peter remembered that he had not gotten his name.

"Jello," the kid said. "Jello Biafra." His band, the Dead Kennedys, was currently unsigned, and this was their first time performing on *New Wave Theatre*. Biafra had taken the gig as much for the opportunity to meet Peter as for the potential exposure.

As Peter narrated his series of clips to the Harvard students, a steady stream of new spectators crowded into the room. In the lecture, Peter set out not only to explain the value and significance of punk and new wave, but to make an argument for their status as noble carriers of the creative flame in a world where the artist had become increasingly commercialized, commodified, marginalized, and neutralized. It was a taste of what the opening and closing *New Wave Theatre* monologues would have been like had they been written by Peter instead of Jove: minus the manic, messianic abstractions, plus some Harvard-trained intellectual rigor and the compelling clarity of a playful but disciplined mind.

Then, at a certain point in the lecture, Peter began to remove his clothes.

"New wave music is the energy and anguish of youth expressed through the vehicle of rock and roll artistry," he explained, dropping his pants and adding that bands must be unruly, antagonistic, and nonconformist to protect their artistic integrity. He added that some of the punk and new wave artists were both full of good ideas and sweet, nice people, explaining that their adoption of unsavory images was just part of the art. "It's the dramatization of an attitude," he mused, "as much as an attitude in itself." He held up Devo and a handful of his other favorite bands as models of sophisticated artistry combined with social and political consciousness.

Under his jacket and pants, it turned out, Peter wore another layer of clothing, and another under that. He removed several more layers while his talk delved deeper into the subterranean cultural landscape.

"The key to the clothes," he said, smiling while stripping down to increasingly casual new wave dress, "is the comfort."

As Peter spoke and stripped, the room steadily filled with students who had got wind something cool was happening. He peeled off the seventh layer of clothes to uncover skintight silver Spandex tights and a T-shirt with the sleeves and neck cut out and a slash painted on the back. He outlined his "Four Laws of the Spermodynamic System," which always boiled down to one absolute truth—"Creativity Equals Fun"—then took out a harmonica and began to play. By the time he finished, close to 150 enthralled Harvard students were ready to follow him wherever he might tell them to go.

A few days later, some of the students inspired by his presentation approached Peter with a small box of business cards.

Please forgive this intrusion.

I am the pathetic victim of a cerebellmun explosion.

Accept this card and help me make a decent living.

Give what you can.

THANK YOU AND GOD BLESS YOU

THE FOUR LAWS
of the
SPERMODYNAMIC SYSTEM

1. *Everything is happening.*
2. *Everything is happening inside my pockets.*
3. *Peter equals Fun.*
4. *I once attacked my counterpart in New Jersey.*

LA, Paradise Studio, 1981, 9:00 p.m.

Tequila Mockingbird and Richard Skidmore reviewed the schedule of bands slated to perform at tonight's taping. Together they drove over to *New Wave Theatre*'s fancy new digs, the state-of-the-art video facility Paradise Studio. It was going to be a big night and a long one: to save money, Jove (who funded the show out of his own pocket) ran all-night tapings, hustling in one band after the next, and then cut them into four or five shows.

Peter pulled up in his Fiat at the same time as Tequila. They gave each other a hug, making for a study in physical contrast: a short, pale muscular Jewish man and a tall, thin, statuesque black woman with dramatic cheekbones, a razor jaw line, and close-cropped hair that changed color every other day. Tequila was a dedicated punk scenester, performer, and fan—for years she had walked around town in a wedding dress in the hope of running into Sex Pistols frontman Johnny Rotten so that she would be ready to marry him at any moment. After answering an ad in a local music magazine, she had become *New Wave Theatre*'s booking agent, talent scout, and overall liaison to the underground.

Jove introduced Tequila to Peter. They liked each other instantly, bonding over a common sense of goofiness. But Tequila noticed that Jove liked to sow tension between people as a way of separating and controlling them. Despite his best efforts, she and Peter became close friends, which seemed to make Jove crazy. She saw clearly that he was using Peter for his Hollywood connections and wondered how long the relationship could last. Though a true lover of everything punk, she also saw that Peter was in a different class, operating comfortably in the grungy wildness that was punk but not quite of it—"a peacock in the middle of a rubbish bin," was how she sometimes thought of it. The punks were kids getting high and partying. Peter was an artist and a self-made man. Peter began to bring Tequila into his own collaborative circle, using her as a vocalist on various video projects. She came to occupy the diva-singer role in his life, a punk rock version of Asha and Yolande.

Working the door at Paradise Studio was a tall, striking young man who could set his face to look hard and intimidating enough to keep things in line. To people who knew him he was a bright, curious kid fascinated by an underground scene he was being exposed to for the first time. A Richard Skidmore connection and subsequently a Tequila Mockingbird fling, Laurence Fishburne was a struggling actor who had caught his big break in Coppola's Vietnam epic *Apocalypse Now*. Fishburne's agent had promised him that the offers would start pouring in, but he hadn't seen any yet.

Peter ducked into the studio lugging a large suitcase filled with costume changes. He exchanged greetings with a goofy, fresh-faced eighteen-year-old who looked as if he had come directly from a meeting of the high school math club. Zachary had been tapped as the latest addition to *New Wave Theatre*'s carnivalesque cast. He had one job, to stand in front of the camera in a tuxedo, smile hugely, and introduce the show and its "talented host, Peter Ivers"—a twisted take on the old-time TV announcer worthy of David Lynch himself.

Jove barked shrill orders across the studio; something in his tone always carried the implication of a threat. He seemed to operate on the principle that it was better to be feared than loved. The cast and crew scrambled to take their places. Meanwhile, the "audience"—a growing convergence of loud punks lured by the promise of good music, free beer, and something to do after most of LA closed down— got drunk and partied. In Jove's vision of barely contained chaos, that was precisely their job.

Tonight's taping was special. After airing for a year on Public Access Theta Channel Three. *New Wave Theater* was about to go national. The USA Network had picked up the show as part of its ambitious, groundbreaking *Night Flight* programming, a bundle of cutting-edge curiosities ranging from live rock concerts to old TV shows to independent and cult films, to a new art form that was just beginning to get the attention of mainstream America: the music video. It wasn't NBC, but cable was promising to be the next big thing and USA's late-night slate was the only programming that catered to the insomniacs, vampires, and teens Jove was interested in converting to his cause.

Jove was ecstatic at the opportunity to take what he saw as his dangerous, revolutionary agenda into the living rooms of Middle America, the front-line in the battle for young minds. Peter was excited for a different reason. This ludicrous character he had created— this outrageous impresario of ambiguous sexuality; maddening foil for the punk subconscious; lightning rod for all the hostility of LA's disgruntled, grunting youth; nurturing, needling patron of new wave—was achieving for him what ten years as a tireless, top-caliber recording artist had not. It was making him a rock star.

Peter had begun to realize the pragmatic value of celebrity. "Fame is equity," he told one interviewer around that time. "If you're famous, you can always get work. I'm just starting to get famous. And that's fun." He told another, "I'm not afraid to have entertainment as part of my artistic portfolio. After all, what is fun but the first half of funding?" It seemed a move away from the artistic purity he had held so dear in the past. Ironically, even perversely—though for Peter it seemed somehow appropriate—this move into the uncompromising, anticommercialism of punk and new wave was for him a move towards commercialism and compromise.

Indeed, people who saw him on the *New Wave Theatre* set noted how businesslike Peter was. Always friendly but professional, like someone punching a clock. He came in, did his job, and left. He didn't interact much with the rowdy crowds and rarely hung out after with the cast and crew. He was still busy, after all, with all his other projects. Foremost among them was a musical stage show called *The Vitamin Pink Fantasy Review*, which Peter hoped eventually to bring to New York and someday shoot as a feature for theatrical release. The show was being funded and executive produced by Harold Ramis and Malcolm Leo, another friend with heavy television credits.

Peter suited up in a pair of leather short-shorts, a skimpy tank top, and a headdress that looked like a dark, glittery chef's hat blown sideways by the wind.

The camera pulled out from a tight close-up framing Zachary's million-dollar smile as he gave his dead-on breezy Las Vegas lounge-king introduction:

"Ladies and gentlemen, your talented host: Peter Ivers!"

Peter stood before the camera next to a beautiful young actress, the first of the night's several Ghost Hosts. This was a label Jove and Ed Ochs had come up to designate a visitor to the show who was known outside of the new wave scene. The Ghost Host's job was to stand with Peter and either simply be seen or have short, often nonsensical conversations. (The more ambitious ones, like Doug Kenney, would display an inane talent or stage a brief scene.) In addition to

Doug, Harold Ramis, Michael O'Donoghue, Tim Matheson (better known at the time as Otter from *Animal House*), and over time, most of Peter's Hollywood friends and connections, especially those affiliated with the *Lampoon,* made an appearance as a Ghost Host. At a taping earlier in the month a preppie-looking guy in his mid-thirties with a nasally voice and bright-eyed apple pie demeanor was asked by Peter to define new wave.

Peter seemed particularly excited about this incongruously clean-cut guest; a special quality of fondness and pride could be detected in his tone as he made the introduction. "It's a pleasure to be here with David Lynch, the director of *Eraserhead* and *Elephant Man.* David and I wrote the song in *Eraserhead.* David is gonna tell us what new wave is." He handed the microphone over to Lynch, who looked back at Peter with the familiarity and respect of an old friend.

"Pete, it's a truck going down the highway at seventy miles an hour. And in the back of the truck there's a hundred smiling cows. Except one of them has got its head stuck through the floor of the truck and its nose is grinding on the highway. And the smell and the scream—that's new wave."

Tonight's first Ghost Host was Beverly D'Angelo, a gorgeous young actress who had been in Los Angeles for less than a year. Her friend Wally Nicita, a casting director who had been tight with the *Lampoon* crowd in New York (Nicita's husband, an agent, represented Doug's girlfriend Kathryn Walker), had come out west with the comedy migration of the late '70s and gone on to cast *Caddyshack.* Nicita was a fan of the punk scene and thought it would be fun for D'Angelo to check it out. She stood next to Peter and flashed a big smile as he introduced the first band of the night.

Like Fear, 45 Grave had become one of the *New Wave Theatre* house bands, making regular appearances and developing an ongoing rapport with its "talented host." Because 45 Grave's members played in a number of different bands, each of which appeared on the show—Don Bolles in the Germs, Dinah Cancer in Vox Pop and Castration Squad—they became especially familiar with Peter and his shtick.

Tonight they opened the show suited up in the ghoulish, skeleton-makeup-painted, fake-blood-dripping costumes of 45 Grave. The crucifix-adorned amplifiers with holy candles dripping wax into their dusty innards fed back the guitars' distorted chords. Dinah's vampiric vocal seduction, voraciously hungry and untouchably aloof, closed the song. She sang her last line, "Dead like a piece of old wax!"

Peter stepped into place next to her and asked her the question she knew was coming and dreaded.

"Dinah, what's the meaning of life?"

Though nervous, this time she at least seemed prepared.

"Buy, sell, produce. I'm a little robot."

After 45 Grave, a lesser-known band called Butch took the stage. To Peter, no band was too big or small to be asked the big questions. Sheri, the lead singer, stepped up next to Peter, who produced a big smile. Sheri seemed entranced, despite the fact that he was covered, at the moment, with enough glitter to wallpaper Alice Cooper's house. Eyes wide, he asked her, "Sheri—what's the meaning of life?"

She blushed. "Your cock." It was two in the morning. Peter was just getting warmed up.

The next segment was going to be a "performance piece" by local punk-rock performance artist Johanna Went. Went was another semi-regular, having performed on the first show. Notwithstanding the wild exhibitionism of her performance pieces, she was personally quite shy and always required some coaxing to come on the show. Her band set up, each piece in a different position around the stage, as Went double checked all her meticulously placed props. Meanwhile, the studio audience, with its sea of faded, multicolored heads, jumped and danced and laughed and stumbled around their designated area. They seemed to make Johanna nervous. Though her performance was far more out-there than most of them ever dreamed of being, personally she was the least comfortable of them all. Also, she wasn't there to have fun. She was there to scream in tongues and whisper ethereally into a microphone while pulling plastic sheeting from the stomach of what looked like a blue poodle, then deliver a jelly baby stuck inside a telephone from her womb, then smear the afterbirth on her face.

Peter introduced Johanna, and her band began pounding out rhythmic, toneless music. Then she went to work. Peter watched, half-gawking, half-grinning, as Went raced around the stage in a tight black leotard, changing costumes and staging violent, abstract little scenes that riffed on the theme of conception—spilling blood all over the stage and herself, for instance, then falling exhausted onto the floor and smothering herself in a slimy residue of sweat, blood, and glop, shrieking and moaning barely intelligible words the whole time. The hyperactive explosion of childishness and dark sex appeal, the mucky sensuality of birth and death, provided an unsettling and riveting spectacle. The audience cheered and stepped slightly back to avoid the occasional splatter. When they saw Peter approach Went, protected in a raincoat and hood, they stepped back again, unaware that the two artists were friends.

Peter began asking his questions, but Johanna remained in character, spewing a rapid-fire barrage of sounds and half-words in a high-pitched squeal, like a five-year-old girl from Mars. Peter quickly changed tactics, pulling out his harmonica and tooting and blowing notes and sounds, the closest he seemed to feel he could come to speaking her language. She responded to the harp's many calls, and while their sparring sounded like nonsense, they also appeared to be communicating with each other.

Then, out of the blue, Johanna grabbed Peter and wrestled him down into her splatter of blood and goo. They flailed about on the floor, each trying to hold the other down, smiling and giggling like little kids. Finally Peter, breathing heavily, smeared head to toe in red and brown slop, took hold of his mic, propped himself up on his elbows, smiled, looked directly into the camera, and said, "That's new wave."

For mere mortals, this would have been plenty of fun for one night. But it was only 2:20 a.m., and there were still half a dozen bands to go.

Keith Morris, an original member of Black Flag, now of the Circle Jerks, was running laps around the studio like a mental patient chasing his own tail, psyching himself up for one of his renowned, adrenaline-spiked stage performances. Jove called out to Tito Lariva, punk royalty as frontman for the Plugz, to "start the vamp"—a lick from the song they were about to play behind Peter as he introduced the band. Peter quickly changed into a pair of army pants, a cut-off *New Wave Theatre* T-shirt, and yet another bizarre, sparkling piece of headgear, this one resembling a pair of glittery bird wings. Backed by the Plugz's driving setup, Zachary ran another intro, signaling that this segment would lead off an episode. Derf Scratch, bass player for Fear, stood respectfully behind Peter to one side, nodding his head to the beat and smiling like someone just happy to be invited to the party.

Keith Morris completed another screaming, flailing lap around the room and settled at Peter's other side, vamping his own big straining Frankenstein grin for the camera while stretching and twitching his neck and then coming to rest it on Peter's shoulder.

"Many luminaries of the LA scene are here tonight to pay tribute to one of our favorite bands. Derf and Keith of the Circle Jerks—"

Peter put the mic in front of Morris, who let out a banshee wail—"Let's Rooock!"—nodded proudly, grinned hugely, then lovingly put his head back on Peter's shoulder.

Peter announced "The Plugz!" The music kicked in with a wailing horn section, and the audience cheered and danced.

Despite all the violence, anger, and contempt he provoked and absorbed on a regular basis, despite how far Peter was from the world that knew him well and loved him more, in some important quarters of the insular, suspicious punk scene, he was beginning to find respect and even friendship. Some of the more mature, sophisticated punks—people like Jello Biafra, Keith Morris, Dinah Cancer, Derf Scratch—appreciated the role *New Wave Theatre* played as clearinghouse, community center, spotlight, and patron of LA punk and new wave. Peter was the ringleader of this underground circus, and some at least were starting to get the joke: to appreciate that underneath the flower-print dresses, hippie questions, and Cheshire grin, Peter was laughing his ass off, at himself and at them, creating a kind of theatre that was uniquely new wave.

As some segments of the community began to embrace him, Peter became more comfortable in the scene, and—of no less importance to him, whose eyes were always on his own creative process and increasingly on concrete career goals—more comfortable every time he got in front of the camera. He was learning things he needed to know, things that would help him become not only a rock star, but also what he saw was clearly the true new wave: a rock *video* star.

At four in the morning, Jove and the crew cleared the studio. Peter packed his costumes into the suitcase. As payment for services, Jove would take select staff out for breakfast at Canter's. Peter had a standing invitation. But this morning, like most, he politely declined. He smiled, waved good-bye, and went his own way.

New York City, Rockefeller Center, *SNL*, October 31, 1981

Saturday Night Live's camera crew finally decided they had enough. Fear was scheduled to shoot their musical guest segment for the show at 5:00 p.m.; midway through their 3:00 rehearsal, the union camera operators pulled the plug. They turned the cameras off and walked out of the studio, leaving the band, and a studio full of DC punks who had been imported specifically for the occasion to "mosh," standing in the empty studio scratching their heads. The next thing they heard was that their appearance had been canceled.

John Belushi stormed into the office of Grant Tinker, Chairman and CEO of NBC, and demanded to know what was going on. He had personally brokered Fear's appearance as a one-for-one swap with NBC: in exchange for booking Fear, he would deliver the signature "Live from New York . . ." introduction and make a cameo appearance on the show. He threatened to walk if Tinker did not intervene.

"Well, the union doesn't want your dancers tripping over their cables," Tinker said. Apparently the union operators claimed that one of the DC imports had tripped over a camera cable and accidentally unplugged it.

Reiterating his threat, Belushi insisted that the dancers were part of the show. In fact, in another expression of how personally significant this was to Belushi, he had booked the dancers himself. Earlier that week, Ian MacKaye of Minor Threat, a leader of the DC hardcore scene, was awakened by a surreal phone call. "Hi, Ian, it's Lorne Michaels of *Saturday Night Live*. I'm calling you because I got your number from John Belushi. He says you might be able to get some dancers up here 'cause we want to have Fear on the show. Hold on a second, I'm going to put John on."

MacKaye strained groggily towards consciousness. "Pardon me?"

"This is John Belushi. I'm a big fan of Fear's. I made a deal with *Saturday Night Live* that I would make a cameo appearance on the show if they'd let Fear play. Penelope Spheeris, who directed *The Decline of Western Civilization*, said that you guys, DC punk rock kids, know how to dance."

After confirming to himself that the conversation had not been some bizarre lucid dream, MacKay rounded up about twenty of his friends and headed up from DC to 30 Rockefeller Center.

Neither they nor the band received a particularly warm welcome when they arrived. While Belushi brought Fear to the studio in a limousine, from the moment they arrived they were met with suspicion and outright hostility from most of the show's cast, crew, and staff. Fear's drummer, Tim "Spit" Stix, felt they were being eyed as if they were the young rapist-murderers from *A Clockwork Orange*. Eddie Murphy seemed particularly pissed off about sharing the stage with such dubious characters. There seemed a broad consensus that punk was not really music and that punks were to be treated like scum.

(There were two notable exceptions. Tim Kazurinsky, the cast member who specialized in playing short, awkward, nerdy types, seemed to appreciate all the pageantry and find the whole situation hilarious. Michael O'Donoghue, *SNL*'s head writer and a good friend of Doug, was considered by Spit Stix a full-fledged comic punk. As a noted *New Wave Theatre* Ghost Host, O'Donoghue liked to stand behind Peter in stoic silence, smoking a cigarette while Peter intro'd the show. On the last word of the intro, O'Donoghue would light a piece of flash paper off his cigarette and lumber offstage as the opening band began to snarl and bang. Before Fear's *SNL* taping, O'Donoghue had let Stix graffiti his entire office with spray paint while he sat at his desk, chain-smoking Nat Shermans.

While the DC punks hung out in the green room giving each other haircuts and showing off their mohawks, the tension in the studio thickened into a hot, stifling steam. The union crew, who saw the rowdy gaggle of grungy teens as a bunch of hoodlums, made a show of guarding their equipment and being irritated by the nuisance and extra work. To the band, they seemed to be looking for an excuse to pull the plug.

Belushi wouldn't hear of it. He reiterated his threat to the head of NBC. By this point in his career, he was *SNL*'s most famous and beloved alum. Tinker relented. The show would go on.

Belushi had been introduced to Fear's music by Peter during the first year of *NWT*. While Peter had been the conduit for many of the "punk comics" to access the underground scene, Belushi had delved in the deepest, turning his legendary appetite to the insatiable consumption of punk rock. Peter and Belushi had initially connected over their love of blues, and both saw the direct line pointing from blues to punk in a way their colleagues—both their musician friends, most of whom had disdain for punk, and their comic friends, who appreciated the attitude and the scene but would never listen to the music on its own merits—did not. It may have had to do with the fact that both were musicians. Or it may just have been that, in their heart of hearts, Peter Ivers and John Belushi were punks. John Landis saw Belushi that way, as interested in all things radical and subversive. He always associated him with Marlon Brando's iconic line from *The Wild One*. Challenged to explain what he is rebelling about, Brando's character shoots back, "What have you got?" Many of the punks saw themselves reflected in Belushi's film personas. Derf Scratch recognized a kindred spirit in Jake Blues. Keith Morris thought *Animal House* was punk rock incarnate.

One night Belushi was watching *New Wave Theatre* on TV. After a Fear song, while Peter was goading Lee Ving to answer his arcane questions with something more than a snarl, Derf Scratch snuck up on Peter from behind and gave him a wedgie. He pulled so hard that Peter fell over. Suddenly, the whole band erupted into violence, descending on Peter and holding him to the ground. Belushi watched transfixed as they viciously punched and kicked him. The screen faded to black. Belushi would have assumed it was all planned and staged, except that, for one thing, it looked disturbingly spontaneous and real, and for another, it was something Fear certainly seemed capable of.

The next day when Belushi called Peter to make sure he was okay, Peter explained that the explosion was ad-libbed but they hadn't really hurt him, the punches and kicks were not real. In fact, Derf Scratch made a point of helping him up and laughing about it, to make sure Peter knew it was all for the camera and didn't take it the wrong way. Belushi thought it was the coolest thing he'd ever seen and decided he had to meet the band.

The opportunity came from one of Derf's bass students, who was friends with Belushi from the Second City days. He informed Derf that Belushi wanted to meet him, and the next thing Derf knew, he was cruising around Hollywood with Belushi and Dan Aykroyd, jamming on bass and shooting the shit in the back of a flatbed truck. They proceeded to make him an Honorary Blues Brother, and shortly thereafter Belushi invited Derf and the rest of the band to a private club above the Roxy, rubbing shoulders with Jack Nicholson and Tatum O'Neal, drinking endless six-dollar beers on Belushi's tab and not getting a buzz because his adrenaline was through the roof.

What impressed Derf most, though, was that Belushi never seemed to be showing off. As soon as Derf walked into the door of the Roxy, Belushi started reciting Derf's jokes from his stage persona, going through the entire litany of *Fear*'s shtick. When Derf admitted that he never really watched *Saturday Night Live*, Belushi said, "It's not about me, man, it's about you." The better Derf got to know him, the more he realized these weren't just empty words, but the code Belushi lived by. Spit Stix felt Belushi saw himself deep down as a musician—a singing drummer of African American descent, to be exact—and all he really ever wanted to do was either talk about music or play it. All he wanted from Fear was to be treated like another player, and they were happy to oblige, inviting him to rehearsals and letting him sing and play drums. It didn't hurt his standing with the band that he was constantly, spontaneously cracking everyone up. Sometimes he was just plain goofy, sitting Stix down on his lap at the drum set, pulling his arms behind his back, and Belushi sticking his own arms out to make it look like Stix was the one playing.

Stix saw Peter and Belushi as peas in a pod: electric entertainers brimming with talent yet more than happy to shine the spotlight on others. Humble enough to enjoy being made fun of, and confident enough, if no one else was up to it, to make fun of themselves. He saw Peter as a grounding influence for Belushi, who, free from the responsibilities of his New York life, tended to go a little crazy when he was in LA.

Pushing for Fear to get a spot on *SNL*, Belushi was doing what he had watched Peter do with *New Wave Theatre* for two years (and which, because of his massive industry clout, he had the power to do on a much larger scale): get mainstream exposure for music he loved and the people who played it. Recently, he had signed Fear to the soundtrack of a movie he was working on. When the studio vetoed the deal, he determined to make it up to them, and this was the most direct cause of the *SNL* hookup and his personal investment in seeing it through.

There were rumored to be other, more indirect causes as well. *Saturday Night Live*, which had made its name on edgy, subversive satire, by 1981 was widely thought of to have gone soft. While Fear gleefully vandalized Michael O'Donoghue's office, O'Donoghue, chain-smoking behind his desk, intimated that Belushi wanted to have some fun with the *SNL* staff, whom he felt were complacent, uptight, and unbearably full of themselves. The musical selections alone were excruciating, a hodgepodge of insipid Top forty acts. The show had lost its direction and its spice, and Belushi wanted to stir the pot— to give *SNL* an infusion of the wild, anarchic energy he had found in the LA punk scene. To make it, perhaps, a little more like *New Wave Theatre*.

O'Donoghue had related all this approvingly to Stix and the band. What he did not mention was he himself was fed up with the show and its producers and planning to leave imminently. There were others on the staff who felt the same way, and they didn't give a damn about saving the show. They just wanted to see Fear wreak some havoc, piss people off, and destroy stuff.

The guest host that night was Donald Pleasance, a British actor in his early sixties who seemed nervously out of his element introducing Fear. Behind him, dozens of punks were already jumping in anticipation. Pleasance had to scream out his introduction over the din of the crowd.

"And now a band . . . [audience shouting] . . . Fear . . . [more shouting] . . ."

After a short, bluesy overture, Ving blasted into a hyped-up hardcore guitar riff. The band rushed in behind him. Ving shook his head back and forth wildly as he belted out lyrics, about half of which made it into the mic. The crowd screamed and moshed and raged. They rushed the front quarter of the stage, knocking down mic stands, jostling monitors, and slamming into Ving and the rest of the band, who kept playing, dead-eyed, seemingly oblivious to the frenzy and indifferent to being violently knocked around. It was punk rock: no different from if they were playing a basement party or after-hours Hollywood dive.

After the first song, Lee Ving lumbered around the stage like a caged animal, eyes to the ground. He went back to the mic, said, "It's great to be in New Jersey!" and launched into a second tune, which did not appear to be part of the plan. The lyrics were as purposefully offensive as his shout-out to the wrong state. "New York's alright,

New York's alright . . . if you like saxophones! New York's alright . . . if you wanna get mugged or murdered! New York's alright . . . if you like tuberculosis!" When the song was done, Ian MacKaye grabbed Ving's mic and screamed "New York sucks!" Despite increasingly frantic signaling from the sides of the stage, Ving broke into a third song. The union crew signaled each other that word had been given to cut to commercial. A carved jack-o-lantern that was being used as a prop—the transitional still shot when the show cut to commercial—sat just offstage. One of the DC kids grabbed it, held it above his head with both hands, and launched it. It splattered across a speaker monitor as the cameras hurriedly pulled out into a wide shot and the punks continued to swarm the stage.

The next thing Ian MacKaye knew, he and his DC contingent were being forcefully shepherded into a room offstage. The doors were locked, and they were quarantined for two hours, berated for their behavior and threatened with lawsuits and criminal prosecution.

During Fear's performance, Belushi had stood and watched just offstage with O'Donoghue, reportedly in hysterics. Next to them stood David Jove, who had traveled across the country to see the show. Jove was not one for big laughs. He watched with his arms folded over his chest and a satisfied grin plastered across his face. In a recent interview, he had referred to *New Wave Theatre* as "the *Saturday Night Live* of tomorrow." Tomorrow may have arrived earlier than expected. The manic energy he had managed to harness into controlled chaos on his scrappy cable access show had overwhelmed the network standard-bearer in a matter of minutes.

LA, Little Tokyo, 1982, 12:00 p.m.

Buell Neidlinger set down the box he was carrying and took in the bare, run-down loft in a factory district of downtown LA known as Little Tokyo. Peter had asked for Buell's help moving all his stuff out of the Laurel Canyon house down to the new loft. Buell had been among the first wave of artists to take a loft in Lower Manhattan, back in '56. He knew about loft living and the trade-offs it involved, the cost-benefit between a big working space and a sketchy neighborhood where you always had to be on your guard. The scene before him was fifteen times worse than any loft he had seen in New York. The immediate surroundings were perpetually dusky and rank. All the outside lights had been broken, leaving a dark alleyway that reeked of piss and a shadowy back entrance to a freight elevator that was often out of service. If Peter had been seeking the grittiest urban scene in LA, he had found it. Neidlinger, for his part, had no idea why.

He knew Peter was hurting for money. Sure, he was becoming a minor celebrity among the punks, but that television show was run on a shoestring and Peter did not get paid a cent. After Lucy moved out, she had continued to pay the rent at Laurel Canyon and send checks to help with living expenses. She also served as the sole investor in Peter Ivers Enterprises, the umbrella corporation they had created together to help fund his various projects, continuing to support his artistic aspirations even after their romantic relationship had ceased. (Their contract stipulated that Lucy would receive 1 percent of all revenue the company generated, Peter 99 percent.) Still, Peter would show up at Buell's house at 8:00 a.m. for breakfast and to talk about gigs because he didn't have work.

Neidlinger wasn't the only one of Peter's friends concerned by the move. For Howard Smith, going to Little Tokyo was like walking onto the set of *Blade Runner*, Ridley Scott's dystopian noir. Rod Falconer thought Peter was making an important life decision based on aesthetics, naïve to the real-life dangers. Johanna Went told Peter point-blank that he lacked the street smarts to live downtown. Even Buddy Helm, Peter's drummer friend, who had himself moved from Laurel Canyon to an "art ghetto" loft in Little Tokyo just a few months before, discouraged Peter from following his lead. "You're a Harvard kid, Peter," he told him, "you shouldn't be in the ghetto."

But Peter was long used to traveling in gritty circles, and he was long used to being misunderstood. Even his friends who were freaked out by Little Tokyo had to admit it was cool. Buddy Helm used his 6,000 square feet and 14-foot ceilings to shoot music videos. Peter had made a few himself, received encouraging feedback from people in the know, and planned to focus on developing his video portfolio. He had been doing a lot of thinking about the intersection of video, live performance, and audience response, which he documented in a six-page manifesto he titled "The Ivers Plan." He was ready to take this new flurry of ideas from theory into practice. For that—and for band and stage rehearsals of his upcoming *Vitamin Pink Fantasy Revue*—he needed space.

Helm also got the sense that Peter was in search of another alternative community to be a part of. Downtown was the LA art scene's Wild West, a seedy no-man's-land with a tight sense of belonging among its artist pioneers. The social infrastructure was exclusively grassroots, which reinforced the sense of community. There were loft parties, bands playing on loading docks, and one-night-a-week clubs where people packed obscure dead venues just by word of mouth.

Jim Tucker, who lived in the loft adjacent to Peter's (they shared a kitchen and central bathroom), was well-entrenched in the downtown scene. He liked Peter well enough but thought it was a strange choice for a kid with a cute little sports car and close friends among the Hollywood power elite. It seemed to Tucker that Peter was a Harvard kid slumming on Skid Row.

Some of Peter's friends thought he was searching for something more than a new group of collaborators and friends. Peter was still Peter—upbeat and focused on his work—but something had changed. His friends sensed that the separation from Lucy affected him more deeply than perhaps even he knew. He seemed lost. His women friends in particular, people like Nancy Drew and Johanna Went, could tell that Peter was sad, that he didn't understand why things hadn't worked out, that he was feeling a sense of failure. He spoke with them about Lucy constantly and seemed to relish just saying her name. He was still in love with her but knew he could not give her the life she needed. Nancy Drew would ride around with him in his Fiat, fielding questions like, "Do you think it's okay for me to borrow money from women?" Sometimes he would call Merle at her office and keep her on the phone for hours, asking, "Why, Mom? What do you think happened?"

If moving downtown had something to do with his separation from Lucy, as far as Steve Martin was concerned, both situations could only be temporary. Peter and Lucy were like family to him, and he could not imagine them being able to stay apart for long. Peter would find a way to make things work; he always did.

He was probably not going to find it, though, in Little Tokyo; the neighborhood was perhaps the one place on earth Lucy hated more than the set of *New Wave Theatre*. Lucy saw Peter's descent into the LA underground as yet another form of self-sabotage—a way of demonstrating that he was not bound by convention. In its benign form it involved him taking his clothes off on a whim; its more malignant expressions included performing in a diaper for a stadium full of people who had come to see Fleetwood Mac. To Lucy, the demons that drove him downtown were the same ones that had plagued him all along. Really, the same one: Paul. Merle, Lucy thought, put it best. She would say that Paul was the kind of person that, if Peter were elected president of the United States, his father would have said, "Yeah, but look at the shmuck he beat."

Whatever the cause, Peter's choices continued to push Lucy further and further away, yet he did not seem to understand why. As far as he was concerned, he was doing what he had always done, experimenting, exploring. What had really changed? He and Lucy still spoke every day and agonized over whether to try to get back together or just acknowledge that it was over and move on. They made plans to find a counselor who could help them talk things out.

At the same time, Lucy had met someone else and decided, gingerly, to test the waters. Doug Wick was a producer in New York who had met Lucy several years before. He had been in touch with her from time to time, and when she and Peter broke up, he stated his intentions. For Lucy, it was still too soon. Soon after, Zoetrope went bankrupt, and Lucy spent some time abroad before starting her next job as a high-level executive at Warner Brothers Studios. She rented a house in Ravello, Italy, with Paula Weinstein, down the road from Gore Vidal. Friends like James Taylor would come around and stay for a few days, and they would ride their mopeds over to Vidal's, who felt it was all "very pleasant." On her way back to start her job at Warner Brothers, she spent some time in New York and began to see Wick.

Peter, meanwhile, was making the most of his new space. Here he did not have to store his equipment under the bed. He set up a TV monitor and video camera and left his personal recording studio open for business 24/7. He began setting up rehearsals and video shoots right away. As in Laurel Canyon, there was a constant influx of guests, old friends and new.

There was also no shortage of female guests. Jim Tucker, though, noted one particularly frequent visitor. He and Peter rarely spoke, save for a cordial hello and good-bye, but sometimes when Peter got home late and Tucker was still up, they would talk. The conversation often came around to Peter's many relationships with women, a subject Peter seemed bothered by.

As Neidlinger stood on the stairs trying to catch his breath, taking in the bombed-out surroundings and unable to imagine how any of it made sense, he had a thought. He stopped Peter as he headed down to pick up another load from the car. "Hey, Peter," he said. "Let's just take this shit back to my car, I'll give you a thousand dollars, and we'll move you to Hollywood."

Things were going well for Buell. He had become the top session bassist for Warner Bros., and was in demand for television and film.

"Oh, no," Peter said. "This is where the artists live."

Neidlinger was an artist, but he could not be more eager to get back to Hollywood after this brief visit downtown. Little Tokyo was the kind of place you try to escape from, not move to voluntarily. He worried about Peter—not only for his safety, but for the mental state that would make someone choose to live amid squalor.

But as he lugged his box the rest of the way up the stairs and into the loft, he saw that Peter was already making himself at home.

close-up:

New Wave Takes Flight

Los Angeles—Only four months after its conception, ATI Video's *Night Flight* took off on the 7.5-million-subscriber USA Network on June 5, offering on the basic cable service some seven to nine weekly hours of music and other youth-oriented programming. According to ATI equities chairman and chief operation officer Jeff Franklin, the package is being aimed at a broad (16- to 45-year-old) demographic base, with a mixture of featured performers ranging from new wave rockers to Lenny Bruce, straight concert footage and cult movies.

—Record World, *July 25, 1981*

STUART SHAPIRO, producer and creator of *Night Flight*
"I was very involved in midnight movies. Pretty much horror films and music films. It was the very beginning of cable and [cable] really signed off by, like, eleven o'clock at night. It's like nobody lives after eleven or twelve o'clock. I was sitting there in New York watching this, and all over the country thousands and thousands of people are going to midnight movies. I just had the desire to put that kind of cultural philosophy into programming on cable. Discovery was the most important ingredient about *Night Flight*. You could come and sit down and know that you would be turned on to discover something, no matter what segment it may be."

DON BOLLES, musician: the Germs, 45 Grave
"When it was picked up by *Night Flight*, everyone was seeing that show. People would come up to me and tell me they saw me on *Night Flight*. Then other videos got picked up by *Night Flight* because we were on that. I guess it had an effect on the programmers, too. So any exposure we had was because of that. Nobody did video back then."

STUART SHAPIRO
"*New Wave Theatre* closed every show. It was a signature of *Night Flight*."

It's a transcendental, earth-moving show, monitoring a gigantic ex-
posion, featuring a variety of creative expression not seen here since
the '60s.

—*Jeff Silberman*, L.A. Weekly, *May 14–20, 1982*

KEN YAS
"The fan mail poured in, and there were bags of it. People said things like,
This is the only television show worth watching in the world."

RICHARD SKIDMORE, booked bands for *NWT,* music producer
"Celebrities wanted to be there. We were the cover story of *Cable News*, like
number-one cable show."

BUDDY HELM
"The first sponsor was Ray Manzarek of the Doors. I went to his house and we
did the only video commercial for the Doors albums, to put on *New Wave Theatre*. He put up a few hundred bucks to keep the show going. He was a supporter of new music, and he was producing X at the time."

The Movement: New Wave of What?

"*New Wave Theatre* is not a music show," [Jove] explains, pacing his
tiny studio in Hollywood agitatedly, "but a rehabilitation program
forcing new life into music and new wave music into life . . . New
wave music is the clarion call to wake up. Wake up or the boogieman
is gonna get us all."

—L.A. Weekly, *August 8–14, 1980*

HAROLD RAMIS
"It was like the optimism of the '60s with flower power, and being crushed
under the boots of the oppressors, and the only response left was outrage and
fucking screaming as loud as you can. Kind of like, Fuck beauty. With a kind
of contempt, I think, for the gentleness of the '60s and the ineffectual quality
of it. There have been other modern revolutions in art that are a rejection
of beauty, a rejection of music, a rejection of melody, a rejection of form.
Punk was like a rejection of everything. I think [Peter] enjoyed it. Secretly

we all probably liked James Taylor. Peter sort of brought everyone into that world."

LUCY FISHER

"Peter glamorized the punk scene because he saw it as people flaunting conventionality, and he always had a soft spot for the danger, the underappreciated, the angry."

DINAH CANCER

"At first it started off being a cult following, but over the years, as it developed, it picked up momentum. They basically sampled the best of the LA underground. One week you would have a punk band, the next week there would be an electronic band, then performance artists. It was an underground variety show, because at that point the new wave was very underground, unlike today where it is very mainstream."

DERF SCRATCH

"I didn't really understand the gravity of it at the moment. Nobody was doing anything like that. I was amazed that people were allowing this to go on."

PETER RAFELSON

"It was the most edgy, unusual, unique scene in LA, literally. This was a consistent three seasons' worth of intense talent, drama, comedy, confrontation, violence, joy, creativity, freedom, and everybody wanted to be there. And the only way you were welcome was if you weren't part of the mainstream. You had to be so fucked up, out there, underground, struggling, punk artist, tattoo, freak buzz head, mohawked out . . ."

MICHAEL DARE

"The audience was everywhere. Behind the band, in front of the band, to the left of the band, to the right of the band . . . it was like being at a party, and not at the shooting of a show. You never knew who you were going to see there."

Your Talented Host

"The Dick Clark of New Wave Music." "Bert Parks in Spandex and shades," "The only TV personality to wear more fright wigs than Milton Berle." A "punk classicist" and "flamboyant guru."
   "Ladies and gentlemen, your talented host, Peter Ivers . . ."

LUCY FISHER

"There was a legitimate artistic aspect for sure, he was trying to create a scene, and part of that was to antagonize them. That was an exaggerated version of him trying to make people feel uncomfortable."

DEE DEE BRIDGEWATER, friend, singer

"I could see that at the *New Wave Theatre,* he irritated all of the punkers, and they thought he was just this jerk. I do remember thinking, Peter you better be careful with these people."

RICHARD SKIDMORE

"David would write the monologues and you would always see Peter wearing sunglasses because he had to read off of this big cue card in front of him."

BUELL NEIDLINGER

"Yeah, that and so he could laugh with his eyes at the total put-on he pulled off. I never watched more than ten or fifteen minutes of that show; I was on it once, I think. I don't know why he was doing that."

HUDSON MARQUEZ

"I thought he was playing along with Jove, and he was just putting out there into the universe, in the context of this mad high energy, and very odd death-rock bands, just throwing out a little poison gas bomb, his own creations. And I thought that was very cool."

HAROLD RAMIS

"In a way, he was kind of a tourist in that world, he was older, he was just fascinated. I think what he strongly related to was their ability, their unfettered self-expression that a lot of those bands represented. Like, do anything you want with your hair, wear anything you want, put pins through your body, whatever. Peter responded to it in a strange kind of way. He wore the weirdest outfits, and they weren't like punk outfits, it was just like every day was Halloween. So he embraced punk because it gave him license."

MERLE IVERS

"He got a kick out of it; he thought it was a hoot. He was an antagonist, that was his job, to make them angry, or test the waters and make it exciting. If you're doing something live, you get weird responses that I suppose could be very interesting."

BUDDY HELM

"He put everybody on the spot by asking them, What's the meaning of life, so everyone would be very embarrassed and uptight, because they knew they were going to be asked that question. So they'd struggle to come up with something clever or, God forbid, meaningful. But Pete was always the raconteur."

STEVE MARTIN

"He was like the host of an open mic night on a space station. What he was doing was providing a platform that made it easier for the square world to interact with this. Like, 'Oh, look at how this guy is dressed, he is so kooky.' It made it easier to digest. Peter knew what he was doing, he had done all those productions at Harvard. It wasn't an accident that he was wearing those clothes."

DEE DEE BRIDGEWATER

"I loved it. I thought it was crazy. It was when punk first came out and they'd have all sorts of piercings, hardcore, and there was Peter Ivers in the middle of all this stuff. He seemed to me to be the person that was always living on the edge and loved to kind of flirt with danger and possible death."

TEQUILA MOCKINGBIRD

"He wasn't a punk rocker, he was like a glamour guy."

MARTY KRYSTALL

"After he broke up with Lucy, he went kind of wild. He was kind of a punk before there were punks, but I thought it was a waste of his talent. Nobody was on his level. They were all just stupid ignoramuses with instruments."

TIM HUNTER, friend, filmmaker

"It's the same reason someone does anything in showbiz: to be seen and get exposure."

JELLO BIAFRA

"A lot of people were willing to go on *New Wave Theatre* just to be on *New Wave Theatre*, but people weren't too down with Peter himself. Some people, like Chuck from Black Flag really respected him as a superintelligent guy, and to me it was more like a wide-eyed fan. Like, Oh my God, I'm going to meet Peter Ivers."

Ghost Hosts

TEQUILA MOCKINGBIRD

"I knew from the beginning that the reason he was put in place was because he had connections. His friends were all too straight for me, but he was great. But like the Ramises and stuff, and Hudson Marquez, were all a lot more adult than we were."

HUDSON MARQUEZ

"Slowly but surely, Hollywood hipsters started showing up. Harold Ramis shows up there, and Harold would get this stuff, he's not threatened by anything. Harold goes, I like this, and is totally sincere about it."

LINDA PERRY

"It was just a lot of fun when Ramis and Doug Kenney would come to the tapings. It's like talent meets talent and mutual respect with Ramis and Peter. They knew he could travel in both worlds as they did."

RICHARD SKIDMORE

"Belushi, O'Donoghue, Chevy Chase, people that were passing through would be grabbed into the show and be called Ghost Hosts. Beverly D'Angelo, Elvira, they were there too."

BEVERLY D'ANGELO

"Ivers was an innovator—when you think about it, he was doing independent TV—no sponsors et cetera. And he communicated a sense of purpose about it—had an attitude of 'not selling out—which was a crucial issue in the late '70s, early '80s, and the basis for huge respect."

STEVE MARTIN
"David Lynch was on *New Wave Theatre*, he was a big star, he didn't have to do that. He did it for his friend Peter."

TODD HOMER
"I can remember shows when David Lee Roth showed up to see us."

BEVERLY D'ANGELO
"I think [*New Wave Theatre*] connected with so many people who were confronted with creative restrictions, and that's why people wanted to be a part of it. Peter was doing something for its own sake, in a medium that allowed anything but that. Like some cowboy video ham operator, he was calling out to the other truckers en route to wherever, saying, there is an underground in LA, and it's alive, well, and hilarious."

Everybody Was Slightly Off: The Bands

TEQUILA MOCKINGBIRD
"He never knew what the kids were going to come up with next. There was no record company to tell them what they could and couldn't do. We used all kinds of music; we didn't limit ourselves to punk rock only. Everybody was slightly off. We were all young."

RICHARD SKIDMORE
"So these are some of the bands that were on *New Wave Theatre:* the Blasters, the Plugz, Fear, and the Rayonics, the Monitor, Red Wedding, Mentors, 45 Grave, Circle Jerks, the Unknown, Vox Pop, Ron Athey in Christian Death, Black Flag, Show Dog, Anthem. Anthem was the band before the Red Hot Chili Peppers with Flea, Anthony, and Hillel [Slovak], one of their founding members, and these little kids that went to Fairfax High School would go up to us at Canter's and say, 'We'd really like to be on *New Wave Theatre.*' They could bring out huge crowds, but they couldn't play anywhere that served liquor. They were really good, but I remember they would ask us if they could play."

DON BOLLES, musician: the Germs, 45 Grave

"The Germs was a big deal at that point in a way. We were spiritually the biggest thing in LA. It was already a legend and a myth. Black Flag would play with us sometimes. We were before all those guys. They were art school guys. Really strange kids who were geniuses. We were weird, smart, acid-dropping, Manson-worshiping freaks, you know?"

KEITH MORRIS, musician: Circle Jerks, Black Flag

"There was a bunch of us that were just Hollywood couch surfers, drug addicts, alcoholics, that's pretty much what we were. We'd hear of these [*New Wave Theatre*] shows and we'd show up because we knew we could get in there for free. That's basically a lure of the scene that was going on with Peter Ivers. It was a big party."

TODD HOMER, musician: Angry Samoans

"It wasn't too chummy, the bands weren't always really getting along anyway, or they were so jaded about each other. Jeff, who sang lead with the Angry Samoans, shot the finger for like twenty minutes to the keyboardist from the Doors. I just remember that there seemed to be hostility between bands. A lot of the bands were just so godawful that we would just have to laugh at them."

SPIT STIX

"At the time, Richard Ramirez was loose, the Hillside Strangler, there were serious serial murderers loose at the time, and there was fear. A lot of people had guns, and there were serious things going on in Los Angeles at the time, and we wanted to kind of, not make fun of it, but take it over the top. This was an opportunity to really act. Peter's goodnaturedness and really androgynous outfit and glasses and whatever, it was a perfect way to just contrast what we were trying to personify, and it was just entertainment. Peter allowed us to go over the top and act scary and ease our own fears of what's going on in society."

TEQUILA MOCKINGBIRD

"I knew Peter and Fear had a real vendetta towards each other, but I didn't fear for his life. I feared more the straight people than the kids, because they had an attention span of five minutes."

SPIT STIX

"It was a more theatrical image that we were portraying, and a hard edge we were playing. We were competing with bands like the Ramones at the time. And Lee [Ving] is just a wiseguy by nature, and David Jove loved that Lee's homophobia was just unleashed on Peter, and I think David Jove got a kick out of that, and he just encouraged us to let it loose on Peter, and he was a good sport about it. We gave him wedgies and did mock beat-ups. We never hurt him or intended to hurt him, but he went along with our tough guy sort of image, and took it tongue in cheek and got it."

DERF SCRATCH

"I was surprised that anyone would behave the way Lee did to Peter. He was a bully. I never was. I didn't care if Peter wore a dress or whatever. I think Peter took the chances that Jove wanted to take but was too much of a wimp to do it himself. I think John Belushi had a professionalism about him to where, anybody had the courage to get up onstage and act like that in front of punks and live through it had his respect. That's the way I looked at it. There were lots of scary people on there. Lee was scary."

SPIT STIX

"I viewed Peter as an equal myself. I guess you'd have to ask the other guys in Fear their opinion. I just looked at him as an equal and said, Here's this entertainer, the host of this television program, and at ease in front of a camera, an entertainer, a professional actor, and could just turn it on for the camera and be a down-to-earth Joe when it's off. Here is the perfect straight man, Peter, wearing sequined dresses and '50s glasses, and it's like, you put those two contrasts next to each other and they really stand out. Peter got it. Peter realized that we, you know, we would laugh with Peter as soon as the camera went off. It was like—boom—arms around the shoulders, good take."

Punk Comics and Comic Punks

HAROLD RAMIS

"I had almost given up on music at that point. I had grown up at a time when I saw Jimi Hendrix live, you know, the Doors' first concert in Chicago, and Cream . . . What I liked about punk and new wave music was that it shattered everything. Rock had become so institutionalized that it was a rejection of that whole, commercialized rock experience. So even though it was intriguing, I still cherished the rebellion of the '60s, but it was over for us. It's hard to want to tear down the establishment when you're living in a big house in Hollywood with a pool and driving a big car and making tons of money. The punks came along and they spit on all of it. They were just, fuck you, and it was great, it was refreshing."

KEITH MORRIS

"I think Belushi was attracted to it because it was so wild and off the hook. So not-mainstream. In his world, he was surrounded by all these square cats, suit-and-tie, play-it-by-the-numbers type of people. Here he's given the opportunity to hang out with these strange, off-the-wall, nutty-type characters. All these wild personalities. I think that was probably one of the main things that attracted him to it."

HAROLD RAMIS

"You know, John was more of a blues guy, but just the nature of his lifestyle took him to all the hot spots in LA, and of course he eventually hooked up with Fear, Lee Ving. One of the last times I saw John Belushi alive, I think Lee Ving was at the party too."

HUDSON MARQUEZ

"Anyone interested in the blues immediately gets punk rock. So John just flew off the deep end for punk because it was another chance to get wild. And you don't have to do any twist dance steps, you can jump up and down. So these comedians were just running on pure emotion, that's why they liked it so much."

JOHN LANDIS

"When I met John, he was into heavy metal. Danny was really into rhythm and blues. John and Judy eventually had a house on Sixteenth Street and John had a music room. They played music so loud that your teeth hurt."

DERF SCRATCH

"Oh yeah, John was a punk."

JUDY BELUSHI

"I remember John talking about Peter and having connected on that level [with music]."

IRIS BERRY

"I remember being at the Whisky to see the Dead Boys and saying to my boyfriend at the time, 'Wow, their drummer looks just like John Belushi.' And it was John Belushi, it was great. He did a whole set."

JUDY BELUSHI

"Belushi even wrote a song and recorded it, 'Fuck Your Neighbor.' "

DERF SCRATCH

"Yeah, John wanted us to do the final song for *Neighbors.*"

SPIT STIX

"[John] wanted to work with Lee and Philo and write something, and I would engineer and produce it. So we cut the movie version of it in the studio. [Mick] Jagger was vocal coaching John in the studio."

DERF SCRATCH

"He thought it would be funny and piss off all the producers. That's what punk was, break down the establishment and let some new people in. He was totally into that. Me, Richard Pryor, and John were hanging out, but John was almost crying to me because he was telling me they weren't going to use the song in *Neighbors.*"

WALLIS NICITA

"You know, comics are not musicians, and writers are just writing what they observe. Peter was such a refreshing breeze for everybody, because he really wasn't a comedy writer in the same sense that they were all trying to be successful comics. He was coming with what was really coming from the street, and I think they wanted to come close to that so that they could get it. Only John and Peter embraced it."

ROBERT ROLL

"Harold Ramis, he too was seeing that this is a new movement, like the Beat movement or rock and roll, this is something we haven't seen before, and there's a part of Harold that always wants to know what the young kids coming up are interested in."

DAN AYKROYD

"Now my theory was that our cover of 'Soul Man' hit number one right in the vacuum of American music which occurred between disco and new wave. John was right there, ready to surf that rising crest in urban culture."

SPIT STIX

"I don't think Peter got enough credit for what he did. These guys *really* aren't ready for prime time. It was underground with a vengeance. There was nothing else happening at the time."

DAN AYKROYD

"Peter Ivers was one of the individuals who introduced John to the creators of this anarchistic movement. Many a night John hauled me to CBGB or its Los Angeles equivalent to audit live performances by Lee Ving and Fear, Black Flag, or the Dead Kennedys. And John may have gained currency in the concert, radio, and recording industry as a bluesman, but in truth he would much rather have been a full-on Henry Rollins–type punker."

> *"I may be gone, but Rock and Roll lives on."*
> *January 24, 1949–March 5, 1982*
> *Inscription on John Belushi's gravestone*

case book *part 7*

DAVID CHARBONNEAU

"I think the first person to tell me that [Peter] was planning to leave the show was Lucy. She was definitely seeing that as a good thing and portrayed it as something that Peter Ivers came to her about. And I got the sense she was happy with that."

KEN YAS

"Peter was part of David's bag of tricks. He was an instrument that David would play. Yet at a point where clearly, the stakes were high, and David had an opportunity to take the show to a whole different level—because he had renewed the interest level in the show, and the eyeballs were on."

JIM TUCKER

"I think Tequila has the best take on the whole thing. Peter was the front, and Jove drove the packaging. And since Peter was going to leave the show, Jove freaked out and followed him back to his place. To me that's the most plausible, but I don't know."

DAVID CHARBONNEAU

"As I started getting more information, I knew [Jove] was somebody I definitely had to go back and talk to. I went back, he invited me to his house, by myself, without Rafelson this time. We talked for a while at his house, I asked him questions about the relationship and Peter leaving, and he pretty much pooh-poohed most of it. He said, 'No, it's not that way, people are just jealous of the relationship Peter and I had together, and Peter would never have gone to the mainstream stuff. We were gonna make it.' There was always a 'we.'"

PETER RAFELSON

"Well, you have to remember that David was focusing all of his energy on pretty much promoting Peter as a celebrity. In fact, they were partners."

DAVID CHARBONNEAU

"He said, 'Let's go out,' so we got a bite to eat. Then we went back to his place, and he cued up, slow motion, Reagan getting shot. And he stopped it right at the point when Reagan was getting shot, and he just played it over and over and over. By the third time, I asked him, 'What are you doing?' And he goes, 'I just love this part.' And I go, 'Great.' He says, 'Can't you just see the realization on his face?'"

KEN YAS

"Jove wasn't only a narcissist. He had no respect for authority because he always got away with everything."

DAVID CHARBONNEAU

"He was fucking with everybody. I knew the guy was the furthest out there that anybody in this group was. In the sense of an alter ego, he was really threatened, and overplaying with everyone. He was overplaying the fact that everyone thought he did it. He was good at it; he just got away with things. It's never a good idea to try and make sense of people that are, in some ways, insane."

PENELOPE SPHEERIS, punk documentarian, producer

"To be honest with you, and you're sure the guy is dead, right? Because he scared the shit out of me. Oh, punk rock didn't scare me at all. The reason he scared me is, people that scare me are people who don't know who they are. He was so psychologically unstable and scrambled up that just looking in his eyes gave me cold shivers. He scared the shit out of me and I'd go to great lengths to stay away from him. I'm not easily scared, okay. I'm pretty tough and brave."

PLEASANT GEHMAN, writer
"I can see exactly why some people wouldn't talk to you unless he was dead."

DAVID CHARBONNEAU
"I knew he was so important, I knew he was fucking with me, I knew everything I saw forensically profiled in a sense was important and he couldn't hide that, so that's why he was putting it in my face. He knew what I was about, he knew what he was about, and he didn't care, and he was basically saying, 'Catch me if you can.' My approach in that second meeting was just much more informal, like yeah, let's hang out and get a burger or whatever. Let's shoot the shit about politics, which is why he pulled out the Reagan stuff. I just had an inkling that the only way I could get him to deal with this in any way was to show me more. And he came up with all kinds of theories. He was spinning more theories than I or anyone else was."

> Everyone thinks I did it, but I didn't do it, it wasn't me, I don't know who did it . . . I remember being in the neighborhood at the time and just hearing things like, it was other bands that did it.
> —*David Jove, Interview with documentary filmmaker Carl Schneider*

PETER RAFELSON
"A lot of other people didn't understand it and didn't want to be around Peter if David had anything to do with him, so it was sort of a monkey on his back, if you will. It made things difficult for Peter in situations where David wasn't welcome. That must have affected him. I'm sure it was a strain, that's probably an accurate word."

DAVID CHARBONNEAU
"Rafelson, he came off to me as a guy who was very low-key, very unassuming. I got the sense from him that he knew a

lot and that he wasn't telling me anything in the beginning. He didn't know what to do with me. I was like, okay, I've got to keep talking to this guy. I really looked at him as a lynchpin from the beginning because of his proximity, and I met with him more than I met with anybody. I got a real distinct feeling that he was close to Peter, protective of Peter."

PETER RAFELSON

"At the time he was about to gain commercial success, all those people he had somewhat legitimized in the noncommercial world resented him and wanted to hold him back. They didn't like that he was about to fly the coop. I never could rule out a few people, and as a result, I stayed friends with them, and I didn't want anyone to feel like I had suspicions, but I did. And I played it very cool, and I would talk to them about their supposed suspicions of other people to appear like I wasn't even considering them."

DAVID CHARBONNEAU

"I had a sense that Rafelson knew just about everything, so that's why he came down on David. There were different reasons that could have happened, and it was a nagging suspicion with him, as well as with other people. But really with Rafelson to a high degree, he felt that nobody could have surprised Peter the way he got surprised that night. He just thought [Peter] was a cat, you couldn't creep up on him and do that. So I come away from Rafelson, and I say I have to keep up with this guy, keep talking to him and use him. He was the closest guy to all the different circles that Peter was in. That's what I understood."

chapter 9

I Could Be Brilliant

He had some powerful ambitions. The thing that bothered me about it was that he had so much energy and so many things to pursue, it was like he was firing them off, one, two, three. Peter would just take my breath away. But he would turn to me and say, "Malcolm, I could be brilliant." And I said, "Peter, you are. You just have to get a bit organized in how you present your ideas."

—*Malcolm Leo*

LA, the Cave, 1982, 7:00 p.m.

Peter swung his Fiat into the alleyway two blocks past Canter's Deli, right off Fairfax and West Hollywood. He parked directly behind the storefront, the one that looked condemned because its street-facing windows were blacked out. The only entrance was the door facing the alley, rigged with a forbidding array of security equipment, video cameras, and listening devices, and thick with decals and posters—California Highway Patrol insignia next to ENTER AT YOUR OWN RISK and VERBOTEN! signs, TOXIC WASTE over a skull-and-crossbones next to a WELCOME! bumper sticker—forming a frenzied chorus of urgent, mixed signals.

Peter and Peter Rafelson got out of the Fiat and approached the door. Rafelson gave the secret knock.

"What is it?! What do you want?!"

"It's Pete and Pete."

Ten deadbolts could be heard unlocking, followed by a two-by-four swinging up off its brackets on the other side of the door.

"Don't let the flies in!" Jove opened the door just enough to let them squeeze through.

It was called the Cave for a reason. Between the blackened front windows and the lack of proper light fixtures, the place was sparse on illumination. While there were homemade knickknacks Jove had out-fitted with miniature lighting, Rafelson knew from experience that you could be there for an hour without knowing there was someone else in the room, then suddenly notice an ominous-looking stranger who had been standing right beside you the whole time. The only real glow emanated from the pulsing monolith dominating the room—the customized editing booth from which *New Wave Theatre* emerged. The walls were covered in antique knickknacks, glass statues, and other art and artifacts. The whole place was stacked with burnt dolls' heads and misshapen dolls' bodies glued together into complex sculp-tures. The sound of crickets chirping ran on an endless tape loop.

Without another word, Jove returned to the editing booth. Fueled by a sense of destiny and a seemingly bottomless supply of coke, this was where Jove spent the majority of each day, cutting the footage from the tapings into episodes, and cutting the episodes into manic joyrides of music and video. He loved to pepper the show with a bar-rage of quick, evocative non sequiturs—his beloved star fields, nuclear explosions, bombs falling from fighter jets, Buddhas being carried through the air by industrial machinery—turning found footage into new wave art. Even those who disliked Jove had to respect his com-mand of the craft. Malcolm Leo, the successful director who was help-ing Peter produce *Vitamin Pink* found Jove insufferable but gave him credit for being a risk-taking innovator at the forefront of video. Paul Flattery, a music video director for major-label bands, noticed some camera and lighting techniques Jove employed to film musical perfor-mance he had never seen before—subtle tweaks he was able to lever-age to arresting effect. Flattery had been so impressed by Jove that he invited him to collaborate on one of his big-name productions.

Peter knew that Jove was a perfectionist. He had come today to record the opening monologue for an upcoming show. (Most of *New Wave Theatre*'s taped segments were shot in the Cave.) He was prepared, if not particularly enthused, to hunker down for several hours and many takes—sometimes Jove would stop him, over and over, on a word he felt Peter was not inflecting correctly. He pulled out the bag of flamboyant "workclothes" he kept stashed at the Cave and started to change. Peter Rafelson pulled up a chair next to Jove at the booth.

To have Jove tolerate this close proximity was, for Rafelson, a sign of progress. The first time Peter brought him over, he nominated Rafelson, who had his own band, for a slot on the show. Jove called Rafelson a Hollywood poser and told him to leave.

Rafelson, though, was hooked. Like so many others Jove brought down into his rabbit hole, he felt strangely, inexplicably elated. Jove did not live by the normal rules, and mere proximity to him infected Rafelson with a portentous sense of the unprecedented: the possibility of living a truly original life.

Sometimes Jove had to work harder to woo people, but he never shied away from a challenge. His standard MO was to identify worthy targets, charm them down into the cave, ply them with cocaine, marijuana, and alcohol, show videotapes, and preach The Message. It was the same message he delivered through Peter on the show, absent Peter's whimsical, ironic touch. For many it seemed to carry the devastating resonance of truth. On any given night Jove's tiny apartment could be found packed with dozens of disciples hanging on his every word, or Jove huddled at his editing booth opposite a potential new recruit, delivering The Message. *There is no time to go to the parties, there is no time to go to the bars, you must determine who you are and why you are here right now.* Spreading The Message, Jove said, was his mission. *Your mission was to make one potentially life-altering decision. Will you help me in that effort? Do you want to join up, or don't you?*

Just because there was no time for parties did not mean there was no time for fun. As far as Rafelson could tell, what bound Jove's group together was a totally unbounded pursuit of new experiences and thrills. There were no rules or judgment, and Jove—whether shooting guns into the ceiling without checking if anyone was upstairs, or careening down Laurel Canyon late at night with no windshield and no lights on the wrong side of the street, ignoring his passengers' screams—led by example.

Peter, too, was known to dabble in the dark, seedy side of LA, especially since moving downtown. Rafelson knew this firsthand. It was not unusual for him to pick up the phone and hear Ivers on the other end: "Come on, Pete!" At this stage in his life, Peter's wide-eyed curiosity brought him to dingy corridors in the back alleys of Hollywood, what struck Rafelson as "weird freaky shit," dark clubs and parties that made Fellini look like child's play and that no responsible person could claim was safe.

While Rafelson, barely out of his teens (a fact that was often overlooked because he came from a cool movie-industry family and had always been exposed to situations beyond his years), loved and respected both men, he did not feel particularly safe either in Jove's Cave or Peter's dusky downtown. There was one key difference, though, between the two pied pipers. Peter was enthusiastic about sharing his experiences, but he never took them too seriously and never demanded loyalty of any kind. He was his own person, and wanted you to be as well. If Peter had a message, that was its sum total.

Jove had a more, well, *comprehensive* agenda, and as the nights in the Cave wore on, Rafelson found himself often feeling less like a guest and more like a hostage. He would agonize for hours over what might be the exact right moment to leave Jove. Otherwise, he knew from experience, he would be attacked, physically and mentally. Leaving was frowned upon.

Peter seemed to be the one person exempt from such concerns. Jove had him in a different category—he didn't preach to Peter as much as use him as a sounding board to sharpen his ideas. When their philosophical discussions became heated, Jove would sometimes playfully exclaim, "I've got you now, Peter!" with a sense of accomplishment that betrayed his respect for Peter's Harvard-trained intellect. When things got tense during *New Wave Theatre* tapings, to lighten the mood they would spar on the set, trading martial arts moves while demonstrating a camaraderie that, for Jove, was rare.

For now, as far as Peter was concerned, it was a mutually beneficial arrangement: Jove used him for his Hollywood contacts, he used Jove for the opportunity to work his acting chops and become known. When it was time to leave, he would leave. In the meantime, he was going to do the best job he could, even if that entailed sitting for two hours on one monologue taking notes from Jove on the proper inflection for particularly significant one-syllable words.

With his pink-sequined dinner jacket and a pair of brown-tinted shades tilted up onto his forehead, Peter stepped up to face Jove and his camera. Next to the camera were the cards with the monologue written out. Peter started every monologue with the shades on his forehead, then tipped them down so that the audience could not see his eyes move as he read. Jove cued him to start.

"In the next few years the video revolution will shift into high gear"—he flipped the sunglasses down off his forehead, blackening his eyes—"offering anyone with a receiving dish and a TV set hundreds of information and entertainment channels from which to choose . . ."

LA, Franne Golde's Home, 1982, 10:00 a.m.

Franne Golde sat at her piano and played the same melody again and again and again. She had come up with it a couple of hours earlier and been repeating it ever since. Every once in a while a hand would thrust out from underneath the piano, by her feet. The hand offered a piece of graph paper with a few new neatly printed lines. She put the paper on the music stand and read the lyrics a few times, let them meld with her melody, and then sang them out loud.

Often she would critique a line or a word here or there, minor points, cut this or move that, a little sculpting. Peter wasn't a natural songwriter—a Carole King or Gerry Goffin—but he definitely had a gift for music and an extremely clever way with words. He was learning, and she was learning, too. Sometimes, he would hand her a lyric from under the piano and her first response would be a skeptical *hmmm*. Then she'd start singing it, and feeling it, and soon it was her new favorite song. Which, as Peter quickly learned, meant it had a very good chance of getting sold.

Franne Golde knew what she was talking about. If anyone *did* have a shot at becoming the next Carole King, it was her. Before meeting Peter, the shy, self-described "Carole King wannabe Jewish songwriter from Chicago" had already seen a number of her songs become R&B hits (most famously Diana Ross's chart-topping 1978 "Gettin' Ready for Love"). She was widely recognized as one of the top up-and-coming songwriters. Having cleared the difficult lower rungs of the success ladder, she seemed poised for a quick climb into the industry stratosphere.

Still, when it was suggested to Golde that she meet Peter, her first response was terror. She agonized about it the entire week prior, unnerved by his Ivy League background, his heavyweight friends, and his reputation as a kind of roving creative genius. But when they actually met, Peter put Golde at ease. She quickly shifted from anxiety to an irresistible urge to mother him. The meeting ended with Franne cooking Peter an omelet, which he loved so much that it became a regular feature of their working process.

The matchmaker responsible for this oddly appropriate pairing was Linda Perry. In 1980, Perry had gone to work in the talent department of ATV Music, a British music publishing company. Her job was to sign writers and match them up with performers to record their songs. There she got to know Franne, who worked for a different publisher upstairs. Perry, the music industry insider whose father and husband were both successful producers, and who had consulted with Durrie Parks over the wisdom of helping Peter get his Warner Bros. contract almost ten years earlier—took it as a given that her brilliant friend did not have the ear for writing commercial music. (Ten years of hard experience had borne out her initial instinct, though she took no pleasure in being proven right.) What she believed was that given the right guidance he was smart enough to learn. One day she sat him down and gave it to him straight. "If you want to make money, this is what you have to do."

It was an offer to which Peter normally would not have given a second thought. He had been offered many high-paying industry jobs—producer, executive, session work on the harp, movie scores—and never seemed remotely tempted. As recently as a year earlier he would have listened to Perry's offer, nodded, gone home, broken out his equipment, and made another new video for another new song.

But something was shifting in Peter, and Linda Perry may have sensed he was ready to hear what she had to say. And the impulse driving Perry to offer Peter this job was born out of a concern shared by many of his friends. While as giving and unpredictable and wacky as always, lately something about him seemed slightly unraveled. It wasn't just his fascination with the downtown underground, though many did see his foray into the fringe as a symptom of desperation and a call for help. What worried them more was that Peter seemed tired.

In the last decade-plus he had recorded four original records and a demo for a fifth, *Nirvana Cuba*, which was intended as not only an album but also as a musical performance to be staged and filmed. He

had created videos for a number of the *Nirvana Cuba* songs and secured a National Endowment of the Arts grant for his video work. He
had written an iconic song for an iconic movie and a handful of other
highly regarded songs and scores for theatre, television, and film. He
had countless other original songs in various stages of completion,
and was in the final stages of tinkering with *Vitamin Pink*, a narrative
song cycle which, like *Nirvana Cuba*, he planned to launch as a stage
show, shoot on video, and eventually turn into a feature film. By age
thirty-five he had generated more creative output than many people
do in a lifetime and had been paid back largely with frustration, rejection, and indifference. Each setback seemed to goad him to focus more
obsessively on his art, to work harder and sleep less; in the last year or
so his creative drive had taken on a kind of frenzied intensity. It was
almost as if he were attempting to make a cosmic barter: rather than
allow for any artistic compromise, he would dedicate himself more
fully, put more hours and more energy into realizing his personal vision.

Meanwhile, many of his friends had chosen instead to focus on
the one or two things they did best, had leveraged their talents, and hit
it big, achieving the kind of success that always eluded Peter. The wear
and tear of constant struggle was beginning to show. Johanna Went,
the *New Wave Theatre* performance artist with whom Peter had become close, got the feeling that as the years wore on, with one friend
after another breaking out in his or her field, Peter sensed he was being
left behind. He still kept in touch with his old Harvard theatre friend
Howard Cutler, and in a conversation around that time Peter told him
point-blank, "I'm tired." Cutler felt that he was talking about spiritual fatigue.

And then there was money. Having mortgaged everything on his
dream, Peter was essentially destitute. The minor celebrity he was at-
taining on *New Wave Theatre* could not pay for dinner. With increasing frequency he started showing up at friends' houses around
mealtime, partially for the company and partially for a free hot meal.
Soon after they started working together, Franne Golde noticed that
Peter seemed anxious about money. He was constantly asking her if he
could borrow small amounts, a five, a ten. His question to Nancy
Drew—"Should I borrow money from women?"—was not hypotheti-
cal and did not apply only to Lucy, who still sent checks and supported

Peter Ivers Enterprises. Peter was also getting scattered financial support from a number of his "ladies in their Mercedes."

Finally, there was Lucy. Peter still agonized over the loss and what he would need to do to get her back. Merle had advised him that Lucy was ready to move on to a new phase of her life, settle down with a family, something he did not seem ready for psychologically, much less financially. Some of his friends felt that around the time of Linda Perry's offer he may have been looking for an opportunity to make himself ready—to prove to both of them, as one friend put it, that "I can be that guy just for Lucy."

All these pressures created the perfect storm for an unprecedented decision. Peter did something he had never done before: he let money figure into his creative process and created art exclusively for the purpose of selling it. His short-term goal was to write a hit single. He asked Linda Perry to set up the meeting with Franne Golde.

From the start, their songs sold. Early on they wrote a tune called "Little Boy Sweet," which would soon find its way to the Pointer Sisters. Another, "Let's Go Up," was recorded by Diana Ross.

Linda Perry promptly signed Peter to a publishing deal with ATV. A quick study, he was nevertheless always sure to refer to songwriting as his "day job." Everything else was his art. Perry could care less. His lyrics were so clever and well crafted he could call his work whatever he wanted.

Songwriting might have been Peter's day job, but Golde was much more than a colleague. From the day they met, Peter and his new collaborator were inseparable. They worked together almost every day, and on days they didn't work they met for lunch. Peter became something like a big brother to Golde, introducing her to new experiences and ideas. He always explained things clearly, thoughtfully, and patiently, and she found herself relentlessly plying him with questions. Her upbringing had been fairly sheltered, and when they first went downtown to work in his loft, Golde became so frightened by the burnt-out cityscape that she refused to step foot in the ominous back freight elevator. Peter cajoled her into the elevator, saying, "Welcome to life!"

She was constantly surprised by all the different projects he was working on, which he would mention offhandedly, incidental to other topics of conversation. Once they were in the studio preparing to record a demo and wanted a particular kind of voice. Peter said, "Let me call my friend Dee Dee Bridgewater and see if she can do it." Franne was flabbergasted. Bridgewater, a world-renowned jazz vocalist, was married to Gil Moses, the Street Choir bandleader with whom Peter had remained friends. The next thing Golde knew, Dee Dee Bridgewater was in the studio, "singing the shit out of" a song she and Peter had written days before.

On a personal level, Golde felt she recognized in Peter something she knew within herself: a deep nagging sadness born out of a difficult family background. She felt he saw her vulnerability and her pain, that he watched over and took care of her.

Nearly every song Peter and Golde wrote together was picked up, a number by well-known artists. Recently one of their singles—one Golde had eyed skeptically when Peter first handed her the graph paper and had eventually come to love—had been signed to be recorded by the Pointer Sisters, for the soundtrack of the upcoming Chevy Chase vehicle *National Lampoon's Vacation*.

Through advances, royalties, and, eventually, copublisher credit with ATV, Peter began to generate income. Strangely, this did not seem to alleviate any of his financial concerns, which as far as Golde could tell, only grew more acute. Often Peter seemed riddled with anxiety. He seemed to need a large sum of money, though for what she did not know. One day the two of them had been over at Peter Rafelson's house. Rafelson played in Peter's *Vitamin Pink* band, which had begun as a collaboration with Van Dyke Parks and then morphed into Peter's next big project. He also worked independently with Linda Perry's husband (the record producer Richard Perry, who also worked on Peter-Golde songs), and had begun to demonstrate some formidable songwriting chops of his own. With so much cross-pollination, it was only natural for Peter, Golde, and Rafelson to strike up a collaboration. That particular day at Rafelson's house, Franne saw Peter ask him for a huge sum of money.

Part of the reason Peter never had any money was that he paid his collaborators well, on time, and always before himself. Once, when Steve Martin was looking over Peter's books, he noticed a huge discrepancy—the band was splitting most of the take among themselves, with Peter barely getting paid at all. "Peter, this is all wrong," Martin had said. "No," Peter told him. "It's right." He also helped many of his struggling artist friends with their rents, or bought their work, even if it meant he would have to turn to his more solvent friends for a hot meal that day. Luckily, he had plenty of people who were happy to feed him.

LA, the Cave 1982, 8:00 p.m.

Peter patiently started again. He was sure he had nailed it, more than a few times, but Jove was still unsatisfied. It was a ritual to which Peter had become accustomed.

> PETER: In the next few years the video revolution will shift into high gear, offering anyone with a receiving dish and a TV set hundreds of information and entertainment channels from which to choose. On the one hand, this will intrigue and delight those with special Interests to the point where—"
>
> JOVE: Interests, it's interests! You're saying int-res.
>
> PETER: Interests.
>
> JOVE: Again.

LA, the Lingerie Club, Vitamin Pink Fantasy Revue, June 8 and 9, 1982

A spotlight shone down center stage at the packed nightclub as the band kicked up a driving rock intro. Peter strutted onto the stage in a short-sleeved shirt that emphasized his biceps, two leather harmonica holsters strapped to his legs like chaps, lined with harps in every size and key. He threw his arms heavenward, crouched to the ground, and let out a sultry, whiny, almost infantile moan. Standing, he held a large harmonica against the mic, pressed it to his lips, and blew some riffs against the intro.

He holstered the harp, swung his hips, and began to sing.

> *My dissonant mother,*
> *S'been thrown out of Russia,*
> *Now I got that hag on my hands.*
> *My sister's a lezzie,*

My brother's a fairy,
And I've got a rock and roll band.
(<>) Song # 9

Vitamin Pink was Peter's showcase, a freewheeling vehicle for his music and ideas. The *L.A. Weekly* called it, "A surreal meeting of the aboveground and the underground centered on two layers whose journey to exotic locales like Iran, Vietnam, ancient Rome and using songs with titles like 'Saigon Rainstorm' and 'Iraq and You Ran.' " A cabaret of original songs staged by a parade of choreographed dancers and oddly named characters in bright outrageous new wave–themed costumes, interspersed with staged dialogue and miniature skits, the show was a kind of live extended music video that brought together many of the influences Peter had absorbed over the course of his artistic life and many of the people with whom he had shared different parts of the journey. An old-time musical review gone berserk, *Vitamin Pink* was vaudeville meets Hasty Pudding meets *New Wave Theatre*.

His main costars included *NWT*'s slick fake-commercial huckster Robert Roll, who played a smarmy announcer (featuring lines like, "I'm Robert Roll, saying: This is Robert Roll, speaking"). Whereas on *New Wave Theatre* Roll's only job was playing the snake oil salesman who tries to sell you "Numrunner" ("So you don't have to find the answers to life. You can just look like you've had them all along!")— now in Peter's show he was singing, dancing, and changing costumes to play different characters in musical numbers and skits. (In one, he played a psychoanalyst questioning Peter's character about his mother. Apropos of nothing, he demanded from his patient, "So, what is the meaning of life?"). For husky backing vocals and slithering sex appeal, Peter used Tequila Mockingbird (introduced by Roll as "Ramona Kimono, thirty-sex acres of fertile female flesh, and it's harvest time in the sand-rock-queen valley") and Rochelle Robertson ("here she is in the flesh—and what flesh—the lovely, the talented, the lithe, the lissome, Nancyyyyy Hopalong. She's just too ambitious to do the dishes, so she's gonna go shopping instead").

To most in the audience, the story line holding all the songs and segments together was not totally clear. In one number, Peter and Rochelle Robertson went back and forth proclaiming their mutual "sex crush." In another, "Oh Jerusalem" (inspired by a trip Peter took to Israel with Lucy's family when her brother was married there), Peter squeezed a toy machine gun under his arm as pretty girls in Arab kaf-fiyehs, with machine guns of their own, crouched and crawled threateningly in the background. Meanwhile, rabbis carried surfboards across the stage.

The only real through-line in the show was Peter—his songs, his gyrating rock star persona exuding equal parts sex and self-parody ("more Brecht than Van Halen" in the eyes of Buddy Helm, who played drums for the show); and especially, as always, his death-defying acrobatics on the harp. For the many Peter Ivers supporters, collaborators, fans, and friends, watching the show that night, that was enough.

Malcolm Leo knew the show wasn't perfect, but as a producer he felt it had achieved his aim, which was showing off Peter's talent. Leo loved many of the songs Peter had written since *Peter Ivers*, knew he could rock onstage, and felt he needed a showcase that featured not only the songs but his whole aesthetic. Peter came up with the idea for a live review, and Leo became a prime mover behind getting the show made, securing investors, and putting in some money of his own. He didn't know where it would lead—the show was too far ahead of its time, he felt, to find a place on Broadway—but it was a step towards getting Peter seen by a wider audience. He knew it would not be simple, and pulling together all the necessary elements had been a struggle from the start. But Peter had come up with a great group of artists and dancers, had pounded the pavement getting the word out, and packed the house. When Leo watched him explode onto the stage, he knew his time, energy, and funds had been well-spent.

Gil Moses, whom Peter had brought on as a producer, watched the show with a somewhat more critical eye. By this time, Moses had become a celebrated director of stage and screen. He won an Obie for the Amiri Baraka play he directed after leaving Cambridge back in '69, was nominated for a Tony a few years later, and won an Emmy in '77 for directing episodes of the groundbreaking miniseries *Roots*. In addition to investing in the show, Moses helped Peter with directorial tips. (Peter had wanted Tim Mayer to direct the show, but after *Aladdin*, Mayer took the plunge he seemed to have been avoiding for over a decade. He signed on to write the book for the Broadway musical

My One and Only, music and lyrics by George and Ira Gershwin, and was unable to take the time away.) After the show, Moses confessed to an interviewer, "There were pearls, but they needed to be strung together into something."

Outside of Lucy, Harold Ramis was perhaps Peter's greatest booster at this point. Ramis impressed Buddy Helm as being extremely savvy about talent—both packaging his own, deceptively offbeat sense of humor to the mainstream and recognizing real talent in others. He saw Peter's talent and wanted to help him figure out how to tweak it to find mass-audience appeal. Ramis also struck Helm as a good friend: he showed up for all of Peter's shows, no matter where they were.

Ramis understood perhaps better than anyone the show's underlying narrative, and in describing Peter's vision for the show to *L.A. Weekly* he also summed up his own attraction to punk and new wave: "The songs could be seen as a history of people who'd come out of the '60s radicalism, been dispersed and demoralized in the seventies, and emerged as the New Wave warriors of the '80s." Ramis was more optimistic than others about the show's commercial prospects, seeing it in the context of another underdog musical that had changed the rules of the game by presenting an underground phenomenon for mainstream consumption: *Hair*. "That was a show which took something alien—hippies—and made them acceptable and pop," he told *L.A. Weekly*. He saw no reason *Vitamin Pink* could not do the same for new wave.

Peter's friends had always rooted for and rallied around him, but there seemed to be a growing consensus that he was reaching a crisis. As one after another they settled into their personal and professional niches, Peter still tread water, splashing around for a break. His work with Golde had given him a foothold in the mainstream. But as he often reminded Linda Perry, that was his day job. Perhaps more than any of them, Peter needed to succeed at his art in order to survive.

Vitamin Pink's two-night stand at the Lingerie was sold out. The guest list included not only friends and connections—names like Stuart Cornfeld, Durrie and Van Dyke Parks, Mark Canton, Linda Perry, Marty Krystall, Beverly D'Angelo, Amy Heckerling, Norman Seeff—but hot rising "baby mogul" producers Don Simpson and Jeffrey Katzenberg.

Peter seemed more ready than ever to embrace the help being offered and step into a new wave of his own. It was hidden in another *Vitamin Pink* lyric, whose personal meaning was not difficult to decode.

> *With half of my life gone*
> *And everything gone wrong,*
> *I find out I don't have you.*

LA, the Cave, 1982, 9:00 p.m.

Peter had been in the Cave two hours longer than he wanted to be. He lost track of what take they were on. But on Jove's cue he smiled wide and began again.

PETER: "On the one hand, this will intrigue and delight those with special interests to the point where total involvement will possibly guarantee their removal from society while on the other hand, we could be courting a new disaster. Network television, with all its shortcomings—

JOVE: It's interests. You're still saying inter-es

PETER [ROLLING HIS EYES]: Okay.

JOVE: From the top.

Hollywood, At Sunset. March 1, 1983, 12:00 a.m.

Peter smiled at the camera, then leaned over the wood countertop of the large restaurant kitchen and held his microphone to a cage occupied by three yellow ducks. Loud background music mixed with the din of what sounded like a large crowd; groups of stylish young people walked through the background of the shot. Behind the duck cage sat a female mannequin's naked bust.

"Hey, are you guys having a good time?" he asked the ducks, holding the mic to the cage and waiting earnestly for their response. The ducks pecked and honked. "How does it feel?" Peter asked. Two of the ducks retreated to a corner of the cage, leaving the third to brave Peter's interview. It seemed to rise to the occasion, puffing its chest and pecking at the mic before retreating coyly into its own collapsed neck. "How does it feel tonight?" Peter pressed. He smiled and looked affectionately at his guests. "Good mix?" The ducks all huddled together. "Are you having fun?" Peter asked. "That's all I care about."

At Sunset was an underground nightclub in the large kitchen of a restaurant of the same name, on Sunset Boulevard. The club attracted a hip but upscale Hollywood crowd, with its share of celebrity guests. John Belushi had been a regular until his death the year before of a drug overdose under circumstances many of his friends still considered suspicious and amid media portrayals (they agreed almost unanimously) rife with misinformation, simplification, and corruption.

(In fact, John had stopped by At Sunset on the night he died, bumping into Derf Scratch, who invited him to meet up later and play some music. Derf had noticed, and become worried, that in the previous few weeks John was experimenting with harder drugs than usual. He often worried about Belushi when he was out in LA, without a support system to give him the occasional reality check. Derf saw clearly now that his friend did not know what he was getting into. He waited for John to show up that night to play, but he never did.)

The owners of the club realized that they did not have any footage of Belushi hanging out there. That part of John's life and At Sunset's history was lost forever. Buddy Helm came up with the idea to shoot live video in the club on weekends, with dancers and DJs and variety. He would shoot continuously from Friday night until Monday dawn. He set up TV monitors around the kitchen, running all the footage from the previous week to create a trippy, self-referential effect as recurring guests watched the old video and commented on their earlier conversations, which sparked new conversations, which were recorded and displayed the following week. After doing this for about a year and a half, Helm decided to try editing the footage down into a TV show. He would call it *At Sunset*.

If it was going to be a show, it needed a host. Helm asked Peter if he was interested in coming in and doing some on-camera interviews. One of his first "audition" interviews was with Jean-Michel Basquiat, the New York artist who was infamously difficult to talk to. Helm was impressed, if not surprised, at Peter's ability to mollify Basquiat and bring out his charm. Soon Peter was shooting *At Sunset* interviews every weekend. Other visitors to the club included O'Donoghue, Timothy Leary, David Lee Roth, Shelley Duvall, Buck Henry, Bret Easton Ellis, Bananarama, writer-director Paul Schrader, and the Clash. But Helm's goal was not just to stargaze. He wanted to create and capture a sense of community. He thought Peter was the perfect man for the job and was happy to be proven right. Who else could pry an interesting interview out of not only Jean-Michel Basquiat, but a trio of ducks?

At Sunset did not interfere with Peter's *New Wave Theatre* work, though Helm sensed Jove did not like sharing his star. Earlier that night, before interrogating the ducks, Peter had been standing with a small group in the kitchen's most popular spot, the meat locker. (Over the year it had become the place to see and be seen. Belushi spent so much time there that someone had scribbled "Belushi's Room" over the doorway.) They were passing the mic, asking each other questions, and playing host, when a young, good-looking guy in a camel-toned sport jacket and dark shades stepped in and joined them. Only Peter recognized the new guest as David Jove.

A gray-haired man currently in possession of the microphone asked Jove how he was doing and held the mic to his face. Jove answered in a quiet, curt tone and stilted foreign accent of ambiguous origin. "*Good. How you? You good?*" He did not appear to be joking or playing, but actually trying to pull off a disguise. When the gray-haired man asked Jove if he knew Peter, he gave a clipped "*No*" and stood awkwardly with both hands shoved hard into his jacket pockets. Peter ventured playfully, if somewhat cautiously, into the pause. "Wait, didn't I work as your interpreter once? I think it was like— where was it—in Athens?" The gray-haired man smiled and echoed Peter appreciatively. "Athens."

Jove turned his head as if distracted by someone calling his name and walked off, deeper into the meat locker, without saying a word.

"You meet the strangest people in a cooler," the gray-haired man mused.

Despite *New Wave Theatre*'s growing popularity, many of Peter's friends sensed he was ready to move on. In his *At Sunset* footage, absent the outrageous persona, the wacky costumes, and confrontational stance, he seemed comfortable playing himself. He still asked difficult questions and tried to engage people in meaningful conversations— and found no lack of opportunities to remove his clothes—but the words, the point of view, the questions were entirely his. He talked about yoga, video, spirituality, art, theatre, sex, *New Wave Theatre*, and Van Dyke Parks, seeming to relish interacting with people. *At Sunset* gave him an opportunity to take his screen presence to the next level, in a more upscale context that held out far greater possibility for commercial success.

Rod Falconer, who had by this point reclaimed his original family name, Taylor, showed up on *At Sunset* from time to time. He and Peter had become close friends over the years and would hang out nights together, adventuring around the city in Peter's Fiat. Taylor felt this was in part because the two of them were facing a similar crossroads in their lives—namely, the need to make money and be grown-ups while also being true to themselves as artists. They decided to attack the problem head-on and together. They chose the most powerful weapon known to the culture in which they lived: a screenplay.

The treatment had Peter all over it. It was a retelling of the Alexander the Great story projected into the sci-fi future with a punk–new wave sensibility. Centered around a teenage conqueror called upon to organize the masses, it was originally given the working title *Teenager the Great*, then *Alexander the Punk*. They settled on *City of Tomorrow*.

The treatment was picked up by Warner Brothers, where Lucy now worked as a high-level exec, for $30,000, which Peter and Taylor split fifty-fifty. Even with such an auspicious beginning, a first treatment by two unknowns was likely to languish in the Hollywood purgatory known as "development." Lucy talked up Peter's talents, and the treatment was fast-tracked onto the agenda for a high-level development meeting to decide whether Warner Brothers would commission a full script.

At the same time, Peter was negotiating with Linda Perry for a songwriting contract with ATV (as opposed to advances and royalties on particular songs). More than any of his other prospects, this held the promise of modest, long-term financial stability—a guaranteed five-figure salary for three years, marking his first-ever regular paycheck—as well as access to a sophisticated recording studio for use on his own projects.

Between the screenplay, the songwriting, and the generally positive reception of *Vitamin Pink*, Peter's fortunes were shifting. Many of his friends noted that his spirits followed suit. Malcolm Leo, who had always believed in Peter's originality and admired his scrappiness, noticed that after the treatment sold, Peter walked around with a perpetual shit-eating grin. To Peter Rafelson, Peter often seemed inexplicably elated and almost hyperemotional. He had asthma, which triggered a nervous cough when he would get excited. He was coughing a lot these days.

Peter's growing list of successes did nothing to ease his frenetic drive. Some friends observed that he was pushing himself harder than ever to translate his art into a stable career. There were different theories but no consensus over what it was that seemed to goad him so mercilessly. Responding to a girlfriend worried he did not take enough time for himself, Peter protested that he had so many things to do and felt he had so little time. Some believed he was finally ready to move on and conquer a new set of life experiences: fame, fortune, and all the doors they would open. Lucy sensed that Peter was trying to prove something to her, frantically racing to make up for lost time. The idea had long been floated between them that if he became successful it might solve their problems once and for all.

Whatever the reason or complex of reasons for Peter's recent single-minded pursuit of "career," one thing was clear: thoughts of Lucy were never far from his mind. A couple of weeks before they were to pick up their second checks from Warner Brothers and hear word about the script, he asked Rod Taylor, "Should I marry Lu?"

The ducks were warming up to Peter's advances. They seemed more comfortable now, almost at ease. Despite the celebrities buzzing around him, Peter was starstruck by the little yellow birds.

Suddenly, midinterview, he became enthralled by something at the bottom of their cage. The camera, the party, the stars—everything seemed to disappear for him as he stared down into the cage and ruminated on the wonder of what he saw. He spoke into the microphone but never shifted his gaze.

"You can't see the veins in these webs, but . . . to think that there's blood coursing through those little purple rivers . . . is a pretty mind-blowing thought . . ."

After a pause, he went back into interview mode, addressing his next question to the bravest of the ducks.

"Hey—what's the meaning of life?"

The duck, which had been silent, started to sing loudly as if on cue. Peter turned to the camera and smiled. It was the most eager, and possibly the most honest answer he had ever received.

LA, the Cave, 1983, Monologue Take 26, 10:00 p.m.

Peter took a deep breath, looked away from the camera, then looked back and began.

". . . Network television with all its shortcomings at least makes some attempts at showing a variety of programs to their viewers, while the specialists' channels will allow the possibility of total withdrawal into their own favorite fantasy world. Is this progress? Some say that man's not ready, that this will only serve to separate individuals further from much needed awareness and cut them off from the solidarity and responsibility they so urgently need to get back on the road to optimum survival. Others say it could be like unloading a box of new toys on a bored kindergarten. Everyone will be so happy, there will be no more time for squabbling.

"The future security of the American people is in the hands of the entertainment programmers. What did you think about today? On behalf of our producer, All World Stage, this is your errant host avis boy Ivers wishing you an Argonaut armistice on the altar of Agnew."

Peter took off his sunglasses, stepped away from the camera, packed up his pink jacket and his patented Peter Ivers smile, said goodbye to Jove, and walked out to his car.

It was late. He had blown the entire night. And he had blown it on something that was becoming clearer and clearer was not in his, but someone else's, best *in-ter-es-t-s*.

Downtown LA, March 1, 1983, 10:30 p.m.

Dear Alan;

Missing you as always. We closed Warners Pic development deal for Peter Ivers' science fiction musical, working title "Teenager the Great"—I will write score, Rod Taylor (remember Rod Falconer?) will do screenplay. Also, to be Executive Produced by me. We'll show 'em who's boss! Also much recording activity on

songs by me and Franne Golde—I've included list on separate
page. Looking forward to our future money biz. I'll continue to
send payments as I am finally joining the establishment. Maybe
we'll lunch at the Harvard Club on me—Thanks, Alan, say hi
to Fam—

    Love, Peter

Peter set his head down on the table of his regular booth in his fa-vorite Vietnamese restaurant in Little Tokyo. It was the first time in a long while that he had good news to report, and now he was too tired to share it with anyone. He had written a letter to Alan Siegal with an update about the recent developments with his screen-writing and songwriting. Siegal had been with him from the start, on a pro-bono basis. He had always been encouraging and never made Peter feel like he was wasting his time. The prospect of taking Siegal out to lunch on his own dime was almost as exciting as finally having the means to send that fuck-you check to his father—admittedly still a ways away but suddenly less the pipe dream, the joke, it had come to seem.

He had yet to share the latest news with the one person in the world who would appreciate it the most. He went to a pay phone in the restaurant and placed a call to Brookline. More than anyone, Merle had been Peter's anchor throughout all his years of struggle and disappointment.

Now she could bask in Peter's excitement about the future that was opening before him. From the restaurant pay phone, he told her about the projects and deals and the money he stood to make. He told her about plans for a future with Lucy. "Mom," he said, "I tell you what we're going to do. Me and Lu are going to build three houses, one on either side of us. One for you, and one for Lucy's mom." While skeptical on the matter of Lucy's consent, Merle responded as she did to every big idea Peter had: "That's lovely, dear."

It was almost midnight. The restaurant, with its fluorescent green glow, was a refuge in a neighborhood that went mostly dark by 9:00 or 10:00 p.m. Peter sat back in his regular booth, completely drained. He hadn't slept much in the last few weeks—or months, or years, for that matter. He'd been going and going, and now, when things were just starting to come together, was no time to let up. Peter found him-self here so often at this time of night that the wait staff treated him as their personal houseguest. Between cleaning and sweeping and wiping everything down, they brought him his regular dinner. He took a few bites but found he was too tired even to eat. He folded his arms onto the table and put his head down again.

It wasn't only work that wore him out. Peter still kept up his intense schedule of visiting friends, mostly unannounced. Lately he'd spent a lot of time with Buell. About a month ago, Neidlinger's good friend Karen Carpenter had died of complications from anorexia. Neidlinger loved Carpenter and was extremely upset. For two weeks, Peter would stop by at Neidlinger's and sit with him at his kitchen table for hours. Sometimes Peter would tell Neidlinger about his life downtown. Each new story added to Neidlinger's growing concern that his friend had moved out to the dangerous edge of the fringe. Then Peter would go to the piano and play a new tune he was working on.

Earlier that day he had hung out with Steve Martin, who told Peter he thought he should get back together with Lucy. Peter said he didn't know, they were such different people; Martin thought he was playing it cool. Selling the treatment with Taylor was the most exciting thing that had happened to Peter in a long time, and it seemed to Martin he might be trying to distance himself from Lucy because he didn't want to feel he was getting the deal just because of her. Probably more than anyone, Martin wanted to see his two friends together. They belonged with each other, period. It seemed an obvious fact of nature. He pressed Peter: "So you're different? So what?"

As much as Martin wanted to light a fire under Peter to get Lucy back before it was too late, the thing he always admired about Peter was that no matter how much he had on his mind, he didn't sit around worrying about it. He was always thinking but never preoccupied. He was the most self-realized person Martin had ever known. He knew Peter was hurting over Lucy. But he was a grown man, and Martin didn't press him too hard.

It wasn't only local friends Peter surprised with his visits. Nancy Drew had left the NEA in Washington and become the head of an artists' foundation in New York. Peter remained a lifeline to her, calling frequently and playing his new songs. Sometimes he just showed up. Only a week ago, on a visit to New York he had appeared spontaneously at the door of her office and asked if she wanted to catch dinner.

Her office was on the sixth floor of a fancy old building with a beautiful antique spiral staircase. Later that evening, when he left, Peter couldn't resist the opportunity to experience it. She watched him descend, following the old staircase's elegant curl. Part of the way down, he stopped, turned, and looked up at her. He waved. "Nance, I will love you forever." She said it back.

A few days ago Peter had spoken on the phone with Tim Mayer, whose long-awaited Broadway debut had not gone as planned. The much-heralded Gershwin musical was scheduled to open in two months, directed and choreographed by Tommy Tune and starring Twiggy. Mayer wrote the book and would be credited as such, but throughout rehearsals, his erratic unpleasant behavior had made enemies of nearly everyone involved with the production, a number of whom he genuinely admired. Mike Nichols was brought in to help smooth things over, but Mayer managed to alienate him, too. Finally, Nichols told Mayer something that many others of lesser stature had undoubtedly wanted to tell him many times before. "Tim, we know you're the smartest person in the room. Now shut up." Mayer was banished from the set.

Peter woke up to the sound of the vacuum cleaner grinding up and down the Vietnamese restaurant's carpeted foyer. He had fallen asleep next to his unfinished noodles. He wrapped up his dinner and went to the register to pay, but found that his wallet was gone. He scoured the booth, then the entire restaurant floor. The whole staff joined in the search. They even checked the vacuum bag. Nothing.

Outside, the streets were empty. He tried to trace as precisely as possible how he'd come the short way from his loft to the restaurant. He knew it was a lost cause. A wallet on the sidewalk of Japantown was piranha food. Not that there was much in it to mourn. He had only really had enough for dinner. Luckily he was a regular; they would take an IOU.

He decided to give up for the night and go home. Tomorrow he was getting paid, a big check for his half of the treatment with Taylor. He wouldn't need anything to hold money in until then.

phone calls

MERLE IVERS

"Lucy had the operator interrupt the call. I guess she said that it was an emergency. The minute she said, 'Merle, are you sitting down?' that was it."

PAULA WEINSTEIN

"Well, it was Harold that called Lucy."

JOE DANTE, editor

"I do remember standing underneath Lucy's window when she heard the news. I might have been with Howard Smith working on the *Twilight Zone* movie. I'll never forget it, it was just a horrible cry of pain. We knew it was her office. Then later we found out why."

HOWARD SMITH

"I was walking towards the postproduction offices, which were let's say, the equivalent of two blocks away on the lot, and I heard this scream, it was just chilling. I just thought to myself, That's Lucy screaming, and I ran into the executive office building, ran upstairs, ran into her office, and her assistant, who I knew—I said, 'Was that Lucy?' And she said yes."

VAN DYKE PARKS

"I remember clearly getting the phone call from Steve Goldman, the guy that was producing my record. So Steve told me. So I put down the phone and I remember being in such a state of shock, because a man that I had trusted and had such high regard for, my producer, is telling me something that is absolutely incredulous, incredible."

BUELL NEIDLINGER

"I was going to play that night at McCabe's with Van Dyke Parks. We were at McCabe's rehearsing."

VAN DYKE PARKS

"And I hung up the phone and I dialed rotary, Peter, and I got Peter's answering service, Peter's voice. I remember hearing his voice and leaving my voice because, if it was so, I wanted my voice to be on his tape, and if it wasn't so, I wanted him to call me back. And then I realized that it might be so, and I called him back, and this time I recorded his voice so I could save it and have it always."

ANNE RAMIS

"Tim [Mayer] said he came home and there were all these phone calls, and he immediately got alarmed, you know, something big. And he was wondering why he didn't hear from Peter."

FRANNE GOLDE

"Peter was supposed to meet me there for the session, and it was very unlike him not to show up. I kept calling and calling, and when I got home I got many messages, on my machine, asking if I'd talked to Peter. I remember when I heard about it, I screamed. I didn't know that was in me, like my reaction, it was almost like this primal scream that came out of me. I was sitting on the floor and my answering machine was on the floor with all these messages."

DOUG MARTIN

"I was supposed to film in his loft, and I was calling on the telephone, and there was no answer. So I was in the valley with my brother, making calls from his office, then saying, 'Fucker, where are you? I've got all these people.' I was frustrated. Then my brother made some calls and found out why no one was answering the phone. I drove home in shock. My brother went down to the loft."

ROD TAYLOR

"I spoke to Peter many times that last night, and he was really excited because we were going to make that movie together. I flew back the next day from Texas, got off the plane, walked to the baggage claim area, and my wife and a very close friend of mine were standing there. They were acting strange and said they had something to tell me. It hit me like a lightning bolt. It was the last thing I ever expected."

TIM HUNTER

"I was in New York working on a project with Diane Keaton. I was in New York when Peter called to tell me Doug died, and I was in New York when I got the call from Howard Smith."

NANCY DREW

"I came in to do an article on LA architects and *Art Forum*. I flew in, I was going to see him that night for dinner, then I got the phone call, and again, it was a phenomenon which I'd never experienced. The world shifts and you're no longer in sync, your timing is gone, and it was just mind-altering."

PETER RAFELSON

"They found my phone number in his belongings. I was the first to find out."

* * *

STEVE MARTIN

"When you see a movie from Universal Studios, you see the globe, the world, and then the word 'Universal' comes flying around it in an equatorial manner and then rests across the planet, stretching across the screen, and on the planet earth, it says *ivers*, and Peter liked that. He would say, 'Look! Ivers covers the world.' So every time we saw a movie, it would be like it was his."

HAROLD RAMIS

"What is tantalizing, and I don't usually think in terms of what if, but if Doug, Peter, and Belushi had survived, what would they be doing, you know?"

MICHAEL SHAMBERG

"They were the first wave of Harvard guys to come out here. You had Tim the playwright, Doug the *National Lampoon*, Peter the musician. Trying to take over Hollywood. Peter may well have been successful, but the cocoon of that gave rise to a lot of creative people and introduced the smart people into Hollywood comedy. You always wonder how that would travel over time. We'll never know."

MARK CANTON

"Music, videos, he wanted to direct a movie, and there's no doubt that he could have been a real force, because he understood the language of cinema."

BUELL NEIDLINGER

"I often thought that he might be a Jean Cocteau, for instance. He would make movies. I guess he was trying to achieve some kind of vision about moviemaking. Nobody would ever really let him in. I always thought the reason that he couldn't be seen was because certain people didn't want him to be seen. He couldn't hook on to the right guy. Can you imagine Peter teaming up with Doug Kenney?"

VAN DYKE PARKS

"He would have evolved, he would have nurtured larger creative work, more collaborative, into film and so forth. He would have grown into a more governmental position in a way. His ideas were that vast and numerous enough, by all odds he would have hit an ultimate commercial success with his ideas that he didn't enjoy in his life. And he left behind an archive of ideas that really were brilliant, but never fully realized. It is tough stuff."

BARBARA SMITH

"I think it's also amazing that when you look back at this stuff, the history of the culture, before the internet, what would it be like now if Peter had the internet? Peter would be this big star, if you really think about it. When you look at the stuff Peter did, it's like so innocent culturally and media-wise, compared to today."

MERLE IVERS

"It's amazing to me, when I look at his output, because he was only out there for twelve or thirteen years. The connections and the things he did, and the things he thought of to do that didn't get done."

ROD TAYLOR

"It was a very different atmosphere that prevailed. I think that one of the reasons we all mourned so deeply was an intuitive recognition that it was the end of an era as well. Peter was definitely a spawn of the '60s and '70s, where expectations were very high. Artists were heroes and they were involved in a cultural and moral revolution, a quest, et cetera. It was all on a great, grand, heroic scale."

JEFF EYRICH

"There was a large community around him, but when he left, it fractured, everyone went their own ways. He was really the catalyst for the whole thing. I don't run into hardly anybody from those times."

PAUL MICHAEL GLASER

"He laid the groundwork, and a lot of people followed."

NANCY DREW

"People are born with a certain degree of magic, and he was born with an overload. What he did is take so many steps in new directions and knew no boundaries, connected all the dots and brought us together."

SPIT STIX

"I think Peter is a crucial icon that has been overlooked. Peter and John [Belushi] were maître'ds for music."

MICHAEL SHAMBERG

"Everyone comes into Hollywood with their peers and because it is looking for the new, you and your peers come to offer the new. There was a whole new wave of comedy and talent in town. As you get older, some of them fall by the wayside, some become very successful, that's how Hollywood works. These guys had everything, you know. They had the brains, they had the talent. I'm always just looking for what's happening now—which is what we were doing then."

VAN DYKE PARKS

"Peter Ivers is somebody who matters to me because of his very character. I thought of Doug Kenney in the same view. A heavyweight with a substantial understanding of what his opportunity demanded. He wanted to do something permanent."

ROD TAYLOR

"There was a universality to his spiritualness. Consequently, he will live on beyond this world. I think we will all meet up again. If I'm wrong, none of us will know about it."

ANNE RAMIS

"It's never seemed real that he's gone. In fact, having known him seems like a dream."

STEVE MARTIN

"I like to think of Pete being out of town, on tour, on the road. It's just a lot easier that way."

NANCY DREW

"I would have loved to see him have some great financial success. Then we would have seen him relax into Peter the man."

HOWARD CUTLER

"I felt then that his courage to live totally for his music had carried him into a deep ocean, where one becomes oneself totally. With no excuses, no blame, and no refuge close at hand. All that he was trading in for a shot at the thing itself: the chance to be living, on target, with the truth."

LUCY FISHER

"From the minute I met him, I was permanently and unceasingly drawn to Peter. His face, his humor, his physicality, his tenderness, his personal mission to make every day a surprise. His penchant for poetics, delight in talent, constant originality, and disciplined devotion to his artistic outpourings. Even the ache that accompanied his edginess. I loved it all."

MERLE IVERS

"I had fun with my kids. There are so many periods of time where the three of us are sitting there being hysterical with tears running down our bodies because he would do something strange, or he would do something funny, or I would do something funny. It's just . . . when you're happy and free with whomever is with you, things happen."

══════════════════*case book part 8*

DAVID CHARBONNEAU
"They called me in, Paula [Weinstein] said they've been rattling the cages of people in Justice, on the federal level. Somebody made a call in again to LAPD and they're going to kick it up a little bit, and I'm supposed to call Petrovsky. So I called him that day and said, 'How about eight o'clock next morning?' And he said, 'Fine.'"

KEN YAS
"David's moment of greatest success, after years of struggling to be taken seriously—even though he argued that it didn't matter—was jeopardized by Peter threatening to leave the show. And three hours later . . ."

DAVID CHARBONNEAU
"So I go back to Rafelson, say, 'I need to talk to you.' I'm starting to be really blunt with people now because I'm frustrated and need to get to the bottom of this stuff. Rafelson and I were talking, I laid it out to him, and I told him, 'I know some people are telling me everything they think they know about David, and I know some people aren't telling me everything, and I think we started on the right foot, but I think you know more.' He got real quiet, said, 'Wait here for a second.'"

HAROLD RAMIS
"Imagine, surrounded by your friends, everyone close to you, and knowing that one of them could have killed him . . . I mean, how do you live with that?"

DAVID CHARBONNEAU
"He comes back in the room and goes, 'Here.' And I go, 'What's this?' And it's just a standard diary. I asked if he read it and he said, 'Yes, I wasn't sure what to do with it.' I said, 'Where'd you get it?' And he said, 'I

took it [from the crime scene] when I went that day or the next day.'

"That whole night I had a friend of mine follow me around because I think I'm dealing with a murderer here, I think he's in this group of people, I'm not sure who or what yet, but I think I'm getting closer, and I think they're all talking about me getting closer because I'm telling them to stop bullshitting me. I'm almost hanging out with these people in these circles, and I know I'm a point of almost gossip amongst them. They were all talking to each other. They were all theatrical people, it's a play, it's going on now, it's performance art. It was real! It was late by the time I got out and I said to my guy, 'Alright, you have to put the damn light on and read this [diary] to me on the way home.'

"Some of it was stream of consciousness, some of it was outright gibberish. It was Peter writing in his diary [paraphrasing from memory], '*There were these guys in San Francisco, and I had to go up there, and we were trying to make a deal.* There was a 'we,' which is where the nexus with David [Jove] comes in. I surmised [Jove] knew a lot about drugs, just from the way he acted. '*The money is important right now to help me do things that we want to do in the future, it matters a lot to the people around me that I do this.*' I remember, he was speaking about being in the room with five guys, and he said, '*This is the only problem I had, these five guys. I was afraid of these people, but—*' and again he was playing both sides—'*I'd have to deal with these people, I'd make money here, it's going to be good money, but I'm going to do a lot of things in my career that are very important and could make me a lot of money.*' "

PETER RAFELSON

"His life was just risk. From the projects he developed, to the music he sang, and the people he hung out with. I'm talking about gangs in the 'hood, artists downtown, to the highest echelon of intellectual and Hollywood icons across the board. He's one of the few guys that ran in just about every circle. And he was fearless, and maybe innocent to a fault. He was never intimidated."

DAVID CHARBONNEAU

"It wasn't a very long diary, maybe fifty pages of writing, and it was very recent, all within the last year, and not daily. There were other references to David, more or less, *'We have to do some parting of the ways here, it is difficult for me, but I know it's the right thing to do. I think of my mortality—'* I remember that term—*'I think of my mortality, I think of what I'm supposed to be next, I know I'm not supposed to be doing what I'm doing now, and I know I need to concentrate more.'* There was talk there about concentration of the career, going in one path and sticking to something to see if it came to fruition, instead of all the different sources."

PETER RAFELSON

"Well, it's possible that, with Peter closing the deal with William Morris [the talent agency representing him on his screenplay with Rod Taylor] and all, that he called off the desperation of doing something else, and that could have in fact been the problem. Like, he was actually finally making his dream come true, and any desperate moves or bullshit he was involved in prior was probably going to be cut off."

DAVID CHARBONNEAU

"I'm driving three hours to get home and go to bed so I can meet Petrovsky back at eight o'clock in the morning. I got home, stashed the diary, slept for three hours, woke up, and went to Petrovsky. And he asks, 'What've you got?' And I said, 'I've got a lot, I got this [diary] last night.' So I said, 'Alright, if you want my theory, here it is. My theory is David Jove psychologically, David Jove with opportunity, David Jove for financial reasons, David Jove because Peter was his alter ego and leaving him, and throw in this Jove [Ecstasy] deal. Peter Ivers was scared.'

"I was dumped off the case at about two in the afternoon. Same day."

LUCY FISHER

"After about a year, I could no longer withstand the agony having my memories of Peter constantly polluted with thoughts of his death, so I quit trying to solve it. I imagined myself walking down a corridor, and when I passed a door that held images of that final night, I would just walk by—no longer opening the door, but instead trying to focus only on thoughts of his life."

DAVID CHARBONNEAU

"I only talked to Peter's mom once. She was not my client. Weinstein/Fisher was the nexus of my employ through the Fonda connection, and I never thought I had a need to communicate anything to the Ivers family."

KEN YAS

"It was a halfhearted investigation. I don't know why they kind of deep-sixed it, I really don't. That was disturbing."

DAVID CHARBONNEAU

"The new detective team was in. I was never asked for findings. I never spoke to either one of them again. *Chinatown*. That's it."

DETECTIVE HANK PETROVSKY

"It's always frustrating when you can't solve a case. And it's not like we get extra money for solving a case; we just did this to get the asshole off the street. It's a cat-and-mouse game and we want to win. With Jove we never got to the point of saying he was the guy. Lucy probably said, 'Look at this guy,' and we did. I can't remember what he said or how many times I talked to him, but we did investigate him as a possible suspect, but we called him a person of interest, because we really didn't have anything."

PETER RAFELSON

"I brought it up once or twice, and I can tell you that I was afraid of Jove thinking that I was accusatory of him, even though he may not have done it. But Jove was also a dear friend, a close friend, and the fact that he claims he blanked out and has no memory of that night doesn't exactly corroborate his innocence. I asked him what happened, he told me he couldn't tell me because he blanked out that night and had no recollection. It doesn't mean he's guilty. The only thing Jove stood to lose was a star for his show. I think that Jove also was a dark enough character that he almost relished the ambiguity, you know? I don't honestly know, in my heart of hearts, that I'd point to him."

STEVE MARTIN

"I had sat at Lucy's place with Jove and other people with the detective. To say I feel foolish isn't really enough, because it goes so far beyond that. No one that I know, or knew, was really capable of something like that. It flipped me out, it made me question everything. Like how could I have not recognized that? That's unfortunately sort of where the road leads. It is such a monstrous accusation. Can you imagine saying that and then being wrong?"

Well, with the Chevy Chase fiasco [on The Top] and Andy Kaufman the replacement host dying a mere two weeks after he did my show, and a couple of other well-placed deaths has caused a certain secret stigma about me and working with me—this is no joke. Having me considered, even for a moment as being the perpetrator is tantamount to putting the cap on an already bad scene. . . . My valiant, truth-seeking efforts seem to be turning against me to the point where I could easily be seen in the light of someone overly concerned with their image etc. Give me a break. Of course I'm concerned.
—*David Jove, draft letter to an editor of*
L.A. Weekly

DAVID CHARBONNEAU

"And what did the new, higher level of cops do with that case? What did the hot-shot homicide guys do? Nothing. And this diary was never found. Never in evidence, never, nothing."

HAROLD RAMIS

"How could they come up with nothing?"

* * *

"We checked in with each other over the years. We had some regard for one another. David Jove was a strong Spirit and an original man."
 —Leonard Cohen

DAVID CHARBONNEAU

"David would call every five years out of the blue. The last time I talked to him, David was still throwing all the theories out there and saying, 'It's too bad no one will ever know, and don't you feel they pulled one over on you.' Just fucking with me. I just said, 'You know, David, there's no statute of limitation on murder,' and that's the last thing I said to him, there was no response. It was a game, always a game. Not long before he died he called me."

ANNE RAMIS

"[Jove] would answer the phone with, 'Did you kill Peter Ivers?' "

PETER RAFELSON

"I wish I had the perfect ending, but maybe the fact is that there is no perfect ending. Whether we know or we never know isn't really the answer. The answer is that Peter knew, and that his life is the answer."

DETECTIVE CLIFFORD SHEPARD

"People want something resolved. They have certain beliefs, and to them, that's what happened, no matter what evidence we show. We can only do what we can do. Did Jove do it? Again, I don't know. Will we ever prove that anyone did it? I don't know. Could someday, someone walk into the police station and confess?

"It has happened."

* * *

David Jove died of cancer on September 26, 2004.

On his deathbed he made no confession, only a plea to his friends to protect the work he and Peter had created.

chapter 10

What Is the Meaning of Life?

I have a childlike view of what is possible and I have tremendous powers of concentration and understanding, which I apply to making my dreams come true. I yearn for love and acceptance, desire to be in harmony with the universe, to know and be known, to explore and adventure. My goal is to change the world. I'm a magician and a leader, and I help people to let go of their rigid frightened viewpoints and to see the common elements and threads enmeshing human existence with the cosmos. I'd also like to bring rock and roll to the White House. I'm a knight of virtue and sex—no, make that I'd like a night of virtue and sex.

> —*Peter Ivers,* American Bachelors Registry *(a compendium of interviews with America's "most eligible" bachelors)*

A silhouetted circus
Introduced by phantom fingers
A hard ringmaster ordering the show
Supplied a comic opera
That commanded my attention
While evening marched it shrinking down the wall.
I saw the autumn come down
And turn the evening golden,
The harvest moon seduced me in his beam,
And you were backdrop
To a private song recital
An audience of one, that wanted me.
> —*"Audience of One" from* Terminal Love *(<>) song #10*

LA, Peter's Loft, March 2, 1983, 9:00 a.m.

The rain started lightly at first, comforting taps against the glass, but now it smacked Peter's oversized loft windows in torrential bursts. A matte of gray cloud smothered the sky. Peter jumped out of bed and checked his clock. Instead of sleeping when he returned from the restaurant, he had stayed up most of the night. Back at the loft, with his recording equipment always out and ready, he had not been able to resist the temptation to make a demo tape of one of his new songs. As usual, he'd crashed out in his clothes.

The meeting was in Hollywood in one hour. If he left right now he could make it, but first he needed to go back to the restaurant and see if his wallet had turned up. It hadn't. He spent nearly an hour retracing his steps. Nothing.

He arrived at the meeting an hour late. It was okay, the meeting really wasn't about him anyway; he was only playing matchmaker. He had put together Alan Sterne, a midlevel producer with whom he sometimes explored the darker corners of downtown LA, and David Jove. Peter had the idea to put the two of them together on a movie based on *New Wave Theatre*. He had little interest in the project; in fact, one of main goals at the moment was to disentangle himself from Jove. Setting him up on something new and exciting that he would see as advancing his career was the surest way to do that. Then David wouldn't need Peter anymore. Jove only cared about people when he needed them.

Despite the show's growing momentum and exposure, Peter was done with *New Wave Theatre*. Not because of Jove's megalomaniacal bullying (though he certainly wouldn't miss it). Peter's own work was coming together. It was time to move on.

Unfortunately, between Peter's lateness and talk about losing his wallet, not much business got done. As Sterne was leaving, he asked Peter if he needed to borrow any money. This gave Peter a welcome opportunity to share the news about selling his screenplay. In fact, he told Sterne, he was picking up a fat check from his agent later that day for the *City of Tomorrow* treatment. Tomorrow the executives at Warner Brothers would be meeting to decide whether to commission a script. If they did, it would mean another $100,000 for Peter and Rod Taylor.

Peter's next stop was to be the William Morris Agency to pick up his check. Just thinking about it made him want to celebrate, and wanting to celebrate made him want to have a friend to share the joy with. He called Peter Rafelson and asked if he wanted to run some errands. Rafelson heard the excitement in Peter's voice. They agreed for Peter to come pick him up at the Rafelsons' house in Beverly Hills.

Beverly Hills, 12:30 p.m.

Before leaving for William Morris, Peter asked Rafelson to play him a tape of a song they had started writing with Franne Golde the week before. It sounded good. They jumped in the car, and Peter turned to Rafelson with his infectious smile.

"You know where we're going?" he asked.

It was a silly question. Hollywood was the living room Peter Rafelson grew up in.

"Well, then: Let us march forth!" Peter crowed.

LA, William Morris Agency, 1:00 p.m.

Peter emerged from the agency waving the check like a flag he was ready to plant in the ground. Rafelson got it: this was uncharted territory. He knew how long Peter had struggled just to stay afloat. He knew that in the last year Peter had hit up a number of his friends for personal loans; he knew because he was one of them. He took Peter directly to the bank, where he deposited the check, keeping only $45 for himself. The rest would have to go towards paying off debt.

Over Rafelson's protests, Peter insisted on using some of his new money to treat his friend to lunch. At a chichi bistro on Melrose, they talked about the missing wallet. Rafelson said he thought it was symbolic. Peter had spent the last year throwing everything he had into transforming his life. It was all culminating for him today, with this first check. Maybe, Rafelson mused, the universe was trying to tell him he needed a new way of holding all the new money he was going to make. After all, his wallet held his identity—maybe that meant he was ready to embrace a new one?

Peter had his own theory: that his lost wallet symbolized his uncertainty about making money. Really, he didn't care about money at all. The less you needed, the less obligated you were to other people, the more control you had. Yet increasingly he had come to realize how much the opposite was also true: how much he *needed* money in order to do his thing at all. He found himself trapped inside a nasty paradox. Maybe his subconscious was rebelling, trying to expel the money virus before it could take hold.

Back in the car, after paying the check and stuffing the change into his pocket, Peter seemed intent on resolving the ambivalence once and for all.

"We're doing it," he told Rafelson. "Fuck 'em all. It's been too long, but we deserve what we're getting. We're going to the top!"

Rafelson offered to drive them downtown, but Peter wanted to make one more stop. They zoomed off down the Hollywood streets slick and dark with oil and rain.

They went to a bookstore where Peter bought a copy of his favorite novel, *Dune*. Then he pulled out a pen and quickly scribbled an inscription.

He snapped the book shut, handed it to Rafelson, and said, "Thank you."

This is what it was like being with Peter, Rafelson thought, totally unpredictable one moment to the next. Before he could read the inscription, Peter urged him towards the car.

"Later," he said. "No time!"

They were off again, back to the Rafelsons' to get Peter's car. They drove downtown separately through the heavy wind and rain.

Little Tokyo, 2:00 p.m.

Back in Little Tokyo, they spent a few hours retracing Peter's steps from the night before. Still no sign of the wallet. Rafelson thought this proved his point: it was time for Peter to get a new wallet to go with his new life. They gave up on the search. Rafelson thanked Peter for the book, and they went over their studio plans for tomorrow. Peter disappeared into his loft.

Back in his car, Rafelson remembered that Peter had scribbled something on the inside cover of the novel. He opened it and read the inscription.

"Every decision you make is a chance to be a hero."

LA, Recording Studio, 5:00 p.m.

Franne Golde was in the studio preparing background tracks for tomorrow's session. During the last few weeks, a number of her and Peter's songs had been picked up by big-name recording artists. Tomorrow they were recording with Brookes Arthur, a big producer who'd worked with Phil Spector and Carole King, and Junko Yagami, a Japanese rock star who had signed on to do one of their songs. Golde was antsy with excitement. It always amazed her how cool Peter was about this sort of thing; when it came to collaboration, nothing fazed him. Making great music with great musicians had always been the easy part for Peter. Selling it was where he'd stumbled, until now.

Peter arrived at the studio just in time to hear a demo of Junko Yagami singing their song, "He's My Kind." It was so exciting even Peter couldn't completely keep his cool.

"We're happening," he said to Golde in the voice of someone trying to convince himself he is not dreaming. "This is it."

To Linda Perry, who was also in the studio, Peter looked positively wide-eyed. Though he never showed it, the years of commercial failure clearly had taken the legs out from under his self-confidence. Time after time, Peter had made music he felt certain the masses would devour—he had thought of *Terminal Love* as an album of teeny-bopper hits teenage girls would chew up like bubblegum. With each new attempt, his instincts had been proven wrong. Now, everything he wrote with Golde was getting snapped up by stars and climbing the charts, and he had no idea why.

"Wow," he sometimes would say to Perry, seeming a bit dazed. "People really seem to like it."

In the studio, Golde noticed that Peter was more lighthearted, less frazzled than she had seen him over the past year. He talked excitedly about the new publishing deal, tomorrow's session with Junko and Arthur. He spoke with Perry about the possibility, perhaps as part of the new contract, of finishing *Nirvana Cuba* and making it his next album. They confirmed the details for tomorrow's session, and Peter was off.

The night is bright as the day is white
And you think it's made for us,

But the people deep who've been asleep
Are surely waking up.
And before I turn into dust
I'd like to see that world
I'd like to meet that girl
I must . . .
Girls of the third world
Take me to your leader.
—Nirvana Cuba: *"Girls of the Third World"*
(<>) song #11

LA, Marco's Restaurant, 8:00 p.m.

After finishing a quiet dinner with one of his yoga teachers at his favorite macrobiotic restaurant, Peter called Lucy. They still spoke frequently, still talked about what they should and would do, how and if they might work things out. They made an appointment to see a couples counselor to help them sort through it all and come to some resolution. Lucy had gotten sick, and they'd had to cancel the appointment. They had planned to see each other tonight, but Lucy still wasn't feeling well. Peter was anxious to know what she thought about the treatment. She told him she was only ten pages in. Peter said he would call again in a few hours, then immediately dialed Rod Taylor, who was working on a movie set in Dallas, Texas.

"Okay, she's got it, she's reading it, she's ten pages in," Peter told Taylor.

"Thanks for the blow by blow," Taylor said. But Peter was saving the best for last. Mark Canton had just read the treatment, liked it, and was going to suggest Warner Brothers commission a full screenplay. If he and Lucy both endorsed it, they stood a very good chance. They buzzed with the sense of a new future just coming into reach and agreed to touch base later so Peter could give Rod another on-the-hour news flash.

"By the way, this is a cool movie I'm doing," Taylor said. "You should get down here, try to get a part." Peter said he would love to be in the movie and would try to come down. Knowing Peter, Taylor would not have been surprised if he showed up the next morning for breakfast on the set.

LA, Howard and Barbara Smith's House, 9:00 p.m.

Peter decided to round out his day with a drop-in at the Smiths. His first home in California, it was the place in LA he'd felt most comfortable since leaving Laurel Canyon. He chatted with Barbara for a while, and when Howard arrived, Peter popped in a demo tape of new songs he had written. He told them about the big-name singers who would soon be crooning Golde-Ivers tunes. To Howard and Barbara, Peter was calmer than they had seen him in a long time. Usually he paced the room, stood on his head, dropped into yoga positions, recited mantras, and phoned home to check for messages. He was always running, even when standing in one place. They were not used to him just talking and sitting still like he was tonight.

He called Lucy again. She had read the treatment. "A little dark," she said, but she liked it. Peter told her he had rescheduled their counseling appointment for this coming Sunday. The truth was that Lucy was not particularly in a hurry to make any final decisions about their relationship. She was enjoying her life and exploring things with Doug in New York. The therapist had been Peter's idea. He missed her. One thing they could agree on, things between them were not clear and not resolved. They said they would speak again tomorrow after the meeting on *City of Tomorrow*.

Peter collected his demos from the Smiths' tape player, thanked them, and said good night. He left around 11:30, with only one more stop before heading back to the loft.

LA, the Cave, midnight

Peter pulled into the alleyway behind David Jove's Cave. It was the last place he wanted to end his day, but he had told Jove he would come by to record a new monologue for the next episode of the show.

Peter slipped into his pink sequined dinner jacket and took his place on the stool in front of the dollar-fifty, dime store planet map backdrop. Jove sat in the darkness behind the camera ready to bark directions, corrections, and the occasional sarcastic joke.

It was a familiar scene, to say the least.

"Ready?"

"Go."

"Hi, video pals, welcome to New Wave Theatre. *Have you ever imagined that the ocean was calling your name or that clouds were spelling out messages for you alone? Guess again, because almost any really frustrated gherkin can hallucinate a mind twister from shackle land. But it takes real blend of vision to not see yourself as being ridiculous, it takes real certainty if you have a dream to resist the doubting opinion of the dull at heart. There's not a moment to waste on anything that prevents us from the richness of our own foreverness. So slap your face, you mental case, and bite your back 'cause nothing can make you anything but what you already are. There is nothing like a believer to believe in believing. Thinking was meant to prevent, not predict. Hey, what are friends for? Enjoy the show."*

Peter nailed it on the first take. Then he told Jove he was quitting the show.

As it dawned on him that Peter might actually be serious, Jove blanched. Then he yelled. Then he raged. Then he pleaded. He told Peter he could not leave. They had worked too hard, and now they were in the perfect position to take off. They were a team, and this was not just a show but a movement, and Peter was the face and the voice of the movement. He started in on his favorite subject—truth—but Peter knew all the words by heart. He had said them all, again and again, in take after take after take. Jove said Peter should go home and sleep on it. They would work it all out. Peter knew he did not need sleep. He told Jove his decision was final, but if he wanted to talk again tomorrow he could give him a call.

Then he slid into his Fiat, onto rain-slicked Fairfax, back towards home to end the night.

Peter's Loft, 2:45 a.m.

Back home Peter picked up the phone and dialed Laurie Riley, a woman he had been getting to know from the *At Sunset* crowd. He apologized for calling so late. She wasn't sleeping. He said that although he felt wide awake, he was going to stay in, meditate, and get ready for tomorrow, which already had arrived. He had a big recording session with Franne, big plans for Nirvana Cuba, a big video shoot with Doug Martin, big news waiting from Lucy and Mark and Warner Brothers. There had been some talks with the director Tony Scott about doing something with *Vitamin Pink*. He told Laurie he would call her in the next couple of days and said goodnight.

Peter sat on his bed. Next to the bed, on the floor, was his journal. Recently he had been recording his dreams, and they were shot through with anxiety and dread. Interspersed with the dreams were agonizing entries about pressing decisions he needed to make, pros and cons, open questions about his future. But tonight, finally, the questions had been resolved, the decisions made, the dread defeated, at least for now. He left the journal in its place on the floor.

Peter was exhausted—he had been on his feet for nineteen hours. He had been wide awake, pounding the pavement, for the better part of fourteen years. It had been a big day, and tomorrow held the possibility to be even bigger. Despite the crushing fatigue, his mind raced (. . . *a real artist, only this time I have a plan, it's gonna work, no more mistakes, no more detours and diddling and no more Mister Nice Guy, I'm Peter Ivers and I take shit from no man, be it giant or midget, producer or director, be it television, music or film . . . Rod and I can knock this thing out and it will be huge, a new cinematic form, the revival of the musical, but can't call it that, but it still comes down to getting the girl . . . did Alexander get the girl? Did the girl get him? Alexander has to get serious too, is that what I'm doing, getting serious, growing up? Never . . .*)

He sat on the edge of the bed and slipped into the day's third and final meditation—that boundless quiet that held the only respite from his demons, the only place he ever truly felt safe. Moving into it was like entering a refuge, coming out often a bumpy, bruising ride. But now, as he opened his eyes from the infinite and found himself back within the four walls of his loft, the transition was seamless, he was not met there by the dark taunting faces of his fears. Today, at least, there were no demons waiting for him on his return to waking life.

Perhaps this was because he had been living, more and more, in line with a call he often used to stir his collaborators, his troops, into action. "We are an army, flags unfurled, racing toward the sunset." Though the sun had set many hours before and would rise only several hours hence, as he adjusted to consciousness even the bare walls of his loft seemed suffused with a warm glow.

Surveying the space from the edge of his bed, he found himself surrounded by his life's work, a comforting hodgepodge of trinkets, clothing, recording equipment, papers, art, photos, audio and video-tapes. His pink sequined dinner jacket, tossed carelessly over a chair across the room, formed a glitter tent over the seat. On the floor lay some goofy snapshots of Peter and Kenney they had taken at a photo booth years earlier. His many tapes, reels of demos stacked in towers according to a logic known only to Peter, told the story of over a de-cade of creative effort. Everything was in its right place and poised to propel him now into an exciting new place of his own.

As anxious as he was for tomorrow to start, Peter could not keep his eyes open. He teetered between fits of conscious thought and wak-ing dreams. In his normal habit, he didn't bother to take his clothes off or turn out the lights before lying down. Outside his window the rain poured down in relentless violent sheets, loud but constant, a rhyth-mic tapping on tin. Peter closed his eyes and fell asleep.

"That's right . . . *Terminal Love*, and a fatal
case of rock and roll. But I wouldn't say I'm suffering.
It's more like, like being in heaven."

—*Peter Ivers,* Billboard, *July 27, 1974*

MERLE IVERS

"I'll never forget, the last call I got from Tim was on Mother's Day, after Peter had died. He called me, and I think it was two years later. He said, 'I was just sitting here and I realized, I haven't got a mother, and you haven't got a son, so I'm calling to wish you a happy Mother's Day.' "

I have just called to say that I am the last remaining Musketeer.
They should make a new candy bar for me.
The One Musketeer.

—*Tim Mayer, from a phone booth somewhere in New England,
around 1988, shortly before dying of cancer.*

Still in Heaven

Peter's album *Knight of the Blue Communion* has been rereleased on HUX Records. His other albums can be found sprinkled throughout the internet, from eBay to obscure Japanese imports. The masters of each album are stored in the Epic and Warner Bros. vaults, waiting to be heard. An artist-in-residency was founded in Peter's name at Harvard, inspired by the residency Peter and Tim shared in 1981. After Peter's death, enough donations were made from friends, family, and fans to keep the residency going for as long as Harvard exists. In the last four years, Peter and Lynch's song "In Heaven Everything Is Fine" was played live round the world to crowds of 40,000 at a time, a staple of the Pixies reunion tour. Merle Ivers still receives monthly royalty checks for this song, and, to her amazement, many others. "Where do they come from?" she says. "How do they find him?"

One afternoon in March of 1983, I was driving to work listening to the radio. The broadcaster reported that there had been a murder in the area of Third Street and San Pedro. The victim was involved with cable television, in a new field of musical entertainment. I had recently signed up for cable and would occasionally watch the music stations. I thought whoever came up with the idea was a genius.

I also had two questions that ran through my mind. Why was he living in an area just bordering Skid Row, an area occupied by the down and out, dope fiends, alcoholics, and people suffering from mental illness? I thought anyone involved with the entertainment industry could live almost anywhere else. I was familiar with the location. I had been a foot beat cop there a couple of years earlier. Violence was not an unknown.

Then my second question: How are the detectives going to solve it? I did not know that they didn't. It wasn't until August 10, 2006, twenty-three years later, that Josh Frank called me and inquired about the status of the investigation. That was when I learned that the murder of Peter Ivers had not been solved. At that time I was assigned to the Los Angeles Police Department's Cold Case Homicide Unit. Our assignment was to review the unsolved murders and attempt to solve them. Since 1960, there were approximately nine thousand unsolved murders in the City of Los Angeles.

As things progressed, I learned more about Peter Ivers. He was a brilliant, well-educated man. He had friends and family who cared for him and loved him. He was part of the nouveau wave that was sweeping the cable networks in the early '80s. And, unlike many of the victims in downtown Los Angeles, Peter Ivers was and is missed. When I have a case involving an innocent victim, I wonder if they had lived, what would be different today? I am certain that Peter Ivers would have been a giant in the music industry. Sadly, his murder is still unsolved, and I am not sure that we will ever be able to prove who took his life. Perhaps we will be able to prove who committed his murder one day, and just maybe, this biography will help.

Cliff Shepard
Detective
Los Angeles Police Department
Robbery-Homicide Division

SELECTED WORKS

THEATRE SCORES
The Bacchae, Charles Street Playhouse, 1968
Everyman, Harvard Agassiz Theater, 1969
Jesus: A Passion Play for Americans, Harvard/PBS, 1969–1972
Aladdin, Harvard with Tim Mayer, 1981

THEATRE: MUSIC AND LYRICS
Nirvana Cuba (unfinished musical), 1977–1979
The Vitamin Pink Fantasy Revue, 1981–1982

ALBUMS
Knight of the Blue Communion, Epic, 1969
Take It Out on Me, Epic, unreleased
Terminal Love, Warner Bros., 1974
Peter Ivers, Warner Bros., 1975–1976
Nirvana Peter, posthumous best-of, 1985

TV AND FILM SCORES
Various scores for AFI, 1972–1974
David Lynch's *Eraserhead,* 1977
Roger Corman's *Grand Theft Auto,* soundtrack, 1977
Long Beach art videos, 1977–1979
Starsky and Hutch episode, "Class in Crime," 1978
Airplane, stewardess's guitar song, 1980
Love Theme from Filmex Film Festival, 1980
National Lampoon's Vacation, "Little Boy Sweet," 1983

TELEVISION AND FILM: OTHER
New Wave Theatre, Host, 1980–1983
City of Tomorrow, story and score with Rod Taylor, unfinished, 1983

In addition to writing his own music, Ivers wrote lyrics for other composers. Peter's songs have been recorded by Helen Reddy, Marty Balin, June Pointer (Pointer Sisters), Taste of Honey, Diana Ross, and Dee Dee Bridgewater. He produced records for Roderick Falconer (Rod Taylor) and Circus Mort as well as a demo for Human Sexual Response.

SOURCES

Ninety percent of the material for this book is based on original interviews conducted by Josh Frank from January 2005 to January 2008. Unless otherwise designated in the "Cast of Characters" section at the front of the book, all those listed in the Cast were interviewed.

Additional sources are also listed below. Any concrete information from these latter sources is indicated as such in the text. Otherwise, these sources were used for time-line or other background reference.

The authors have folded certain stories into a condensed time frame for the sake of the narrative's dramatic flow. Several instances of dialogue (only in the narrative sections—not in the oral "close-ups" or "case books") have been re-created based on the author's interviews with original sources.

The "Case Book" and Cold Case investigation research is based on new original material collected through live interviews by Josh Frank (January 2006–December 2007).

NARRATIVE, CLOSE-UPS, AND CASE BOOKS
Interviews conducted between January 2005–January 2008

BOOKS

Karp, Josh. *A Futile and Stupid Gesture* (Chicago: Chicago Review Press, 2006)

Schmidt, Paul, ed. *Running from America: The Poems and Plays of Tim Mayer* (Washington, D.C.: Seven Locks Press, 1992)

WEB PAGES

http://www.irscorner.com/ijk/ivers.html (Peter Ivers, general)

http://www.rockinboston.com/peterivers.html (Joe Harvard on Ivers and Pixies)

http://www.dareland.com/emulsionalproblems/kaufman.htm (The Top)

http://en.wikipedia.org/wiki/Peter_Ivers (Peter Ivers, general)

http://www.poormojo.org/pmjadaily/archives/007062.php (Fear on *SNL*)

PHOTOGRAPHS

Peter Ivers promo shot, 1980—courtesy of Dennis Keeley

Peter (center) on his high school prom committee, 1964—courtesy of The Peter Ivers Estate

Peter and Tim Mayer, 1969—courtesy of Lucy Fisher and The Peter Ivers Estate

Peter in his studio in Laurel Canyon, 1974—courtesy of Tim Hunter

Peter with Devo at the Santa Monica Civic Center, July 1979—courtesy of Steve Martin

Peter with John Cale at the Whisky a Go Go, March 1980—courtesy of Steve Martin

Peter in Jerusalem with Lucy Fisher's family, 1978—courtesy of the Fishers

***New Wave Theatre* video stills**—courtesy of Lili Haydn, Stuart Shapiro, and Research Video Inc. Copyright New Wave Theatre/Night Flight. Night Flight is a registered trademark of Digital Download Inc.

Left to right: Tim Mayer, Doug Kenney, Peter, Lucy Fisher, and Harold Ramis, 1978—courtesy of Merle Ivers

Left to right: Roderick Taylor, Peter, Lucy Fisher, Jody Uttal, and an unknown woman, 1979—courtesy of The Peter Ivers Estate

John Belushi with The Dead Boys: Jimmy Zero, Johnny Blitz, Cheetah Chrome, and Stiv Bators, 1978—courtesy of Judy Belushi

Peter and the *New Wave Theatre* regulars, 1981—courtesy of The Peter Ivers Estate

Peter and Tequila Mockingbird on *New Wave Theatre* with Vitamin Pink, 1982—courtesy of The Peter Ivers Estate

Polaroids—courtesy of Michael Dare, www.dareland.com

Peter on *New Wave Theatre*, 1982—courtesy of The Peter Ivers Estate

Poster for Peter Ivers's *Vitamin Pink Fantasy Revue,* June 8 and 9, 1982, Lingerie Club, Los Angeles, California—courtesy of Merle Ivers

Peter and Lucy at their Laurel Canyon home, 1974—courtesy of Tim Hunter

VIDEO

New Wave Theatre clips and episodes—courtesy of Ian Marshall at Research Video

NWT and The Top archive footage—courtesy of Research Video

"The Top"—courtesy of Paul Flattery

"At Sunset"—courtesy of Buddy Helm

"Vitamin Pink Review"—courtesy of Malcolm Leo

ALBUMS

Knight of the Blue Communion—(originally Epic) Hux records: Re-released
   2007
Take It Out on Me—(Epic): Paul Lenard personal collection (out of print)
Terminal Love—(Warner): Lucy Fisher personal collection (out of print)
Peter Ivers—(Warner): Author's personal collection (out of print)

PETER IVERS' LYRICS
Courtesy of Franne Golde, Harvard Archives, Alan Siegel

TIM MAYER LYRICS
Schmidt, Paul, ed. *Running from America: The Poems and Plays of Tim Mayer*
   (Washington, D.C.: Seven Locks Press, 1992)

ARTICLES
Collected from the Harvard Archives and the personal collections of Merle Ivers,
   Lucy Fisher, Richard and Robbie Greene, Tim Hunter, Tom Barron, and Char-
   lie Haas.
"Salute to Times Past: The Lampoon Ibis" by Betsy Nadas. *The Crimson,* Monday,
   June 3, 1968.
"A Hit and a Myth" by Timothy S. Mayer. *The Theatregoer,* Friday, March 10,
   1967.
"Everyman at Agassiz," by Tim Hunter. *The Crimson,* Friday, August 16, 1968.
"From the News Land Poons," by Samuel Z. Goldhaber. *The Crimson,* Tuesday,
   April 7, 1970.
"As Strange as 1969 Ever Got," by David Fricke. *Rolling Stone,* August 17, 2007.
"Review of 'Terminal Love,' " by James Spina. *Women's Wear Daily,* July 24,
   1974.
"Harmonica Player Turns Composer." *Buffalo Courier-Express,* February 4, 1970.
The Nichel review. Syracuse, New York, January 16, 1970.
"Listening, Knight of the Blue Communion," by Hal M. Hughes.
Peter Ivers, July 1974 WB interview
Peter Ivers (Circular), vol. 6 number 25, Monday, July 29, 1974: "The Happy
   Victim of 'Terminal Love' " and (Circular) and April 10, 1976. Warner Bros.
   Records Publications.
"Lampoon's Lemmings a Rock Musical Review." *Time* magazine, February 19,
   1973.
"Review of *Peter Ivers,*" *Rolling Stone,* July 1, 1976.

"Playback" by Tom Von Malder. *Chicago Herald,* September 3, 1976.

Philadelphia, the week of September 14 through September 21

"From the moment of his arrival . . ." *LA Times.*

Philadelphia, the week of September 14 through September 21

"On the Werewolf Circuit," by Jack Knoll. *Newsweek,* September 11, 1978.

"The Lampoon Goes Hollywood." *Time,* August 14, 1978.

"City Punk, Surf Punk, New Existentialist-anything new can usually find its way onto New Wave Theater . . ." by Patrick Goldstein, *Los Angeles Times.*

"People around the country will know what a real punk show is like."
    LA Weekly, May 14–20, 1982.

"Television/8am: New Wave Theatre: High Low Tech TV," by Melodie Bryant, January 30, 1981. Los Angeles—It's around 10:00 o'clock on a Sunday night . . . "A flamboyant figure whose clothing ranges anywhere from transparent vinyl . . ."

Peter Ivers in *Home Video* magazine, 1982: "I play a character, I try to tease everybody, but still stay supportive"

Video Won't Swim in Mainstream: "New Wave Theatre" Cable Show exposes Rock in Major Markets," by Cary Darling, Los Angeles, 1982.

"ATI Video's 'Night Flight' Builds a Cable Music Audience." *Record World,* July 25, 1981.

"New Wave Television," by Jeff Silberman. *LA Weekly,* May 14–20, 1982.

"New Wave Theater is not a music show." *LA Weekly,* August 8–14, 1980.

"That's right, Terminal love and a . . ." Peter Ivers. *Billboard,* July 27, 1974.

"The Ivers Plan," by Peter Ivers (unpublished), 1979.

The American Bachelor's Register, by Celeste Fremon and the Editors of *Playboy.* New York: Simon & Schuster, 1982.

"Peter Ivers: A Death of Innocence," by Michael London. March 27, 1983.

"Forever Young," by Tony Schwartz. *New York* magazine, September 5, 1983.

"Who Killed Peter Ivers," by Michael Bygrave.

"In Praise of Peter Ivers," by John Leone. *LA Weekly,* March 18–24, 1983.

"Cable's Top 25 Stars." *Home Video Reader,* 1981.

Review of Sept. 23rd live show at SF's Savoy promoting *Peter Ivers,* by Jack Badger, *Rock and Roll News.*

Review of Live Show for *Peter Ivers SF Examiner,* Friday, September 24, 1976.

Review of *Peter Ivers,* by Howard Klein. *Bay Area Review.*

"Rolling With the New Waves on TV," by Jeff Spurrier.

"L.A.'s Vanity Video—Hey, Mom, I'm on TV," by Bronwyn. *LA Weekly,* December 5–11, 1980.

"'New Wave Theatre' Cable Show Exposes Rock in Major Markets," by Cary Darling. [No name of publication.]

"Cable's Theatre of the Absurd," by Patrick Goldstein. [No name of publication.], February 1982.

"New Wave Comes to Beverly Hills," by Laura Daltry. *LA Weekly,* August 8–14, 1980.

ACKNOWLEDGMENTS

Thanks from Josh Frank

My friend and collaborator Charlie. Rebecca Ramirez, my research assistant and web designer. Michael Harriot and David Vigliano. Wylie O'Sullivan, Elizabeth Perrella, Dominick Anfuso, and everyone else at Free Press.

This book would not have been possible without the generous and overwhelming support of the expansive community of Peter's family, friends, and fans.

Merle Ivers and Ricki Lopez. Lucy Fisher and Meghan Snyder. Harold, Violet, and Anne Ramis. Clifford Shepard, Steve Forman, Josh Karp, Ian Marshall, and Research Video. Steve Martin, who guided me lovingly through all things Peter. Same for Buell Neidlinger and Van Dyke Parks. Charles Thompson, David Lynch, Paul Lenard, Malcolm Leo, Buddy Helm, Paul Flattery, Richard Skidmore, Ken Yas, and Michael Dare. Mel Rodriguez (Dr. Watson to my Sherlock in Los Angeles). Greg Nodler, who told me to go with Peter, and Jodi Bart who told me to call the Vig. Tom Lee, Rachel Howarth, and the Harvard Archives. Wallis Nicita, Durrie Parks, Howard Cutler, Rod Taylor, Peter Rafelson, Michael Shamberg, Mark Canton, Deb Newmyer, and Paula Weinstein. Franne Golde, Tequila Mockingbird, Asha Puthli, and Yolande Bavan. Judy Belushi, John Landis, and Dan Aykroyd. Derf and Spit. Eric Nederlander, Isaac Levy, and Resolute. Didier Gertsch, Caryn Ganz, Josh Weiss, David and Rachel Wyatt, Heather Zicko, and all my other creative collaborators: Peter reminded me how much I miss them and long to be surrounded by such a community of wonderful creators again and forever.

My father, Steve; my mother, Marcia; and my sister Rachel. Yvonne; my grandmother Shirley; Merrill and Helen Tracey; Rich Wasserstrom, Dennis, Patty, Sarah and Rebecca, the Rosens, and Dogbaby. My grandfather Joe Frank. I will miss you in this life, but we will carry on your name and all that we have learned from you. You not only made us, you made us great, and we thank you forever.

A most important thanks to everyone who took the time to talk to me about Peter; to send me music, articles, and media; to be available at a moment's notice to answer my questions at all hours; and to revisit both wonderful and difficult memories. The simple fact that there are more names to mention than would fit on this page is a testament to Peter and to you. Your stories have changed my life and taught me to never give up on my dreams, and for all this I am forever grateful. This book only exists because of you.

Thanks from Charlie Buckholtz

Josh—for introducing me to Peter and all his friends, and for knowing only two old friends could tell his story.

Lucy—for the chance.

Mike Harriott—for being mind-bogglingly sharp in helping us shape and sell the concept, steady in your support, and gracious throughout tricky negotiations.

Uncle Ed—the sweetest bulldog a nephew could ever need—for having my back always and with no questions asked.

Wylie O'Sullivan—for getting excited about Peter's story; trusting us to tell it; exuding an unbroken flow of positive, encouraging energy while we did; and bringing it home with the steadiest and smartest editorial hand I can personally imagine.

Elizabeth Perrella—for being brightly and awesomely on top of everything at all times.

Mom, Dad, D, Josh, Hill, Nana—to thank you is like thanking my lungs for taking in air. For your unconditional everything.

Peter—for giving so much, so vividly, in such a short period of time, that I can find in you a brother, a teacher, an artist, a trickster, a prophet, a tzadik, and a friend.

And Sara—my compass needle. I made this book for you. As it turns out, I could not have made it without you—your steadfast support, dead-on suggestions, and wise counsel. Our story, Godwilling, is just beginning.

ABOUT THE AUTHORS

Author of *Fool the World: The Oral History of a Band Called Pixies* (St. Martins Press USA/Virgin Books U.K.), writer, producer, composer, director, and pop-culture dramatist Josh Frank has penned numerous plays (including an authorized adaptation of Werner Herzog's *Stroszek*), screenplays, and musicals (including *The Jonathan Richman Musical*). He is presently writing the authorized adaptation of Kurt Vonnegut's son's memoir for the screen and a TV show called *One Hit Wonder*. Josh lives half his life in Austin, Texas, and the other half "in the hearts of the people."

Charlie Buckholtz is a freelance writer living in the East Village of New York City. He received an MFA from Syracuse University and is currently working on his first novel.